FINANCING
THE SMALL
BUSINESS

A Complete Guide to Obtaining Bank Loans
and All Other Types of Financing

Robert Sisson

Adams Media Corporation
Avon, Massachusetts

Published by
Adams Media Corporation
57 Littlefield Street, Avon, MA 02322. U.S.A.
www.adamsmedia.com

ISBN: 1-58062-681-5

Printed in Canada.

J I H G F E D C B A

Library of Congress Cataloging-in-Publication information
available upon request from the publisher

This publication is designed to provide accurate and authoritative information
with regard to the subject matter covered. It is sold with the understanding that
the publisher is not engaged in rendering legal, accounting, or other professional advice. If legal advice or other expert assistance is required, the services
of a competent professional person should be sought.
— From a *Declaration of Principles* jointly adopted by a Committee of the
American Bar Association and a Committee of Publishers and Associations

Cover photo by Getty Images/Dick Luria.

This book is available at quantity discounts for bulk purchases.
For information, call 1-800-872-5627.

Visit our exciting small business Web site at businesstown.com

Contents

Foreword

If you are an owner of a growing company, or if you are thinking of starting a new venture, one of the greatest challenges you must face daily is financing your business. Whether the financing will be used to fund your startup, provide necessary working capital for your current operations, or fund your growth, it is critical to your success that you obtain the appropriate amount of capital from the right sources and with terms that are properly structured for your business requirements. But how?

Robert C. Sisson has written an outstanding guide—*Financing the Small Business*—to assist you in this process. He provides meaningful tips on how to navigate the numerous, and often complicated, paths that can lead you to successfully securing financing, not only from traditional banking sources, but also from "out of the box" alternatives that should (no, MUST) be seriously considered.

This highly relevant guide will help you better understand the banking environment and the process banks and other credit grantors utilize to review and, hopefully, approve your loan request. In addition, Mr. Sisson openly shares his banking experiences to help you better understand what financial and other data a lender expects from you and how to present such data, as well as what expectations you should have from your new "business partner," both in good times and bad.

But what if bank financing is not an acceptable answer for your business requirements, possibly due to a lack of a track record, erratic financial performance, you operate in a cyclical industry, there is insufficient collateral, and the list goes on and on?

Financing the Small Business will help you clearly see the viable financing options that will allow your business to continue to survive and thrive.

Howard B. Allenberg
Vice Chairman and Chief Operating Officer
BDO Seidman, LLP
Accountants and Consultants to Growing Businesses

Banking the Small Business

There are 24 million small businesses in America, and almost 600,000 new businesses join those ranks each year. Most business owners will spend more time, energy, and money designing their business cards than planning for their companies' banking needs. Yet, without sufficient cash with which to pay bills and buy working assets, the company suffers gridlock, or worse, bankruptcy.

When the needs for banking services arise, too many entrepreneurs limit themselves to one option—banks—and follow the age-old custom of throwing everything they have against the wall to see what sticks. Of the thousands of loan applications that I have personally declined over the last two decades, the vast majority died due to self-inflicted wounds caused by uninformed or careless business owners. Entrepreneurs, who shine brightly in every other endeavor, have an uncanny ability to shoot themselves in the foot when it comes to loan applications.

The simple fact that small business owners largely come from every walk of life but banking—like engineering, sales, and tool-making—explains the collective lack of financial education among them. I cannot remember one month passing during my career when a successful business owner did not tell me, "If I knew then what I know now about business finance and banking, I never would have started my business." Since 90 percent of all American jobs are provided by small businesses, it is fortunate for us as a society that most people are unaware of what it takes to properly finance a small business!

Just like a pending fender-bender seems to happen in slow motion, the thought finally occurred to me that a resource guide for business owners that covered all the bases of small business finance would be helpful. This book provides the information that business owners want to know, need to know, and must know. The information is a blend of lessons learned from all those thousand-plus loans that I have declined, answers to questions most asked by loan applicants, and an insider's perspective of how best to navigate the various channels of small business finance.

"Thinking outside the box" is a hot catch phrase in corporate boardrooms and business school classrooms. *Financing the Small Business* applies a philosophy of "Banking outside the box" to small business finance. When owners of small businesses limit themselves to one financing option—namely, banks—they effectively box themselves in. Once a person enters a bank, he is cornered by four walls: conservative credit standards, regulatory bureaucracy, investment averse philosophies, and lack of creativity. This book ushers the reader through the corridors of the bank and points out more than a few back doors that lead to creative financing alternatives.

This chapter sets the stage for the remainder of the book. Two topics are discussed. The first is the effect of changes in the banking industry on small businesses. The second topic is the power of business credit—why small businesses need to borrow money.

The Changing Banking Industry

The bad news for even wizened owners of companies who have spent a lifetime perfecting their banking relationships is that banking today is not what it was just one year ago. Big changes have arrived and more are on the way. It is absolutely incumbent upon every business owner from the person who is planning to start a business to the person who is nearing retirement and the sale of his or her business to keep abreast of these changes. The alternative is to watch financially competent and savvy competitors blow the spectator out of business.

Change, inevitably, has a stranglehold on the banking industry and has forever altered the way individuals and businesses conduct their financial affairs. Long gone are the days when a handshake and a signature were all that were required for a loan. If a person last borrowed money from a bank just one year ago, he or she might be in for a rude awakening upon the next visit to the bank. Today, it seems that the primary business of banks is to avoid lending money—at least to the uninitiated bystander and unprepared business owner.

Much of the change that has occurred is positive. Banks are no longer stodgy bastions where anal-retentive men in dark suits while away their days in richly paneled offices perusing the *Wall Street Journal*. In fact, mandatory sales training is almost universal for employees of all levels of every type of bank! The stereotypical banker embodied by Mr. Mooney from "The Lucille Ball Show" and Mr. Drysdale from "The Beverly Hillbillies" has been modernized in the mold of stockbrokers and real estate salespeople.

Small business owners are just as likely to transact business over the telephone, at in-store branches located in neighborhood supermarkets, or on the Internet. Technology has made it possible to handle an entire banking relationship without any personal interaction with a flesh-and-blood banker. There are fears within the banking industry that the next wave of change will include the creation of a coast-to-coast branchless bank by an information technology giant like Microsoft (and bankers are trembling because of it and proactively seeking preemptive strategies).

The pace of change has been and will continue to be fast and furious. Business owners cannot rely on an old-fashioned two-hour interview in a bank loan officer's office to state their case for a loan. Bank officers are hard-pressed to keep up with their workloads, so they must perform triage of a sort with loan applications. Those applications that need too much work or assistance are placed at the bottom of the pile most likely never to see the light of day again or are simply rejected and returned to the hapless small business owner. The rules have changed and only entrepreneurs who prepare the appropriate game plan will succeed.

Why is it so difficult for small business owners to obtain loans for their small businesses? The answer is simple: Businesses fail. In fact, four out of five new businesses fail within five years of opening their doors. With odds like that, it really is a miracle that anyone is interested in lending money to small businesses. Naturally, bankers try to weed out the 80 percent of business owners that will not be successful at the time of the loan application. Bankers who do not develop an aptitude for this skill are quickly shown the door by their employers.

A successful business loan applicant can prove to the banker that he or she is the one out of five. Again, changes in the banking industry rarely allow for an applicant to wear a banker down with a half-day monologue or impress the banker with personality-by-Dale Carnegie. That's why small business owners have to stay on top of changes and trends in the banking industry. Financing is just as crucial for a tool-shop owner as is the latest laser technology. A company's financial structure is like a skeleton that we flesh out with a unique identity, be it retail, manufacturing, or service. Every business has a financial structure that needs periodic and frequent adjustment.

The Power of Business Credit

Business credit, money borrowed for a business purpose, is a powerful tool that can make the difference between success and failure. It can make the difference between a business that merely is in existence and one that is achieving and growing. There are three basic, broad things that business credit does for an entrepreneur: start up a business, provide working capital with which to operate the business, and provide money to fund growth. There are as many ways to structure credit as there are banks and bankers, but there are just these three general uses of funds. The ability to compartmentalize these categories will enhance the preparation of loan applications, money management, and discourse with bankers.

STARTING A BUSINESS

More than sixty years ago, my maternal grandfather partitioned off a portion of the family's living quarters with a curtain to serve as a retail flower store and used the family's milk money to buy a few bunches of fresh-cut flowers for his starting inventory. Grandpa, an immigrant from Germany, spent his days working in a paper mill and evenings propagating geraniums on the back porch. Grandma minded the kids and the store. Almost three decades later, they borrowed their first loan from a bank in order to build a separate, modern store. That store survives today and is managed by a second generation of family members. The story of Hodapp's Flowers in Plainwell, Michigan, is a true American success story and is the fruit of hard work and years of dedication; unfortunately, it is a rarity today.

Business owners today do not have the luxury of launching a business on a shoestring budget and cannot afford to slowly build a business over the course of decades, years, or even months in the case of technology businesses. Any good idea will quickly be copied by competitors if better funding will allow them to leapfrog over the existing business. Startup credit allows business owners to launch their businesses with the necessary firepower to be immediate forces in their respective markets. Oddly, another common problem for brand-new businesses is too much growth too fast. Without proper startup capital, a new business can quickly find itself out of cash with no way to pay wages or replace inventory. Employees jump ship to companies that can cover payroll, and customers leave the fold to find a more reliable source of service. Suddenly, euphoria turns into despair and another promising small business closes its doors.

Another reason to borrow money to launch a new business is to spread the risk of financial loss to other people besides the entrepreneur. It is anathema for a banker to utter those words and heresy to do so publicly. Most entrepreneurs leave a job or career with a regular paycheck and put their life savings and homes on the line to start businesses. Anything an entrepreneur can do to lessen the risk of total ruin is to his or her advantage. In a perfect world, banks would assume no risk of loss when they made loans. In the real world, though, banks do take considerable risks. The amount of risk a bank will assume is dependent upon many factors that will be discussed in later chapters.

The businesses that can be started without any money can be counted on one hand. A paper route immediately comes to my mind. Even an Amway Distributorship requires an outlay of a few hundred bucks for the purchase of the starter kit of products. Obviously, opportunities are extremely limited for anyone who hopes to start a business with no or little cash. Startup loans are required in nearly every instance to bridge the gap between personal savings and the cost of opening and running the business. Consequently, the ability to convince people to loan money to you is paramount to starting a business.

OPERATING A BUSINESS

If the financial structure of a business is its skeleton, then the money used to operate the business on a day-to-day basis is its lifeblood. This money is called working capital. It cycles through the business in different forms. Obviously, it starts out as cash. Some of the cash is used to purchase inventory that a business will sell in normal course. Sometimes, when the inventory is sold, the buyer promises to pay the price later, so the business creates an account receivable. Cash, inventory, and accounts receivable are also called liquid assets because cash can be spent immediately, and inventory and accounts receivable will convert to cash (we hope) very quickly. The term *liquid* helps us visualize the cycle. Think of water. When it is in liquid form, we can drink it; but when it is in a solid or gaseous state, we have to wait for it to convert back to a liquid.

Of course, we do not see our neighbors standing in their backyards, palms up, buckets at their feet, waiting for the next rainstorm to replenish their water tanks. We borrow water when we need it from ground or surface sources, and it is replenished later by precipitation. Likewise, we would not expect to see a shopkeeper close his or her store and post a sign out front that reads, "Sorry, all my cash is in inventory and accounts receivable. Check back later." Working capital loans are available to ensure a consistent flow of cash through the cycle so a business never has to worry about the cash register going dry. These loans are often overlooked by business owners because of the intangible nature of the underlying assets and the failure to view the latter two categories as liquid assets that can be converted into currency. Business owners that have not provided a permanent source of working capital or lined up a source from which to borrow working capital face continuous financial dilemmas ("Which bill do I pay today?").

As alluded to earlier, a provision for working capital is a must for a brand-new business, or else the business could screech to a halt very quickly. Think of startup working capital as a bucket of cash. Soon after opening the doors of a business, the bucket is emptied to buy inventory that is converted into accounts receivables. The easiest way to replenish the bucket is to borrow working capital funds that would allow further purchases of inventory and increasing levels of accounts receivable. As receivables are collected or cash sales are pocketed, the cash proceeds are either added back into the bucket or sent to the bank to pay down the loan. The key reason for using working capital loans is they give the business's management control of the flow of cash through the business and take it out of the hands of a fickle public (that may change buying habits and certainly is in no hurry to pay accounts owed to businesses).

Even mature, older companies that have not grown sales one cent in years have need for working capital loans. Standard terms offered by vendors are a 2 percent discount of the purchase price if payment is made within ten days of invoice (terms vary, but let's use this as our example). Under the assumption that the company continuously purchases an identical monthly amount from the vendor throughout the year, it could save 24 percent in purchasing costs by taking advantage of the discount. When a company makes a purchase on account, the selling company is really lending an amount equal to the sale to the purchaser. Let's assume a company buys $100,000 of product monthly from one of its suppliers. The company pays its bills every thirty days and, therefore, on any given day, probably owes the supplier $100,000. Of course, it is not the same $100,000 from one month to the next month, but the average amount owed to the supplier nevertheless is $100,000.

Let's do the math to flesh out this example. If the company buys $100,000 of product from its vendor, it could save $2,000 by paying its invoice within ten days of purchase. The typical cash cycle employed by most businesses requires receivables to be paid no later than thirty days after billing. The accounts receivable for the example company are collected, on average, at about thirty days. So, the example company will have no problem keeping its account at its own supplier current, but it will never be able to pay the account early enough to net the 2 percent discount.

The inability to save $2,000 per month adds up to $24,000 over the course of one year. The $24,000 of discounts not taken divided by the $100,000 average account payable balance equals 24 percent. That 24 percent is paid to the vendor for the privilege of borrowing $100,000.

The 24 percent cost is very much like bank interest, except it is paid to the vendor in the form of higher prices. The autumn of 1982, when interest rates topped 20 percent, was the last time banks could charge a customer $2,000 per month in exchange for loaning the customer $100,000 and get away with it. Businesspeople still gripe about that long-ago time. Yet, businesses lose money at that rate all the time from the failure to take advantage of terms offered by vendors.

Working capital loans can save a bundle of money for businesses. If the company in our example borrowed $100,000 from the bank at an interest rate of 10 percent and used the money to pay its supplier in time to take the discount, the net result would be annual savings of $14,000. This result is the difference between saving $24,000 in purchase costs by taking the vendor's terms and the annual interest expense of $10,000 for the bank loan. The savings could be invested in the business and yield further savings or promote increased income. The $14,000 could make the difference in hiring or keeping a great employee or in a decision to buy new technology for the business. Table 1-1 compares the two methods of financing inventory purchases, discussed earlier, using annualized numbers.

Table 1-1

Method	Average Debt	Interest Cost	Cost of Purchases	Total Costs
Accounts payable	$100,000	$0	$1,200,000	$1,200,000
Loan	$100,000	$10,000	$1,176,000	$1,186,000
Savings realized by using working capital loan:				$14,000

This category of loans is of foremost importance for highly successful businesses that are experiencing rapid growth. Just like startup ventures, a fast-growing concern can quickly tie up all its cash in inventory or accounts receivable. Although a startup company might have the right mix of owner's cash equity and bank funds, rapidly growing companies typically are highly leveraged. That is, sales have grown at a rate much faster than the company's net worth. Sales might double over a short period, but profits increase only by 10 percent. The only way to keep cash in the checking account with which to pay bills or replenish inventory is to borrow more money. The more borrowed money that is invested in a business in relation to the actual owner's cash equity or profits, the more highly levered the company. Higher leverage means higher risk for a variety of reasons that will be discussed in a later chapter. Suffice it to say this is why even the most successful companies often have problems convincing bankers to lend more money to them.

Whether a company is brand new, mature, or speeding to record results, working capital loans are the key to running a business and staying in business.

GROWING A BUSINESS

A business owner's nightmare is to turn away customers because of insufficient capacity to meet the demand. Will the customer come back later? Will word spread that the business can't take care of its customers? Will the word turn into rumors about pending bankruptcy? I have seen many business owners get into financial trouble because they could not bring themselves to turn away customers. They stretch their companies beyond the breaking point and end up scaring customers away with shoddy performance and products.

The third major use of borrowed money is to help companies expand to meet or prepare for growth. Almost every company will need to improve or expand at some point in its life. It might be something seemingly inconsequential like a new computer system or something huge like a new building. Expansion is usually driven by two factors: growth and competition.

A company might experience growth in sales such that it sells everything it can produce. The next logical step is to create the ability to produce more product to sell. Or a savvy manager might anticipate growth with forecasts, market data, or any of many other reasons and build excess capacity in order to meet the expected increased demand. It is not uncommon for significant customers of a company to promise a large increase in business if the company would add capacity or some special abilities. For example, one of my former clients manufactured boxes to package small items made by another local manufacturer. The boxes, made of plain white coated cardboard, were shipped by my customer to another company that imprinted the product design on the boxes. The end user suggested to my customer, who was chugging along making decent profits, that he might consider purchasing a four-color printing press and performing the printing job as well as producing the plain boxes. We financed a beautiful Heidelberg four-color press for our client. His sales nearly doubled and profits climbed to unforeseen heights.

Competition, or the threat of competition, forces a good percentage of business expansions. One of the best marketing ploys is to always be the biggest, best, fastest, first, or newest. For this reason, many business owners are eager to buy new technology or product capabilities. Retailers love to plug holes in markets by being the first store of their type to open in a town. Immediately, the retailer can lay claim to first and newest. If the market is relatively small, the mere existence of the store may prevent any other business owner from moving in. Another example is the simple relocation to another building—one better configured for present circumstances—that affords the business cost efficiencies that allow better, more competitive pricing.

Bank on It

+ Every small business owner is also his or her own chief financial officer.
+ Banking is changing rapidly, and successful managers will stay on top of those changes and trends.
+ Starting a new business requires enough up-front capital to allow the business to run properly, or else it risks alienating customers and employees and opening a door for competitors.
+ Cash is the lifeblood of an operating business. Working capital loans ensure a steady source of cash with which to operate the business.
+ Business credit can help grow a business that faces high demand or competitive pressures.

t w o

2

Understanding Banks

Before a successful saleswoman calls on a prospect, she spends a lot of time and energy learning all that she can learn about that prospect. The knowledge gained ahead of time helps her determine the prospect's needs, what products or services she will show to the prospect, and the character of her sales presentation. Make no mistake about it, when an applicant approaches a bank (or nonbank alternative), he or she is selling his or her business's ability to repay a loan. Why then do most applicants not go to the trouble of learning anything about banks?

Loan applicants need not earn PhDs in banking in order to have success. This chapter provides a quick overview of information that will help you select a bank, apply for a loan from that bank, and deal with the bank.

Popular Misconceptions About Banks

There are two popular misconceptions about banks that get in the way of doing business with banks. First, a huge number of Americans actually believe that banks are quasi-governmental institutions. There are several reasons why people believe this misperception. Bank buildings look like federal government buildings. Big, cavernous, expensive pieces of real estate, marble floors, rich woodwork; they bear the hallmarks of spending an unlimited budget. Transacting business with a bank is reminiscent of tangling with government red tape. Given the milquetoast personalities associated with bankers and government bureaucrats, it is easy to see why people might think that they were hired by the same human resource department. Probably more than anything else, though, is the fact that nearly every action taken by a banker is governed closely by federal laws. Every page of literature or documentation that consumers receive from banks has the imprint of more than one government law or regulation. The similarities between banks and government are striking; however, no one is entitled to bank services simply because he or she pays taxes. Calling your congressperson to complain about a bank's services is not of much use.

The second misconception about banks is that they are charitable institutions. Granted, in just about every community in America, banks are the single largest source of corporate contributions to every nonprofit organization or fundraising cause. Bankers are ubiquitous members of the board of directors for all kinds of charitable, service, and community groups ranging from the United Way to Girl Scouts to church building fund drives. In fact, the requirement for participation in these do-good groups is written into many bank job descriptions. Obviously, it is good marketing for a bank to insist on its officers' participation in those causes since the higher the visibility the more business generated for the bank. Little known outside the banking fraternity, though, is the fact that the government basically requires bankers to roll up their sleeves and become involved in charitable organizations and projects. The government provides this little push in the Community Reinvestment Act (CRA). The CRA and how to take advantage of its provisions are discussed in Chapter 10.

Over the years, I have faced loan applicants across my desk who try to convince me to make the loan to them because, "if I can't pay it back, you can write it off as a charitable contribution." Alternative logic would have me believe that the loan will have all sorts of positive ripple effects throughout the community, and therefore, the bank should simply give the money to the applicant with no pretense of looking for repayment. Others have issued commands for loans, "I'm a taxpayer and I demand this loan!" Needless to say, I never really warmed up to those types of applicants.

Banks are businesses and are no different from any mom-and-pop business. Banks that do not make profits do not stay in business. Banks that are publicly owned and do not perform up to the stockholders' standards are sold and folded into other banks. Banks whose businesses are not managed properly are sanctioned or taken over by the government. It is a simple mantra, but one that is invaluable to any businessperson who wishes to transact business with a bank: Banks are businesses.

The Business of Banks

At their core, banks are ingeniously simple businesses. They are financial intermediaries; that is, they borrow money from one person and lend it to another person. They actually rent the money from someone called a depositor. The bank then rents the money to another person known as a borrower. If all goes according to plan, the rent the bank receives from the borrower is higher than what it pays to the depositor.

It is such a simple business, it is a wonder that everyone does not get into the act. There are basic advantages that banks enjoy and that make them the ideal intermediary for money transactions. Banks offer complex record keeping and reporting, a central location for transactions, safekeeping of records and the underlying cash, and the expertise to deal with the innumerable complications that usually arise in financial transactions. Personally, I would not want to call my neighbor, to whom I have loaned a sum of money, to ask, or demand, its repayment. Similarly, I would hate to ask my grandmother for collateral to secure a loan to her. Even if a depositor had the fortitude to locate a willing borrower to whom to lend a nest egg, the costs of making the loan would more than likely lower the net income on the loan below the rate a bank could offer the depositor due to its economy of scale.

For these reasons, banking is one of the world's oldest professions, ranking right up there with you-know-what. It is one of the few professions to merit a mention in the Bible (you know the verse about casting the money lenders from the temple). Bankers originally dealt in commodities before currency was invented. At some point, someone decided it would be easier to value all commodities, goods, and services in one base unit. The textbook example uses clamshells, hence, the nickname for dollars: clams.

BANK INCOME

Banks earn two types of income: interest and fee. Interest income is actually rental income received by the bank from people or companies who borrow, or rent, money from the bank. Interest income has always been the primary source of revenue for a bank. The interest rates for loans are determined in a variety of ways. Most banks today sell their home mortgage loans and student loans to secondary market investors. These investors represent huge pools of investable cash and buy loans nationwide. Thus, whatever rate those secondary market investors wish to realize on their investments dictates the rates that bank charge their customers. There is no secondary market (in the same vein as home loans) for commercial loans yet. That is why when you call a bank and ask for the going thirty-year home mortgage rate, the bank can give you a specific answer, and why when you ask for the rate on a five-year commercial loan, it cannot answer you.

Commercial loans historically have been priced according to individual risk. Traditionally, banks charge their very best customers the prime rate of interest. These customers are considered the best credit risk among the bank's customers. Customers with perceived higher risk have rates incrementally higher than the prime rate. Many factors are considered when determining a particular loan's risk. These include the applicant's credit history, length of time in business, industry, and market. Other factors include the length of the term of the loan (the longer it is outstanding, the more that can go wrong) and the collateral or guarantees behind the loan. The bulk of commercial loans will fall between the range of the prime rate and the prime rate plus 2½ percent.

Banks may charge a variable rate of interest or a fixed rate of interest. Generally, when the loan is going to remain on the bank's books, the rate will be variable. That means that as rates change in the marketplace, the interest rate on the loans will be adjusted. For many people, it may appear that banks get away with robbery when they raise rates. The variable rate structure simply allows banks to compensate for the increased rates they will have to pay to depositors in order to continue to attract funds to the bank. Fixed rates signal a loan that might be sold to a secondary market investor, thereby removing the risk that the bank might be stuck with a loan earning less income than the bank has to pay a depositor for the use of the money. Fixed rates are also set by matching loans of specific periods to deposits of the same length. For example, if a bank is paying 5 percent on five-year certificates of deposit, it might fix a rate of 8.75 percent for five-year loans. That covers its cost of the deposits plus builds in a gross profit of 3.75 percent. (This is one reason why CDs carry penalties for early withdrawal—to compensate banks for the loss of the matching funds.)

Fee income is a relatively new pursuit for banks. Every bank sets different fees for different products or services. One bank received huge amounts of negative publicity when it began to charge its customers $3.00 for the privilege of speaking with a teller. That fee was not designed to generate vast quantities of income for the bank, but to direct business to automated teller machines, which have a lower cost per transaction than do flesh-and-blood tellers. Fees, though, are fast becoming vital sources of revenue for banks.

Transaction fees are small amounts charged for items that require processing by the bank. These transactions include checking account debits (processing checks that you write) and credits (deposits that you make), wire transfers into and out of your account, issuance of cashier's or certified checks, purchase of blank checks, and so on. Businesses that accept credit card payments from their own customers know that banks charge fees for processing credit payments. These fees range from less than 1 to 5 percent of the purchase. The higher the volume of credit card deposits, the lower the fee usually charged by the bank. Individually, these fees seem quite small and insignificant. Cumulatively, though, there is no doubt about the value of fees to banks.

Let us assume that a small-town bank has 10,000 customers who write an average of 10 checks every month. The bank charges fifteen cents per check written. That means that the bank earns $15,000 every month just to process checks. Imagine what that fee income is for larger, national banks with hundreds of thousands of customers; it quickly becomes very significant.

The largest source of fee income for banks is commitment fees. These fees are usually a flat percentage of a loan amount. Homeowners will recognize these fees by another name: points. When a person obtains a home loan, the lender will charge 0 to 2 percent of the principal amount. Because there are no direct offsetting costs, the fee income drops directly to the bank's bottom line. Similarly, commercial loans are usually accompanied by commitment fees ranging up to 2 percent. Because of the effect fee income has on a bank's profits, they have received increased focus from bank managers.

Another source of fee income—albeit invisible to customers—is generated by the sale of loans. The sale of an individual loan or a group of loans is common practice among banks. There are always other banks, individual investors, or institutional investors who have a surplus of cash to invest or cash underinvested as far as rate of return. They can purchase loans from banks and put their cash to work earning higher rates of return. Those buyers are even willing to pay more than the face amount of the loan sometimes. For example, the bank makes a $100,000 home loan to you and sets the interest rate at 9 percent. An investor who has his or her money invested in a United States Treasury note at 4.5 percent might be willing to pay $110,000 to the bank for your loan. For simplicity sake, let's assume that you pay only interest on your loan. At 9 percent, that's $9,000 per year. It doesn't matter what an investor paid to buy your loan; you still pay 9 percent of $100,000.

That $9,000 earned on the investor's $110,000 is equivalent to 8.2 percent to him or her. That is a whopping improvement over the 4.5 percent the previous investment had earned, and that is why investors are hungry to buy loans from banks. The $10,000 premium earned by the bank on the sale of your loan is treated as fee income—it goes straight to profits.

Contrary to popular opinion, banks do not make money by foreclosing on businesses and homes and auctioning off those assets. Interest income and fee income are the two ways banks bring money in. Now, let's see how banks spend money.

BANK EXPENSES

The most significant expense for a bank is similar to any other business's—cost of goods sold. Although the cost of goods sold for other businesses can be composed of many items, including purchases, direct labor, and commissions, the bank's version of cost of goods sold is limited strictly to interest expense. The bank purchases money from depositors; the cost of those purchases is measured in interest expense.

The difference between a bank's total interest income and interest expense is called its net interest margin and is equivalent to a nonbank company's net profit margin. The percent of net interest margin to interest income is a key performance gauge in the banking industry. Just ten years ago, the top performing banks posted net interest margins of 4 percent and higher. Today, banks with net interest margins at 3.5 percent are high flyers. The reduction is the result of competition from other banks, particularly the major banks that have expanded into new markets. To put this into perspective, let us look at a single loan. If a bank has deposits on which it pays an average interest rate of 5 percent, it must price the loan at 9 percent to hit a net interest margin of 4 percent, or 8.5 percent to achieve a net interest margin of 3.5 percent.

Minor fluctuations in a bank's net interest margin can have a huge impact on its net profit. A one-tenth of 1 percent change is equal to $10,000 per $1 million of interest income. Now, you understand why bankers get so wound up about squeezing as high an interest rate as possible out of you!

Banks have other expenses, too. Salaries, utilities, benefits, advertising, and so on, just like any other business. There are government-mandated expenses like Federal Deposit Insurance Corporation (FDIC) fees and the costs of paying for government agents to visit the bank for periodic audits. Another fee that is important in understanding banks is the allowance for loan loss. Loans go bad and sometimes cannot be collected either from the borrower or via liquidation of the underlying collateral. It is just part of the banking business. In order to smooth out loan losses, banks accrue a noncash expense called allowance for loan losses. This accumulates into a balance sheet account, just like other companies accumulate an allowance for bad debts to counter any accounts receivable which may become uncollectible.

Banks typically expense an amount equal to 1½ to 2 percent of their loan portfolios annually. Historically, this is enough to cover any loans that will go bad in the normal course of business. Once in a while, a surprise loss will require a bank to charge the loan loss directly to profits. The importance of this detail to borrowers will become more relevant when issues like selecting a bank and negotiating with a bank are discussed later in the book.

Income minus expense equals profit. The higher the profit, the better the bank—at least in the eyes of the investing public. Bank customers, though, must never lose sight of the importance of the major components of a bank's income statement, including interest income and loan loss allowance. A bank's success or lack of success in managing any of those components has a direct impact on individual loan customers. If the market forces an overall reduction in interest rates charged on loans, banks will try to maximize rates on individual cases to make up for lower rates charged to other clients. Heavy loan losses can make a bank very conservative in its credit standards; that is, it might be darn tough to get a loan approved at a bank that just charged off a huge loan. Conversely, a bank with few loan losses might be more willing to accept risk and approve loans other banks would not touch.

BANK BALANCE SHEETS

Balances sheets are simply a listing of assets that a company owns and liabilities that it owes. The difference between the two is the equity in the company. Banks have fairly short balance sheets. Assets are composed of cash, investments, loans, buildings, and equipment. Liabilities are composed largely of deposits and short-term loans from money market lenders (for example, the Federal Reserve Bank). Two things should jump right off the page at you. Loans are assets and deposits are liabilities. Isn't that the opposite of what we all learned in Accounting 101? It is confusing. Even bankers have difficulty remembering the mirror-nature of their own balance sheets.

Deposits are easiest to explain. When a customer walks into a bank and deposits $100,000 that customer is making a loan to the bank. The interest rate and the conditions under which the money will be returned to the depositor are the terms of the loan. A depositor's savings account, checking account, or certificate of deposit are assets for the depositor. Thus, it stands to reason that they must be liabilities for someone else: the bank. The bank offsets the liability created by the deposit by increasing the cash account on its asset side of the ledger.

Loans, on the other hand, are a bank's primary assets. The bank takes cash from its own vault and loans it to you. Its cash assets are reduced but offset by an increase in the loan account. Loans are not assets like equipment or buildings. Since they are financial assets, they exist solely as accounting records. All the documents a person signs at a loan closing simply represent or govern the loan. The actual loan is intangible, and all physical evidence of it evaporates once the borrower spends the money.

On a bank balance sheet, loan assets might be lumped all together in one line, or they might be broken down into types of loans: residential, commercial, agricultural, consumer, and credit cards. Those subcategories might be broken down into smaller categories based on length to maturity, geographic location, fixed or floating rate, or any other identifiable characteristic. It is a good place to peruse to find out what kind of business a particular bank likes to transact.

The last section of any balance sheet is the equity or capital section. One of the major measurements used to grade a bank's performance is return on equity (ROE). ROE is calculated by dividing net profit by equity. Fifteen to 20 percent is considered average to above average. Any bank president who posts a lower return than that might consider freshening up his or her resume. A bank's equity position can offer strong clues to a potential borrower. A higher-than-average equity position might signal the bank's need to make more loans and, therefore, lower its credit standards until the right amount of capital is deployed in loans.

Later, in Chapter 7, we will learn how to use a bank's financial statements to target banks for loan applications.

Types of Banks

The financial community has divided banks into several classes: money center banks, national banks, super-regional banks, regional banks, and community banks. Following is a quick overview of those categories.

MONEY CENTER BANKS

These are the largest of all banks and usually have a global presence. The term *money center* comes from the fact that these types of banks are usually headquartered in the world's money centers. Historically, those places were New York City, London, Frankfurt, Hong Kong, and Tokyo. It is difficult to comprehend the scope of their activities. When news of impending foreign currency crisis or collapsing third-world markets sends the stocks of American banks down, it is these banks that will bear any brunt of those disasters. Money center banks lend money to countries like Russia, Argentina, and China. They lend money to General Motors, Volkswagen, and Honda. They also lend money to the local donut store through small business banking units.

Because the banks are located amid the densest concentrations of people and corporations in the world and because foreign governments and just the top 100 companies in the world are their target customers, they have no need to develop vast networks of branches in the hinterland of America. The economies of scale that are levered by key locations and huge customers guide their business philosophy. Why seek out 1,000 customers to whom to lend $100 million when it can all be lent to just one company? It is much less expensive to keep track of one client than 10, 100, or 1,000 customers. Money center banks do not typically have branch offices anyplace but in major metropolitan areas.

NATIONAL AND SUPER-REGIONAL BANKS

In America, we do not yet have a truly national bank, that is, a bank with offices blanketing every state. With every merger, banks move closer to that goal. Super-regional banks are banks that do business in one or more of our well defined regions: Northeast, Southeast, South, Midwest, and West. These banks have fully penetrated the specific region and probably have offices and operations scattered outside their primary markets in places like Florida (to take care of their clients who migrate there for winter) or Europe (to take care of customers who transact business there).

In many ways, these are the banks that drive innovation in the industry. Since their customers include huge, global corporations, mom-and-pop businesses, the wealthiest of the wealthy, and schmucks like me, they have had to create a niche and all-encompassing products. And they have had to create systems with which to deliver those products efficiently. These are also the banks that drive consolidation in the industry. Money center banks are not interested in merging with a bank that might do business in Minnesota, Wisconsin, and Michigan; but a super-regional based in Indiana, Ohio, and Illinois could buy that bank and deploy its successful products and systems immediately in a very similar market. After all, there are not too many corporations in Michigan's Upper Peninsula that could use a $250 million line of credit issued by a New York-based money center bank; there are plenty, though, that could use a super-regional bank's merchant credit card product.

REGIONAL BANKS

Regional banks are smaller institutions than their super-regional brethren. Regional banks might concentrate all of their business in one well-populated area, like Boston or Chicago; or they might cover one entire state or parts of several states. They tend to act a lot more like old-fashioned banks on the local level. Part of the appeal of regional banks is that their area of coverage is usually homogeneous. For someone who lives in a rural area, there is a comfort in doing business with a bank that caters to rural areas elsewhere. Likewise, banks based in the Rustbelt seem to have a competitive advantage with manufacturing companies.

Regional banks are stalked prey these days. Because of their size, they are like pieces of a giant puzzle. Larger banks scout out which pieces might fit best into those already assembled. Economies of scale and the cost of "keeping up with the Joneses" all conspire against this size of bank. Pundits have forecast the demise of this class of banks within the next decade as truly national banks are put together by today's super-regional banks.

COMMUNITY BANKS

Community banks are as much a part of the American landscape as the local post office and church steeples. Just a few years ago, they were an endangered species. No one, the author included, thought that there would be a single community bank left anywhere in America after the merger-wave poured over the country. Thankfully, as big banks have become bigger and other banks have been gobbled up, entrepreneurs have filled the niche with startup banks. New, single office banks are opening at an astounding rate, faster than in any period since the Depression, and are finding great success.

Community banks cannot possibly compete with products and services that are provided by larger multi-state banks. Their edge is in personal service. Every customer is known by name. Every bank officer lives in the same town as the customers. Their kids go to the same schools. Their families fill pews at local churches. The officers and the members of the board of directors are accessible. The president of the community bank where I began my career met with a continuous stream of little old ladies everyday. It was not unusual for him to help one or two to balance their checkbooks or for him to field complaints about "tarty tellers."

Nowhere is the cost–benefit dichotomy more pronounced than at a community bank. Because of the economies of scale enjoyed by the larger banks, they offer products and services that cannot be offered by community banks and at prices that cannot be matched either. The comfort level afforded by the human touch of community banks is something with which large banks cannot compete.

The bank that is everything to everybody does not exist. Every bank has its strengths and weaknesses. Both are by design and determined by the market that the bank's management decides to target. Money center bank strengths include the abilities to handle huge financing needs, complicated transactions, foreign currency exchange, and international trade transactions. Super-regional bank strengths include the ability to finance large deals, facilitate cash and loan transactions for businesses with multiple locations, merchant services, and services to individuals like mortgage and automobile loans. Regional banks can enjoy some overlap with the super-regional bank strengths and community bank strengths especially in areas like small business loans, mortgages, and specialty lending like marine or agricultural finance. Community bank strengths are largely in personal relationships with their customers.

There may never be a perfect fit between bank and customer, but there certainly is a "best fit." As customer or consumer, it is up to you to decide.

Bank Mergers

With nearly two decades' experience in the banking industry, I have more than once woken in the morning and learned from my local public radio news report that my employer had acquired another bank or been acquired. As you might guess, the former is easier on the stomach than the latter. For consumers, though, the news can even be more anguishing. One bank in the town where I live has been acquired three times in the last three years. It started out as a community bank that was acquired by a larger, multiple-office bank in our area. Then that bank was bought by a statewide regional bank that was in turn bought by a super-regional bank based in the Midwest. I know several of its clients who are still using up checks from the community bank's existence!

Major mergers have become a part of our daily news. The primary reason for the activity is economy of scale. The largest, more successful banks can afford to push technology, products, and services by investing incredible sums of money. Other banks must spend equal sums of money to remain competitive. A great example is the Y2K problem that plagued everyone in the late 1990s. Some banks simply could not afford to invest the cash to fix their systems. Their only solution was to merge with another bank that could afford to prepare for Y2K.

Banks agree to be acquired because the cost of competing in their market will adversely affect their bottom lines. Acquiring banks buy others in order to spread those costs over a larger market base. This is manifested in one of two ways. The first way is for a bank to buy a bank with a different geographic presence. The new bank can then use the acquired bank's delivery channels (branches) to move its successful products and services to a new customer base. The second way is for two banks in the same geographic location to merge. The acquiring bank can close duplicative branches, eliminate the backroom (accounting, human resources, operations, and so on) departments at the acquired bank. The surviving bank effectively gains a huge increase in the number of customers and lowers its overall cost per customer significantly. To illustrate the theory behind this merger activity, imagine that there are two grocery stores located at opposing corners in your town. The larger of the two stores acquires the other store. It closes that store down and eliminates all the overhead and employee expenses associated with it; yet, the closed store's customers all cross the street to shop at the surviving store. Sales might double, but expenses barely rise at all.

Mergers will continue to occur until no possible economy-of-scale benefit remains in the economy. Experts now predict that we will end up with a couple of dozen very large banks and thousands of community banks (many of which will open to fill that personal service niche vacated by merged bank offices).

Bank on It

+ Banks are not branches of the government.
+ Banks are not nonprofit charities.
+ Banks earn income by charging rent to borrowers for the use of money.
+ Every bank has particular strengths and weaknesses.
+ No bank tries to be everything to everybody.
+ Bank mergers are driven by the desire for economies of scale.

How Banks
Approve Loans

Banks use different methods to review loan applications. An applicant that is ill prepared to tangle with a specific approval method might as well use the loan application for birdcage lining. Failure to understand how the target bank approves loans and to tailor an application or presentation for that particular process greatly increases the odds that the loan request will be declined. This chapter outlines the four basic methods used by banks today and points out the advantages and disadvantages for applicants of each method.

To illustrate the importance of understanding with what process you will deal, here is a story told to me by a peer at another major bank. A customer recently visited a rural branch of his bank in the backwoods of Michigan and applied for a $250,000 commercial real estate mortgage loan. The loan proceeds were to be used to purchase a party store. Now, party stores do very well in lonely outposts of Michigan, and this was no exception. The simple two-page application, which had been given to the customer to complete, reported a good track record of earnings which, for the last half-dozen years, were ample enough to more than cover the proposed debt service. The branch manager gleefully thanked the customer for the opportunity to consider the loan application and told the customer that he would have an answer within forty-eight hours.

The customer left the branch with confident thoughts of soon running his very own party store! Little did he know that no sooner had he climbed into his pickup truck out in the bank's parking lot, the branch manager was in the backroom of the branch, hunched over a fax machine, electronically sending the application 425 miles away to a credit-scoring facility. All the bank's applications for business loans of $300,000 or less automatically go to this same facility. As the fax printed out in the credit-scoring office, it was pulled off the machine and handed in random fashion to an anonymous analyst for scoring.

The analyst tallied up the business's cash flow, the applicant's credit history, liked what he saw, and issued an approval. Eureka! Within hours, an approval was faxed back to the branch manager who, in turn, telephoned the customer with the good news. There were conditions, of course, just like any other loan: an appraisal of the real estate, survey, copies of this and that, and insurance coverages. The customer leaped into action and placed orders for everything required by the bank. He spent nearly $4,000 of which $1,200 was for the appraisal.

The appraisal was completed and mailed to the credit-scoring department for review. That's when the dream of small business ownership came crashing down on our customer. The appraised value of the store building and real estate was just $85,000. The bank's approval required a loan-to-appraised value ratio of 75 percent or less. This meant that the building had to appraise at least at a value of $334,000. The credit-scoring analyst called the branch manager with the bad news. The branch manager's response was along the line of, "Duh!" You see, the branch manager, who drove past the party store every day, could have told the credit-scoring folks that the building was no more than a simple Quonset hut and that land in that part of Michigan can be purchased for a few hundred bucks per acre. Unfortunately, since the purchase price of the business was $350,000, the credit scorer had assumed that the hard assets would provide the necessary collateral.

The customer was out several weeks of valuable time and $4,000 and still was no closer to getting the loan he needed. In credit scoring, subjective information, pro or con, can be missed entirely by omission of the applicant or banker. As we will see later, credit scoring does have its benefits. The fault in the example lies in poor communication between customer and banker, which can be a disadvantage in credit scoring. Had the applicant known that his loan application would be decided nearly 500 miles away by people who did not know him or his business, he could have provided more detail in the application or sought out a bank with a different approval process.

Loan Policies

Every bank has a written loan policy that governs all aspects of its lending business, including what types of loans the bank wishes to pursue, those it wishes to avoid, its underwriting and credit criteria, and its methods of loan approval. Bank employees must adhere strictly to the policy or face dismissal. A copy of a bank's loan policy manual would be an excellent source of information for business owners who plan to apply for a loan at a particular bank. It would provide a blueprint of the approval process and allow the business owner to design a proposal that complements the bank's process. Unfortunately, banks do not share their proprietary loan policy manuals since other banks could use it to emulate successful banks or to develop predatory business practices aimed at the competitor's weaknesses.

Applicants, though, are entitled to ask questions of the bank representatives, whose answers will provide a rudimentary outline of the bank's loan policy. The most important question is the subject of this section: How do loans get approved at your bank?

There are four ways loan applications are approved or denied today: credit scoring, individual loan officer authority, lines of business loan authority, and loan committees. None of the processes is foolproof or without disadvantage. The advantages and disadvantages of each will be pointed out.

Credit Scoring

Credit scoring was unheard of five years ago. Today, it has become one of the dominant methods that banks employ to consider commercial loan applications. Borrowers are more likely to find this system in larger banks with multistate operations. The philosophy, which drives big banks today, is to identify its best clients, provide those clients with a host of products, and give tremendous service to those companies in order to retain them as clients. "Best clients" are those that require large loans, letters of credit, payroll services, retirement plan management, and cash management services. These types of clients typically transact much of their business electronically, which saves their banks considerable overhead expense. That eliminates nearly all non-Fortune 2000 companies from best-client status. Big banks cannot justify allotting the same manpower per account to small businesses as they do on large accounts. It takes just as much time to service a giant customer as it does a small mom-and-pop business. While one large customer may pay a bank $1 million per year in interest and fees, it is hard to justify dedicating the bank's capacity to serve a local gas station that might pay just $20,000 in interest and fees to the bank. So, banks that have achieved a certain size are more profitable when they focus on the larger sources of income. Fortunately, the federal government requires banks to meet the credit needs of the entire community in which it has a presence. That means large banks must provide, at a minimum, some cursory method to meet the needs of small businesses, too. Credit scoring is that method.

Credit scoring is an automated system of accepting loan requests. Banks design proprietary software or purchase canned programs with underwriting standards embedded in the code with which to screen loan requests. The software programs use only objective measures like debt-to-worth, cash flow, and collateral coverage ratios, and credit ratings supplied by popular rating services like TRW, Dun & Bradstreet, or local credit bureaus. Because of the reliance on hard numbers, loans for the purpose of starting new businesses rarely qualify under a credit-scoring system. Likewise, one bad year of financial results—no matter the reason—may kill applications. There are no such things as leg loans or accommodation loans in credit scoring. Since the loan application is "scored" in a far-away location, no benefit of local knowledge, like in the preceding example, can be used to the applicant's advantage.

The basis of the credit-scoring system is normally a one-page application, which the business owner must complete. A 3-inch thick business plan is worthless because it will not be used in the scoring process or even perused by any bank representative. Letters of recommendation from customers, other banks, and past creditors are likewise worthless. In fact, the application will probably be taken by personnel from the bank's retail division—the same people who make car loans, resolve checking account problems for little old ladies, and sell certificates of deposit. The person with whom the business owner meets will probably be located in a branch office, far from the commercial lending nerve center. The banker will fax the application to the credit-scoring center or keystroke it into a computer terminal. Presto! Within minutes or hours, the computer will spew out an approval or denial. Most banks will not allow second looks at denied applications as a precaution against "fixing" applications to circumvent the elaborate software program.

The five multi-state banks that have offices in my community credit score all loan requests under certain sizes. One bank credit scores all requests of $100,000 or less; three credit score all requests of $250,000; and the fifth bank credit scores all requests of $500,000 or less. Some national banks are now scoring loans up to $1 million! The majority of accounts with which I have worked over the years fall into the under $250,000 range. Indeed, $250,000 is sufficient to open and operate most of the top franchises now available to investors.

Credit scoring is an efficient way for banks to deal with a high volume of applications. It allows the bank to spread its manpower over a wider base of customers, which goes a long way to keeping costs lower for small business customers. When my bank converted to a credit-scoring system for its smaller business customers and applicants, I was skeptical. My whole banking career revolved around spending hour upon hour with each of my clients annually. I simply could not see how the system would be a benefit to my clients and me. After a few months, though, I became a confirmed fan of credit scoring. Frankly, the vast majority of small businesses stand to benefit from credit scoring because of the minimal paperwork involved and fast turn-around time for decisions. The reduction of paperwork both in the application and backroom processes allows the loan officer to spend more quality time to meet the needs of the customer. Startup companies and businesses that are experiencing financial difficulty, though, will find it a difficult process because of the inability to satisfy the objective measures required to get an approval.

To its credit, Wells Fargo Bank uses credit scoring in an innovative way. The bank, over the last several years, has hired dozens of sales-people, given them laptop computers, and sent them out to call on businesses across the United States. The newly minted bankers usually do not have banking backgrounds, but do have sales experience from other walks of life. Their duty is to go door to door in their markets and ask business owners if Wells Fargo could provide a competitive proposal for the business's banking requirements. The banker inputs financial information into the laptop and sends the data to Wells Fargo's headquarters via modem; within minutes, a proposal is electronically sent back to the laptop, on site, in the business owner's office. The business owner can take it or leave. Obviously, the number of times that Wells Fargo lands a new client is dependent upon the total number of doors on which its salespeople knock. This use of credit scoring can only help businesses that already have loans in place, but may be able to acquire them at lower costs through Wells Fargo.

The key to success in the credit-scoring system is to know the parameters of sound credit-granting criteria (Chapter 5). If the business does not look good on paper, it will likely have difficulty flowing through the credit-scoring system.

Lines of Business Loan Approval Systems

Lines of business loan approval systems are also growing in stature among larger banks. This method eliminates overhead by shifting management of specific bank products—like commercial loans—to one corporate-wide management chart. Rather than have local managers for each department, larger banks have eliminated levels of local management in favor of regional and national managers who operate across state lines, in their area of expertise. This means that an applicant may meet with a bank officer who must pass the request onto a manager outside the community or state.

The lines of business method offers two distinct benefits to loan applicants. First, the applicant's request can be turned around immediately. The loan officer does not have to wait for a loan committee date; he or she can simply call the appropriate underwriter—be it his or her boss, department head, or a credit staffer—and pitch the applicant's proposal for approval. The second benefit is that only bankers with strong experience in commercial lending are placed in underwriting positions, and they are the people who will consider the application.

These experienced decision makers can see past minor flaws in an application, can offer very productive advice, and can consider subjective information in support of the request.

The negative aspect of the lines of business method is that local conditions and experiences do not impact loan decisions. An underwriter located in another state or locality will not be familiar with the applicant, the applicant's history, local market conditions, and other pertinent information that may otherwise aid an application. Fortunately, supporting information that is often attached to applications can be forwarded to the decision maker for consideration.

The key to a successful loan application in the lines of business method is to work with a good loan officer. The applicant must find someone who is willing to go to bat for the small business and advocate the request. A loan officer who merely passes the request along without a modicum of enthusiasm does the applicant no favors.

Individual Loan Officer Authority

Believe it or not, it is difficult for the most hardened loan officer to turn down a loan request. Imagine yourself sitting before an earnest applicant with the task at hand to pop the customer's bubble. I know many loan officers who always turn loans down by stating, "I really like your loan request and would love to help you out, but the loan committee (or my boss) turned it down. I'm terribly sorry." Most applicants do not realize that their loan officer does have some level of authority to approve loan applications. They accept the lender's comments and walk out of his or her office and into oblivion never the wiser.

Always ask the person with whom you meet—right up front—what amount of loan authority they have been granted by the bank. Bankers have precious little to brag about today. They do not earn much money. Banker's hours were eliminated in the early 1980s. Most even have to pay the same ATM fees regular customers now pay. Believe me, it would be a very unusual banker who would not gladly expound upon his or her own loan authority with great pride.

Most banks, large and small, still employ some level of individual loan officer lending authority. This method simply means that the banker with whom you meet can approve loans up to a certain dollar amount with no further bureaucratic messing around. Larger banks will invest larger loan authority levels in its loan officers. Smaller banks may give loan officers just enough authority to approve overdrafts or car loans. More experienced lenders will have larger loan authorities than younger lenders. Traditionally, newer lenders "cut their teeth" on walk-in or non-solicited loan requests as part of their training. These rookies may have little or no loan authority until they have proven their ability to make sound credit judgments. Banks that pay commissions or incentive compensation to loan officers for loan production may not give lenders any authority at all to prevent the loan officers from "writing their own paychecks" by granting weak loans. It is key for an applicant to find out what size loan his or her banker may approve under individual authority. My preference, if I were a business owner, would be to deal only with a banker who could sign off on my entire loan requirement.

Individual loan authority gives the applicant the ability to meet face-to-face with the decision maker. The applicant's subjective attributes will play an important role in the decision. The applicant's enthusiasm, experience, references, and persistence can make a difference. Human nature plays an incredibly important role in this type of system. I am the first to admit that I have made many loans over the years that I should not have approved because I simply could not say no to the applicant or because of the squeaky-wheel persistence of an applicant.

The applicant must somehow endear himself or herself to the loan officer. A Dale Carnegie course would be beneficial to any "personality-challenged" business owner prior to visiting banks. The loan officer must be made to feel part of the business's team. Applicants who emphasize some personal connection to the loan officer will, at a minimum, find a loan officer who is willing to go to some extra length to help out. Those personal connections may be a shared interest in Civil War battle reenactment, shirttail relatives, mutual friends, common church membership, children's schools, and so on.

Many owners of successful, growing businesses may also outgrow their loan officer's loan authority. These business owners should try to include their original loan officer in any future meetings with bank representatives since that banker is most familiar with the business and probably already knows the answers to questions that will inevitably pop up. The original banker can play the role of internal advocate for the business. Over the long run, though, business owners will be much better off by insisting that their loan requests be taken in face-to-face meetings with bank officers who have the authority to approve the requested loan amount. Should that not be possible, the applicant is still in better shape than in any other form of loan approval since his or her loan officer will probably be required to present the application, personally, to the proper approval authority. More than likely, that keeps the application in local hands, and the presenting loan officer still has firsthand knowledge of the applicant business and its principals.

Loan Committees

Loan committees were once ubiquitous in the banking industry. In general, all loan requests (in this type of system) over the amount of the individual loan officer's loan authority must be approved by a committee composed of bank officials. Most banks employ a tiered committee system with three distinct committees. All loans must be approved by the loan officer's committee, which is composed of the bank's commercial loan officers and the commercial loan manager. Loans of certain size that are approved by the loan officer's committee must then go to a senior or executive loan committee, which is composed of the bank's executive officers. Finally, applications for the largest loans, which have been approved by the prior two committees, must be reviewed by a directors' loan committee, which is composed of members of the bank's board of directors.

The loan size cutoffs for each loan committee are determined by several factors, including a bank's average loan size, its legal lending limit (how much it can legally lend to any one borrower), and the size of the bank's loan loss reserve. The authority of each committee is stipulated in the bank's loan policy manual.

Several obvious complications for borrowers are inherent in the committee system of loan approval. Committee meetings are usually scheduled one year in advance. If a customer's request misses the cutoff time for a specific meeting, it may have to wait one, two, three, or four weeks for the next committee date. Director's loan committees are normally held no more often than once a month and on rare occasions only quarterly. Delays caused by the committee system can cause problems and lost opportunities for businesses. For example, if an applicant needs loan approval in order to execute a purchase agreement on a prime piece of real estate or to accept an order from a large customer, the opportunities could be lost without quick action by the applicant's bank.

Another problem is office politics. Over the years, I have witnessed the warped personalities of more than a few loan officers wreak revenge on other loan officers by voting down presented loan requests. The biblical verse that begins, "An eye for an eye, a tooth for a tooth" has a home in loan committee meeting rooms. Some committee members may wish to slow down a particular loan officer's success rate as a way to make sure that incentive compensation of one officer does not dwarf that of other officers. Naturally, there will be members of the committee who are not familiar with an applicant, who do not like the applicant's type of business, who have one of the applicant's competitors as a client, or who have suffered a loan loss to a similar business. These members will not be supportive of specific applications or businesses. Such is the realm of the loan officer's committee.

Executive or senior loan committees are most effective. Loan applications that arrive in this committee have had the bugs worked out in the lower committee. At least one person on this committee is probably familiar with the applicant in the capacity of the loan officer's supervisor and will champion the loan request in committee. Normally, several members of the committee will represent other areas of the bank, like consumer loan, real estate mortgage, and trust departments. Because of their limited experience in commercial loans, they tend to quietly vote with the bank president or senior lender. The movers and shakers on the committee know their lending and go about it with surgical precision. Unfortunately, most executive committees are not composed of local bankers anymore. They are composed of state or regional personnel who, again, will not weigh subjective information very heavily in their votes.

Directors' loan committee used to remind me of the familiar skit from *The Muppet Show* where the two old codgers sat in a theater balcony making sarcastic remarks. Bank directors are generally successful businesspeople or community leaders. The chance that any one member has experience in the same industry as the applicant's is fairly slim. Conversation in the committee room during directors' meetings usually revolves around such diverse topics as with whom the customer is sleeping, who knows the applicant's neighbors, where the customer was last seen drinking in public, and other sordid details. Fortunately, this is a problem only with banks in smaller communities. Larger, multi-state banks are likely to use directors' loan committees only for huge loan packages. Then, the committee will be composed of CEOs of Fortune 500 companies. These executives exercise a much more discernible level of knowledge and professionalism. Most fortunately of all, the committee system is fast falling to the wayside as banks restructure for cost and customer service effectiveness.

In order to properly prepare for a loan request to a loan committee, the business owner should be sure to pare all fat from his or her application material. Do not prevaricate, and eliminate anything that could be construed as such. Rosy projections will not fly in loan committees. Too many eyes have seen too many real-life situations, and those same eyes will see through the smoke screen of poorly thought out projections. The business owner should bear in mind, too, that directors on the directors' loan committee likely transact business with many of the same companies as does the applicant. Any falsehood or nonfactual information is more than likely to be uncovered. Skeletons in the closet have a habit of finding their way to the light of day in the committee room, too. Applicants should mend any bridges that need mending and check all facts that need to be checked prior to releasing information to the bank and its committees.

Loan committees do present an opportunity for a borrower to tailor his or her application to appeal to more than one voting member of the committee. This is particularly true in small communities where the applicant probably knows several of the members. The application should be designed to appeal to the "leg loan" weaknesses of as many voters as possible. For example, if a farmer sits on the director's loan committee, the applicant should include information on agricultural customers or suppliers or the importance of that industry to his or her business. An example of the reverse is eliminating blame for losses on increasing medical costs if a doctor or hospital executive sits on the committee. This tailoring can be done for all levels of a bank's committee system if the applicant has knowledge of the likes and dislikes of the voting members. A good loan officer can provide direction on the "hot buttons" of each committee, but it is the business owner's job to ask the question of the loan officer.

Conclusion

The method or combination of methods that a bank uses to approve loans is critical to loan applicants. Prior to writing a loan proposal or submitting an application, it is crucial for the business owner to discover how each bank in his or her community approves loans. This information will help the business owner to tailor the loan application, prioritize the list of banks that will receive the application, and manage the application through the approval process. The business owner's first choice of banks should be those that invest considerable loan authority in individual loan officers located in the same community as the business. The next most favorable banks are the ones that use the lines of business loan approval method. While it is difficult to label banks that use loan committees as "more favorable" than any other, they are preferable to banks that will require an applicant to submit to credit scoring.

Applicants who take their chances by applying for a loan without the knowledge of how the particular bank approves the loan have the same odds of success as does someone trying to beat the house in Las Vegas. The unprepared or uninformed applicant will have little chance of obtaining loan approval via credit scoring. If an applicant assumes that someone other than the banker with whom he or she meets must approve the loan, the applicant will miss a great opportunity to use human relations skills to gain favor of the loan officer if he or she does, indeed, have the authority to approve the subject loan. If the applicant assumes that the loan officer has adequate authority to approve the request and leaves it on the lender's desk, it may die a quick death when the loan officer runs it up his or her boss's flagpole. Under no circumstances should an applicant accept the following replies from a loan officer:

"My boss turned it down. Sorry."

"Our loan policy won't let me make this loan. Sorry."

"Committee didn't like it. Sorry."

In each case, the applicant should request evidence of the denial and a meeting with the loan officer's supervisor. Don't accept the first or second no without explanation or verification.

Bank on It

+ Always find out how a particular bank approves loans before you make an application.
+ Try to present your request to an individual who has the authority to approve the loan.
+ If your business has been in existence for more than two years and earnings have been stable or growing, credit-scoring systems can save you a lot of time.
+ If the loan officer with whom you meet does not have the authority to approve the loan, he or she will be your advocate inside the bank; leave him or her enthusiastic about your business and plan.
+ Avoid loan committees. If you cannot, solicit your loan officer's help to tailor the presentation for the eyes of the powerbrokers on the committee.

Types
of Loans

The easiest way to signal a banker that you are clueless about finance (and, therefore, incapable of managing a business) is to march into a bank office and request the wrong type of loan. This is a subject area where the adage "just enough knowledge to be dangerous" applies to the loan application process. This chapter explains the different types of loans and the proper uses of each.

The principle to which bankers adhere in establishing loan terms or amortizations is to match the repayment period of a loan to the useful life of the asset that is acquired by the loan proceeds or the asset that secures the loan. This theme is evident throughout the following discussion.

Short-Term Loans

Short-term loans are loans of one year or less in duration. The underlying assets associated with these loans are typically current assets like cash, accounts receivable, and inventory. Lines of credit, construction loans, floor plans, and regular loans with durations of twelve months or less fall into this category.

Until the 1970s, most short-term loans were structured as thirty-, sixty-, or ninety-day loans that required all principal and interest to be paid at maturity. Nearly every industry had cyclical periods every year when sales peaked. If a company planned ahead, it might borrow money for a brief period in order to increase inventory in anticipation of the annual spike in sales. Conversely, a company might need to borrow money shortly after the peak in sales because all its working capital was invested in accounts receivable. The first company would repay the loan with cash proceeds from sales and the second company would repay the loan from collections of accounts receivable.

Businesses experienced profound fundamental changes during the 1980s as computers, unabashed consumerism, and access to worldwide markets supercharged our economy. Companies no longer experienced annual peak periods of sales activity. Sales either were maintained at a higher baseline or continued to climb to new heights. Banks found that they were renewing thirty-day notes over and over again. The processing of a loan costs banks a lot of money, and renewals of existing loans are not any less expensive than originating a new loan. It did not take them long to find a more efficient way of providing for the short-term loan needs of their clients: lines of credit.

LINES OF CREDIT

If you have a credit card, then you already grasp how a line of credit operates. A bank will establish a line of credit limit—the maximum amount a customer may borrow—and allow the customer to borrow or repay money at will. The line amount is determined in a delicate balance between the client's financial strength, actual need or usage of the line, and collateral. Bankers joke among themselves about their customers who harbor "line envy." Those customers ask for increases in their firm's line of credit limit at every opportunity in the belief that the bigger the line the more important the company. My eyes have rolled back into my head many times when a customer said to me, "I was talking to Sam at the golf course the other night. He says his line of credit is $100,000 bigger than mine. I want another $200,000 on my line."

Certainly, the financial strength of a company plays the most pivotal role in determining the size of a line of credit. Business owners have the right to be proud of the financial success of their companies. Factors other than the financial might of a company, though, limit the line of credit amount a bank will commit to any company.

Banks have costs directly associated with the amount of loans committed, whether the available dollars are used or not by customers. It behooves banks to keep lines of credit at the lowest possible level that meets the customer's needs in order to minimize those expenses. If a customer is adamant about maintaining a line of credit level well above what is required to manage his or her business, the bank is likely to impose a facility fee on the unused portion of the line. This fee either offsets partially or entirely a bank's actual cost of reserving the specified loan amount for the customer. The bank would make more money if the line of credit is used—any facility fee is collected solely to help the bank break even on the cost of providing the line of credit.

Consumers may use credit cards as evergreen five-year loans, but commercial lines of credit are designed specifically for short-term uses. An advance from a line of credit can fund working capital requirements like payroll, accounts payable, and inventory purchases. Banks expect that once cash sales or accounts receivable are collected, the line of credit will be reduced on a pro rata basis. Understandably, a customer may have a steady balance outstanding on its line of credit as borrowings are paid back and reborrowed constantly as cash cycles through the business. In order to assess the continuing creditworthiness of a customer or to enforce proper usage of the line, lines of credit are set to expire annually or are on a demand basis.

Lines of credit are reviewed annually by the bank to consider any changes in the customer's financial status during the past year. If actual usage is different than originally believed, the line of credit can be decreased, increased, or canceled at this time. Other terms can be changed, too, like the need for more or less collateral or interest rates. The annual maturity date allows the bank to escape from customers, terms, or conditions without messy lawsuits or negotiations. Fortunately for business owners, the current trend is toward lines of credit that are due on demand. Any loan that is due on demand can be called in by the lender at any point in time, and the borrower would be forced to repay any outstanding principal balance. In reality, banks are shy to the extreme about enforcing the due-on-demand feature unless a customer is on the verge of bankruptcy. The advantages to businesses of the due-on-demand structure are reduced paperwork and lower costs of borrowing. Because the bank does not have to redocument the loan, the bank can pass the savings on to customers in lower interest rates and fees. A borrower should not be frightened off by demand language since its purpose is bank expense reduction and not to take advantage of borrowers.

Basic lines of credit are intended to help businesses sustain a consistent cash cycle. As cash cycles through the checking account to inventory to accounts receivable, a line of credit smoothes out bottlenecks and affords a business regular cash inflow and outflow in its day-to-day operations.

FLOOR PLAN LINES OF CREDIT

Floor plan is a term that applies to a line of credit that is used to purchase specific inventory items. Advances on the line of credit are paid back by the proceeds of the sale of the specific item. The classic example is a floor plan line of credit for an automobile dealer. A bank establishes a line of credit for the dealer. The dealer borrows an amount equal to the wholesale cost of a vehicle or several vehicles. The bank puts its name on the vehicle title(s) to indicate that the vehicle is collateral for a loan at the bank. The vehicles are sold at a retail price, and the dealer remits the wholesale price to the bank to pay off the underlying advance on each specific car and the bank releases its lien on the vehicle. The amount above the payoff balance is the dealer's gross profit on the sale.

Floor plans have a built-in safety valve called curtailment. Assume that our car dealer bought a lime green hatchback for the sales lot. The thing does not sell because taupe, not lime green, is the color of the moment. After a period predetermined by the bank, it will begin to require monthly payments of principal on the money borrowed to put that specific vehicle in the showroom. The payment, or curtailment, is usually a standard percentage based on the type of inventory being financed. Vehicle floor plans might require a monthly reduction of debt equal to 12 percent of principal. Any car that cannot be sold in one year, before the new models arrive at the lot, probably cannot be sold at a profitable price. This practice precludes stale or obsolete inventory from the bank's collateral assets and shifts the burden of poor inventory management to the business owner.

Appliance stores, boat and recreational vehicle dealers, and large-ticket furniture stores are likely to use floor plan lines of credit. The ability to specifically identify each piece of inventory is the key to qualifying for a floor plan line. Anything that is labeled with a serial number, vehicle identification number, or other permanent, unique mark can be floor planned. Larger merchandise is sold from a sales floor—hence the term, floor plan.

CONSTRUCTION LOAN LINES OF CREDIT

Bankers fervently hope that any construction project will be completed in less than one year's time. Construction lending is a very specialized practice. Many banks simply refuse to make construction loans and avoid making loans to construction contractors, in general. There are too many things that can go wrong in construction and cause financial ruin for the bank's client and loan losses for the bank. Except for basic single-family home construction, I have never been involved in a project that did not include my client in actual or threatened adversarial legal action.

Here are ten reasons why bankers avoid construction project financing:

1. Clouds or claims on the title of ownership of the property.
2. Cost overruns and accumulated change orders that force the bank to lend more money than it intended to do.
3. Environmental problems ranging from spilled cans of paint to hidden underground storage tanks.
4. Subcontractors who do not follow specifications.
5. Property encroachments.
6. Neighbors who are upset at the noise, aesthetics of the new building, or any of a myriad of other minor inconveniences.
7. Acts of God, like a rain shower over a stack of yet-to-be installed drywall.
8. Borrowers who are upset at the contractor, banker, subcontractor, or the like.
9. Zoning and other local officials who like to stand on their soapboxes and show their plumage of power.
10. The time commitment required to manage the project is not commensurate with the financial reward for the bank.

In a perfect world, the bank would lend its customer the entire amount of the project up front and commence the principal amortization. A number of problems make that practice improbable. Borrowers do not like to pay interest on money that they have not used yet. Since a contractor bills a client several times over the course of a contract, the customer really has no use for all the money until the very end of the construction period. By borrowing just enough to cover the contractor's progress payments, the customer minimizes interest expense.

There is also a problem of expertise. Small business owners might be experts in manufacturing or retailing, but clueless in construction practices and law. The customer is at the mercy of the contractor and must accept every word from the contractor as gospel. How many laypeople can actually tell how much of a project has been completed, know the ins and outs of the Americans with Disabilities Act, recite the technical aspects of both national and local building codes, and understand the forces at work in the prices of construction material commodity markets? Simple miscommunication on daily change orders, finish details, and site plans can cause hardships in construction projects.

Then, the fact that anyone with a hammer holster and the ability to sit through a daylong contractor's license program can hang up a shingle further increases the risk of this type of lending. (Most banks have "approved lists" of local contractors with whom the bank has had past, favorable experiences. Bank clients are usually required to use an "approved" contractor.)

In an effort to reduce risk as much as possible, banks have, on staff, specialists to act as a buffer between contractor and client. The money spigot is guarded by the bank, which keeps all parties on their toes. Before any change orders or overruns can be incurred, they must be approved by the bank. Before any advances can be made to the contractor, the bank will make a site inspection to verify that the work has been completed. The inevitable disputes can be mediated by the bank, which can save time and money. There are, literally, daily decisions that must be made and that must involve the approval or input of the banker. It takes a special person to be a construction loan officer . . . and I am not one of them!

Of course, the culmination of a construction line of credit is completion of the construction project. The local building inspector issues a certificate of occupancy, which is the final seal of approval. At this point, the construction line of credit is paid off by a permanent financing source, which is usually provided by the same bank.

Long-Term Loans

Logically, long-term loans are repaid over a period of time greater than one year. The term of the loan is intended to match the useful life of the underlying collateral, usually the asset purchased with the line. For example, car loans range from two to five years in length. New cars can be expected, under normal conditions, to be used for at least five years; consequently, banks provide five-year loans for new car purchases. Used cars generally qualify for loans of shorter durations dependent upon the expected remaining life of the vehicle as measured in mileage and model year.

EQUIPMENT LOANS

Business equipment can run the gamut from a desktop computer to manufacturing machines the size of a city block. Through experience, bankers gain a working knowledge of the useful life of a wide variety of equipment. Some assets, like computers, can be expected to become obsolete in a matter of a few months. Others, like metal stamping equipment, might last twenty or thirty years. Curiously, the advent of computer-operated machinery has reduced the useful life of many types of traditional equipment which are now subject to the vacillations of software development.

The theory is that by the time that the loan is paid off, and no sooner, it is time to replace, update, to euthanize the financed piece of equipment. Customers cannot stand making payments on a computer that they replaced three years ago. Bankers hate collecting those payments because it means they did not do a good job at the loan's front end. (The two reasons why someone would have payments on a retired asset are either that the asset is obsolete or damaged as a result of a disaster for which insurance was insufficient to cover a replacement.)

Loan terms can range from one year for assets like computers to three years for small woodworking equipment to ten years for major industrial equipment. As appetizing as it may be to stretch payments over a longer period of time, borrowers should always strive to retire any debt associated with an asset well before the life expectancy of that asset expires.

REAL ESTATE LOANS

Real estate by its very nature would seem to have an infinite useful life. In America, we have buildings dating back to the 1600s still standing and in livable condition. So, why are there not 100-year mortgage loans available for real estate purchases? For one thing, the term useful life also applies to the borrower's life!

Loans for the purchase of homes can have a maximum term of thirty years for two reasons. First, by the end of the loan, there will be a long list of updates, modernizations, and redecorating projects required to keep the home competitive with other homes in the market. Potential buyers have the choice of many homes in any one marketplace; all things being equal, they will choose the one that is most current in tastes and conveniences. A homeowner who has resided in one residence for thirty years will have to invest a lot of money in the home to keep it up to date. A continuing mortgage payment would hinder the owner's ability to make that investment.

Second, most of us, God willing, will have about forty years of productive, income-earning years prior to retirement. That means we really have time to pay off only one thirty-year mortgage while we have income from employment. Bankers would be stupid to give anyone a fifty-year mortgage with the knowledge up-front that the borrower will not have the necessary income to make the payments for the last ten or twenty years of the loan amortization. (German lenders are experimenting with just such an animal. They expect fifty-year mortgages to be inherited by successive generations of family members in tandem with the family homes.)

Commercial real estate is an entirely different animal than residential real estate. More often than not, it is cheaper to simply build a new building than to reconfigure or update an older building. New manufacturing efficiencies may even prevent an older building from being considered as a viable option by most companies. Even multipurpose buildings like office complexes may become outdated and unusable. The incredible advancements made in computer technologies have allowed builders to create "smart buildings" to enhance security, automation, utilities management, and communication. It is much less expensive to start a new building from the ground up than to retrofit many older buildings. Older buildings that are unusable because of the preceding reasons are termed functionally obsolete.

Buildings can also become locationally obsolete. This has never been more true than the present time. As suburban areas continue to grow farther and farther away from urban cores, older, once successful locations can easily become useless. Hudson's, the major midwest retailer, closed its downtown Detroit flagship store several years ago. Finally, after years of trying to find a suitable buyer, the store was imploded upon itself and the land left vacant for a future use. Like-wise, manufacturers might find customers moving farther away, which increases costs of delivery. Competitors, located closer to the customers, gain price advantages. For example, if Ford closes a Michigan automotive plant and shifts that production to a southern state, midwest-based auto-mobile parts suppliers might find it necessary to move south, too.

Highway planners can render miles of buildings locationally obsolete simply by rerouting a highway or changing a strategic exit ramp. The view from our nation's highways is blighted by hundreds and hundreds of rundown gas stations and fast-food establishments that, due to new interchanges or highway improvements, have lost any competitive edge. Meanwhile, shiny, brand-new stores, often under the same name brand, open up within a few minutes drive time. Location, obviously, is one of most vital factors in commercial real estate finance.

Thankfully, municipal authorities, economic development groups, and entrepreneurs all across the country have vested interests in finding uses for older buildings. Rarely, though, can those older, gentrified buildings be expected to produce the capital or income of former years. This is one reason why banks limit the amortization on commercial real estate loans to fifteen or twenty years.

The life expectancy of the borrower is much more crucial in commercial real estate loans than the life expectancy of the building itself. We know that the average life of a human being is somewhere in the vicinity of seventy-five years. Can anyone guess the life expectancy of any business? Many companies in America are more than 100 years old, but they are the exceptions. Remember from the first chapter that four out of five new businesses fail within five years? Businesses cease to exist for many reasons: poor financial results, mergers, changed consumer tastes, death of owners, and changes in relevant laws are but a few reasons. It behooves banks to accelerate repayment of long-term loans, like real estate loans, as fast as possible.

For this reason, a straight, bullet loan of ten, fifteen, or twenty years is rare. The normal industry practice is to extend a real estate loan with a maturity of three or five years in length with payments calculated as if the loan was a fifteen- or twenty-year loan. The loan matures in its predetermined term, and payments are based on a longer amortization. The maturity date is the date of the balloon payment when all the remaining principal is due and payable.

Normally, the bank simply commits to renew the loan for another three or five years and to continue the same amortization schedule. That is, if the original loan was a five-year term loan with a fifteen-year amortization, it would be renewed as a five-year term loan with payments now based on a ten-year amortization. The shorter term (compared to the amortization) allows the bank the chance to review the borrower's economic status at more acceptable and practical intervals and to make decisions based on new information like market conditions and new laws. In the mid-1980s, a bank for which I formerly worked decided that it did not wish to have any commercial real estate loans in its portfolio anymore because of changes in federal laws pertaining to environmental liability and appraisal requirements. As loans matured, many with substantial principal balance balloon payments, the bank simply told its customers "No thanks" and sent them packing to other local banks.

Real estate lending also entails a whole other set of due diligence that must be performed by lenders and requires application of extra documentation. Some of these issues are discussed in Chapter 8.

Letters of Credit

A letter of credit is a liability of the bank. It tells the recipient, the beneficiary, that under a specified set of circumstances, the letter may be presented to the bank in exchange for a sum of money up to the maximum amount established within the letter itself. Customers ask their banks for letters of credit to facilitate business transactions across distances or with vendors who may not be familiar with the customer. For example, travel agents are required to give letters of credit to the Airlines Reporting Corporation (ARC), the company that processes all airline ticket purchases. If a travel agent fails to make the proper payment to ARC in the required time frame, ARC will present the letter of credit to the bank and demand payment under the terms of the letter of credit.

Letters of credit facilitate trade. A seller sells only when it believes that it will be paid by the buyer. Since many transactions take place between unfamiliar parties, letters of credit substitute for a track record based on successful past experience between the parties. This is especially true in international trade. A company in China is not likely to agree to sell you its product unless you pay up front or provide some guaranty of payment. You are not likely to pay up front unless the company provides some guaranty of delivery of acceptable product. If you provide to the company a letter of credit from an American bank, the Chinese firm is guaranteed payment if it delivers as promised on goods and satisfaction.

Prior to issuing a letter of credit, the bank performs the same credit evaluation on an applicant as it would for any other loan. Even though the expectation is that the letter of credit will never be drawn upon, it is documented just as any other loan to protect the bank's security interests. If a letter of credit is presented to the issuing bank with all necessary documentation, the bank must immediately cash it for the beneficiary.

Small banks are at a disadvantage when it comes to letters of credit. The name and credit of a small bank does not carry any weight outside its immediate marketplace. A company in Germany is not likely to accept a letter of credit from Plainwell State Bank but it would accept one from a major bank. Thus, small banks often must issue a letter of credit payable to a larger, correspondent bank, which, in turn, issues the actual letter of credit to the vendor.

Similarly, a beneficiary of a letter of credit, especially a foreign company, is not going to send a courier to the office of the issuing bank (in America) in order to cash the letter of credit. A German company would take the letter of credit to its own bank and cash it there. The German bank would then, through its own network or that of a larger correspondent bank, present the drafted letter of credit to the American bank for reimbursement.

If a letter of credit is actually drawn upon, it usually means there is some dispute about either the delivery or quality of the goods and that the issue is headed for court. For this reason, banks are very cautious about issuing these documents.

Import letters of credit are used for purchases of items from overseas. A letter of credit may either be revocable or irrevocable. Revocable letters of credit may be canceled at any time by the bank; irrevocable letters of credit cannot be canceled by the bank under any circumstances. Obviously, most letters of credit that are issued are of the irrevocable kind. See Figure 4-1 for an example of a letter of credit.

A letter written to "Whom It May Concern" by a bank officer that states that checks written by a certain customer up to a specific amount are good or are covered by deposits in the bank is not a letter of credit. Frequently, bank customers need just such a letter to take to out-of-town dealers or auctioneers to prove that their checks are good. These are informal communications that state only that at the moment that the letter was written, the customer had credit available or deposits available up to the specified amount. It has no legal bearing whatsoever and cannot be presented to the bank should the customer bounce a check.

Letters of reference are also not to be confused with letters of credit. Letters of reference are simply a bank officer's statement about the character, employability, or work ethic of a customer. Often when a customer develops a new source of inventory, supplies, or equipment, the supplier will contact the bank for a credit reference. Again, a letter of reference is not a liability of the bank.

Other Types of Loans

The previous discussion categorized loans by structure or purpose. There are two other terms with which the reader should be aware. These loans may fit into one or more of the foregoing categories and are included here for easy reference.

Figure 4-1: Letter of Credit

OLD FAITHFUL NATIONAL BANK

IRREVOCABLE STANDBY LETTER OF CREDIT

Letter of Credit:
Date: November 12, 2000
Number: 091862
Amount (USD): $200,000
Date of Expiration: 12/31/2001

Issuer:
Old Faithful National Bank
One Geyser Square
Yellowstone, WY 43209

To Beneficiary:
Gmbh. Global Hops Supply
896 Dasensteingweg
Kappelrodeck
Federal Republic of Germany

Applicant:
Lewis and Clark Brewery, Inc.
4427 Idaho-Wyoming Highway
West Yellowstone, WY 43210
U.S.A.

Date: November 12, 2000

Gentlemen:

We hereby establish our Irrevocable Standby Letter of Credit No. **091862** in your favor for account of **Lewis and Clark Brewery, Inc.**, 4427 Idaho-Wyoming Highway, West Yellowstone, WY 43210 for a sum not to exceed **Two Hundred Thousand and No /100 Dollars ($200,000)** available by your drafts on **Old Faithful National Bank** at sight when accompanied by the following documents:

1. A signed statement reading as follows:
   The undersigned is an authorized representative of Gmbh. Global Hops Supply. Gmbh. Global Hops Supply certifies that the amount demanded represents amounts due which were invoiced to the applicant and which were not paid in full in accordance with the terms of payment.
2. A copy of the invoice(s) referred to in the signed statement.
3. Copies of all shipping documents that prove delivery of the invoiced materials.

All sight drafts drawn under this Credit must be marked "Drawn under Old Faithful National Bank Irrevocable Standby Letter of Credit No. **091862** dated **November 12, 2000**.

L/C No. 091862, p.2.

This Credit shall be governed by the Uniform Commercial Code as enacted in Wyoming from time to time, and to the extent not modified by said law, the Uniform Customs and Practice for Documentary Credits as most recently published by the International Chamber of Commerce.

This credit is subject to the following special conditions:

A. Within reasonable time, after your presentation, we will provide you with a statement of all defects in your presentation by telecopier or such other method as specified by you in your presentation.

B. Partial and multiple drawings and shipments are permitted. Invoices may exceed the amount of this credit, but payment may not exceed the credit.

C. Payment will be made by wire transfer of immediately available funds, free of any wire transfer charges, to the account stated in your presentation.

The original of this Letter of Credit must be submitted to us whenever a partial draw or cancellation of this Credit is requested. In every case of partial draw the Letter of Credit shall be promptly returned and remain valid for the balance unused.

We hereby agree with bona fide holders that all sight drafts drawn under and in compliance with the terms of this Credit shall meet with due honor upon presentation and delivery of the documents as specified if negotiated at our offices on or before **December 31, 2001**.

Very truly yours,

Old Faithful National Bank

_____

By: James T. Bridger, Vice President

ACCOMMODATION LOANS

I once knew the president of a small community bank near my home who carried blank promissory notes in his coat pocket. He would write out loans for folks on the hood of his car, at the lunch counter, or wherever someone with a need bumped into him. Many, if not all, of these borrowers were accommodated by him. That means that in any textbook sense, they did not qualify for the amount of money loaned to them. The loans were made simply to accommodate a friend, a recognized person, or the friend of another customer. My then-employer found this out shortly after we bought that little bank! Those borrowers felt a sense of debt to the local president since he had, after all, accommodated them; but those feelings did not accrue to the new, big bank. Although they would have gone to the ends of the earth to repay the person, the customers felt no such obligation to the new owners.

Community bankers still make accommodation loans. The key to "qualifying" for an accommodation is some relationship with a banker who has the authority to make such loans. Most larger banks have eliminated the ability to make these loans either in specific loan policy language or by removing individual loan authority. Although the ability to make these loans is nice for a handful of bank customers, the move to eliminate them by banks is positive. The adage, "just enough rope to hang yourself" holds for loan authority. Too many loan officers find themselves mired in problem loans once they start to make accommodation loans.

LEG LOANS

Once, a very long time ago, a female applicant sat on the other side of my desk and presented her business plan to me. Twice during the presentation, she stood up and leaned across my desk to point out to me a particularly vital piece of information in the plan. The first time she did this, I noticed that her blouse was unbuttoned much lower than it should have been, and it was obvious from my point of view that she was not wearing any undergarments. The second time, she affected an obvious, contorted pose to provide to me the full benefit of her (lack of) attire.

Her business plan stunk. Had I made the loan to her (I did not), it would certainly have been classified as a leg loan. Leg loans are a relic of past times when all bankers were stodgy old men who found pleasure in casual flirting. The name implies that the only reason a loan is or was made was due to the legs of the female applicant. Obviously, times have changed since this type of loan received its moniker—legs are the least of the temptations bankers are presented with today. And that is not to say that the temptations are all of the flesh, either.

Leg loans still exist in the modern world of banking although defining legs has changed. A "leg" can be anything of interest that increases the heartbeat of a banker, be it business or hobby related. Every business might be the recipient of a leg loan. The key is to find a loan officer who has a soft spot in his heart for the products or services of the company or some other factor related to the business like its location or season tickets to the ballpark. I know one commercial loan officer who has a private pilot's license and will do almost anything to hang out at airports and in the offices of fixed base operators. If I had a business related to aviation or located near an airport, I would seek out this lender over all others. Golf is a more common "leg" than are actual human legs today. Personally, I would pull every string possible to make a golf course loan!

Bank on It

+ Loans are either short term or long term.
+ Short-term loans are used to supplement working capital in the cash cycle of a business.
+ Construction loans are complex and are one of the most risk-filled types of lending practiced by banks.
+ Long-term loans are used to finance assets with useful lives of one or more years.
+ Leg loans are loans made by a loan officer because of some special interest that the officer has in the applicant, its principals, or some ancillary reason like location, perks, and personal interests or hobbies.

five

The Six C's
of Commercial Lending

Bankers can speak for hours about credit and loans and customers. The whole discourse, though, boils down to a checklist of six points: character, cash flow, capital, capacity, collateral, and credit history. If a business passes muster on all six points, it will get a loan. Loan applications must be tailored to prove that the applicant meets the criteria for each standard. This must be the focus of a loan application, and all other fluff should be removed. This chapter explains each of the C's and its relevance to a loan application. The next chapter then ties them together into a loan application.

Character

In 1912, J. P. Morgan, perhaps the most influential American banker ever, appeared before a United States Congress subcommittee hearing on the concentration of power on Wall Street. The following dialogue between Morgan and Samuel Untermeyer, a committee attorney, is taken from *The House of Morgan*, a book written by Ron Chernow and published by Atlantic Monthly Press.

Untermeyer: Is not commercial credit based primarily upon money or property?

Morgan: No, sir, the first thing is character.

Untermeyer: Before money or property?

Morgan: Before money or anything else. Money cannot buy it. Because a man I do not trust could not get money from me on all the bonds in Christendom.

Character is the foremost of the C's. The fastest way to loan declination is to have any cloud of character hovering over a business owner or management team. At a former employer, I was told by my manager to send an applicant packing because of rumors that he was the money man behind a exotic dance club in town—and he had a certificate of deposit to fully secure his requested loan amount! Another long-time client of mine was a hard worker who had struggled for years and stayed with his business so that he could repay the bank. He would have been better off to liquidate his assets, stick the bank with a loan loss, and get a job at someone else's shop, but he believed that a man's word was his bond. Unfortunately, his character flaw had to do with the inability to recognize the age of majority in our state as it applies to certain behavior with the opposite sex. He spent six months in jail, and we made the decision to close down his business for him when the problem came to our knowledge.

Gauging a person's honesty and integrity is difficult at best. Think of all those gullible people who sent checks to Jim and Tammy Baker at Heritage USA. Bankers deal with business owners who evangelize about their own businesses. Bankers are not immune from gullibility. One fellow in our town had borrowed large sums from every bank and was the epitome of success in the public eye—that is, until his office equipment Ponzi-scheme came crashing down on all of us. His quip in the local newspaper was, "I just wanted people to like me."

Character is measured largely on a person's reputation, both personal and professional. A person known to file lawsuits at the drop of a hat, to litigate matters that should be the province of polite, reasoned interpersonal communication, will not register high on the bank's character meter. The manner in which someone has managed his or her private life is a key to this issue. Someone who is consistently late on house, car, or credit card payments is not likely to handle his business any differently. Even disputed medical care bills can cause problems. Unpaid medical bills commonly pop up on credit bureau reports. The usual answer to my question about the unpaid bill is "it's between my insurance company and the hospital." A person of good character and sufficient resources would pay the bill and then fight the insurance company for reimbursement.

Most character issues are things that a person can avoid by simply doing the right thing all the time. The one subjective channel of information that cannot be controlled by living right or taking corrective action is the local rumor mill. I have sat in loan committees and listened to other officers or board members pass along little tidbits, probably completely without basis, about bank customers or loan applicants. Within seconds, an applicant's name can indelibly be linked with no-no words like "drugs" or "affair" or "deadbeat." I fought many battles over one very successful client of mine who was rumored—at least by certain high-ranking executives of the bank—to be involved in a monthly bacchanal in a leased apartment kept just for this activity. Those rumors were baseless and founded only in the envy of other people.

Although the national standard of morality has eased over the years, a known extramarital affair is likely to fell your loan application. A friend of mine is fond of saying, "If your spouse can't trust you, who can?" Your banker? In the same category is delinquent child support debts. If you won't take care of your own child, I will not expect you to take care of me.

Professional character is more easily measured by bankers. The way you have handled past loans is of primary importance. Bankruptcies, uncollected accounts, lawsuits, and loan losses are surefire reasons to turn down a loan request. Tax liens that result from unpaid taxes will absolutely kill a loan application. Banks will often ask for business references, people we can call to discuss how you handle business transactions. More frequently than not, the bank already knows with whom you do business and can do some snooping around without your knowledge.

There is a class of hard-nosed businesspeople who are extremely successful. They drive hard bargains with vendors and customers. They are absolutely honest, yet they beat the smallest horses to death. No one wants to deal with a customer who will continually nag for concessions, changes, discounts, refunds, and freebies. Some of the aggressive practices used by these businesspeople can be viewed as being mean-spirited. If so, a reputation is quickly earned and spread around town. These folks, as bank customers, cost more money to service than any others. If the potential for income from the customer is not there, most bankers will simply pass up the opportunity to make the loan.

Never, ever, present your tax returns to a banker, wink at him or her, and say, "There's more than what shows here. This is just what I want Uncle Sam to know about." I have heard this dozens of times in my career. First, if you are willing to cheat the federal government, with its omnipotent powers, you would be willing to cheat the bank. Second, the banker probably has at least one relative who has died fighting for this country and all its laws, including the tax code. If you don't like our laws, work to change them rather than ignore them. When you cheat at business, you unfairly tilt the playing field in your favor. To the majority of the owners of the 22 million small businesses in America, business is not a game, it is life. When you cheat, you are messing with other people's lives, and that riles bankers to no end.

Another way to let your banker know that you might be a character risk is to play one bank off another. It is common practice to take a commitment letter from one bank to another bank to see if the second bank can improve upon the deal. Even long-time customers of one bank will ask another bank to make a proposal for the company's business from time to time just to keep the current bank where it transacts business honest. What is not good practice is to completely make up or even embellish what another bank might be willing to do for you. Banking is a fraternity. Most bankers in any given town will know each other from past stops in their careers, professional organizations, charitable activities, service clubs, and private lives. Bankers, at social functions, band together; a casual observer would never know which ones are colleagues or competitors. Bankers know each others' styles and limits at a minimum. Bankers know who each others' major customers are and

how those loan packages are structured. An applicant fools only himself
or herself when making up terms and conditions not actually offered by
another bank as a way of negotiating. Anyone who abides by this practice is likely to be told by the banker, "Gee, I can't beat that deal. Thanks
for letting me look at your proposal," and find the door shut in his or
her face. Without a solid commitment in hand, an applicant risks alienating at least one bank in town and finding himself or herself standing
out in the cold with no loan package.

It seems odd to say this, but unfortunately, good economic times do
not allow bankers to measure perhaps the greatest test of a business
owner's character. How a manager handles his or her financial affairs
during a time of crisis is the best measure of professional character.
Banks will open the vaults for an old client who had a business failure
if that person had worked hard to protect the bank's interests and to
repay the business's loans. In good economic times, everyone's a hero.
Don't get cocky just because you are riding the crest of good times!

Cash Flow

Cash flow is the stream of money that repays loans. It is not to be confused with profits. Profits are numbers written down on paper. Cash
flow is money in the bank. It is even possible, and common, for a company to have good cash flow and a net loss. After character, cash flow
is the focus of bank analysis. Indeed, cash is king.

The definition of cash flow varies from place to place. Financial
statements prepared by certified public accountants include a statement
of cash flows, which is a complex method of balancing a company's
cash account from the beginning to the end of a certain period.
Bankers use a simple formula:

Profit (or loss)
+ Noncash expenses
+ Nonrecurring expenses
+ Long-term interest expense
= Cash flow

The source of the numbers that are plugged into the formula is usually year-end financial statements, tax returns, or interim financial statements. The purpose of this arithmetic is to determine how much cash a company has available to cover principal and interest payments on debt. Without turning this into an accounting lesson, let's look at each component of the formula.

PROFITS

A firm's profit is the amount of dollars left over after subtracting all expenses, including taxes, from its revenues. If the number is negative, it is called a loss. The whole concept of profits has lost some luster in recent years. Most financial analysts are now more concerned about cash flow and free cash flow. Free cash flow is the money a company has available after all debt service with which it may make capital investments, pay dividends, or buy back its own stock (in the case of publicly owned corporations). We, as individuals, are familiar with free cash flow, although we do not call it by that name. Free cash flow held by individuals (basically, what is left over from our wages after all living expenses and taxes) is called disposable income.

NONCASH EXPENSES

Accrual accounting systems include noncash expenses; the two main expenses are depreciation and amortization. The ability to take these deductions from income is granted by tax laws. There are two reasons why the government allows us to write off a portion of asset costs every year on our income statement. First, the ability to reduce taxes encourages business owners to buy assets and to boost the economy. Second, in an ideal world, the business owner would actually set aside an amount of cash equal to the depreciation, like a sinking fund, which could be used later to replace the specific asset. In the real world, though, businesses use the cash made available by the depreciation gimmick to fund other, ongoing needs.

Depreciation is not billed or invoiced. The business owner does not write a check payable to anyone for the amount of depreciation. It is a noncash expense that reduces net income and the resulting income taxes. Even though the money has been expensed, it is still in the company's account and available for use elsewhere. Thus, to determine how much cash a business generated in a given period, these noncash expenses are added back to the net profit or net loss number.

NONRECURRING EXPENSES

Almost every business will experience an expense or cost from time to time that is a one-time expense. Examples include the costs of relocating to a new place of business, the settlement of a lawsuit, and other expenses that can be argued will never occur again. What might be a nonrecurring expense in one industry might be an ongoing cost of business in another. For example, we would not expect a retail store to be involved in any lawsuits that would cause large expenses for legal help or settlements. On the other hand, a security firm might have dozens of lawsuits pending at any given time and might have a high level of legal costs every year. An example of what expenses would not be eligible to be added back in for cash flow purposes is utility expense. Since the weather is never predictable over a long-term period, bankers will never allow a company to add back higher than expected utility expenses due to harsher than normal winters or hotter than normal summers. A business might have to plow its parking lot every day in one winter and not once the following winter. Utility costs are recurring expenses—we just don't know when they will recur.

LONG-TERM DEBT INTEREST EXPENSE

Interest expense is added back because the cash flow sum is usually compared to a debt service figure that includes principal and interest payments. Short-term interest expense is not added back. This is interest that would be paid on lines of credit or other loans used for day-to-day operations and can be expected to recur every year and would not be available to make term debt payments.

CASH FLOW COVERAGE

Once cash flow has been calculated, the banker subtracts all expected principal and interest payments on existing debt for the next twelve months from the sum. These payments may or may not be to the bank that is considering the new loan request. The amount left over is net cash flow and is the amount of cash available to make payments on any new debt. The banker then calculates the annual principal and interest payments required on your requested loan amount and compares it to the net cash flow.

For investor real estate loans, where revenue is generated by rental income, bankers typically require net cash flow to be 110 percent of debt service. Simply, if your total principal and interest payments in a year will be $100,000, then your cash flow must be at least $110,000.

For operating businesses, including real estate loans for buildings occupied by the borrower, banks generally want a cash-flow coverage of at least 120 percent of debt service. Why the difference in coverage between investor real estate and operating companies? Income from investor real estate tends to be much more stable than that of operating companies. We know the greatest risk to income of investor real estate businesses is vacancies. Based on experience, we also know that established rental properties usually do not have vacancy rates in excess of 10 percent—hence the 110% coverage requirement. Operating companies face so many risks to income that may vary profit levels from year to year. Thus, a larger coverage factor is built in to provide a cushion should revenues drop or expenses increase unexpectedly.

CASH FLOW ANALYSIS

If all a person had to do was compare last year's cash flow number to the payments of a new loan, banking would pretty much be a cut-and-dried business. Alas, it is not that simple. Bankers look at historical financial information for several years. They compare year-end results for three to five years to gauge earnings stability, trends upward or downward, and to compare past management projections to see how management performed based on those projections. We look at interim financial results from comparable periods over the past several years to look for any seasonality in a business, to look for early clues that point to eroding sales or profitability, and to anticipate capital needs of the customer. Many small businesses that approach banks are brand-new start-ups with no historical financial information. Banks then rely on projected financial or cash flow statements.

HISTORICAL CASH FLOW

As alluded to earlier, historical cash flow is calculated from information derived from past financial statements that may include management prepared direct income statements, accountant prepared compilations, reviews or audits, and tax returns. Increasingly, banks rely on tax returns as the most accurate source of information. Applications should include copies of a business's last five year-end statements. Those statements should be supported by copies of the tax returns for the same periods. The bank will use one or the other for its purposes; at a minimum, the presence of the tax returns speaks to the veracity of the numbers in the financial statements and sends a subconscious message to that effect to the banker. Further, a current interim financial statement, as up to date as possible, and the statement from the same date in the prior year should be included.

The applicant should provide a brief narrative memo to highlight any nonrecurring or unusual items of expense, cost, or income that appear on the statements. If a business is not yet five years old, it will be able to provide financial information only for fewer periods, and that is understandable.

PROJECTED MONTHLY CASH FLOW

Seasonal businesses that have peaks and valleys in sales (and therefore profits) and startup companies should provide a one-year monthly cash flow projection. Figure 5-1 is the format used by the U.S. Small Business Administration and is standard for this task. In order to complete this type of projection correctly, everything you may have learned in Accounting 101 needs to be brushed aside. The format looks daunting, but it is very simple to complete.

See Reverse Side for Instructions and Public Comment Information

NAME OF BUSINESS		ADDRESS		OWNER							

	Pre-Start-up Position		1		2		3		4		5
YEAR MONTH	Estimate	Actual	Estimate	Actual	Estimate	Actual	Estimate	Actual	Estimate	Actual	Estimate	A
1. CASH ON HAND (Beginning of month)												
2. CASH RECEIPTS												
(a) Cash Sales												
(b) Collections from Credit Accounts												
(c) Loan or Other Cash injection (Specify)												
3. TOTAL CASH RECEIPTS (2a + 2b + 2c = 3)												
4. TOTAL CASH AVAILABLE (Before cash out) (1 + 3)												
5. CASH PAID OUT												
(a) Purchases (Merchandise)												
(b) Gross Wages (Excludes withdrawals)												
(c) Payroll Expenses (Taxes, etc.)												
(d) Outside Services												
(e) Supplies (Office and operating)												
(f) Repairs and Maintenance												
(g) Advertising												
(h) Car, Delivery, and Travel												
(i) Accounting and Legal												
(j) Rent												
(k) Telephone												
(l) Utilities												
(m) Insurance												
(n) Taxes (Real estate, etc.)												
(o) Interest												
(p) Other Expenses (Specify each)												
(q) Miscellaneous (Unspecified)												
(r) Subtotal												
(s) Loan Principal Payment												
(t) Capital Purchases (Specify)												
(u) Other Start-up Costs												
(v) Reserve and/or Escrow (Specify)												
(w) Owner's Withdrawal												
6. TOTAL CASH PAID OUT (Total 5a thru 5w)												
7. CASH POSITION (End of month) (4 minus 6)												

OW PROJECTION

Form Approval:
OMB No. 3245–0019
Expires: 8–31–91

TYPE OF BUSINESS	PREPARED BY	DATE

6		7		8		9		10		11		12		TOTAL Columns 1—12		
...ate	Actual	Estimate	Actual	Estimate	Actual	Estimate	Actual	Estimate	Actual	Estimate	Actual	Estimate	Actual	Estimate	Actual	
																1.
																2.
																(a)
																(b)
																(c)
																3.
																4.
																5.
																(a)
																(b)
																(c)
																(d)
																(e)
																(f)
																(g)
																(h)
																(i)
																(j)
																(k)
																(l)
																(m)
																(n)
																(o)
																(p)
																(q)
																(r)
																(s)
																(t)
																(u)
																(v)
																(w)
																6.
																7.

The first column is an accounting of cash put into and taken out of the business prior to opening your doors. Examples of cash into the business are your cash equity, bank loans, and any other cash not received though actual sales. Cash taken out of the business prior to formally opening the doors for business might be supplies, paper products, licenses, initial inventory, equipment, and so on. These might not be expenses in the double-entry accounting sense, but are items for which you paid money. Line 7 at the bottom of the page is the amount of cash you have on hand after you have adequately prepared your business to open. This figure is carried up to line 1 in column 1 and is your starting cash the day you throw open your doors to the public. The next step is the only tricky thing about the form.

Line 2 asks you to predict how much cash will be generated by sales for the first and each succeeding month of operations. This cannot be a number plucked from the sky. You must really think these numbers through. If you have completed a business plan, it might provide some clues to expected sales levels. The assumptions that led you to believe that your business would succeed are the foundation of these projected numbers.

You must make specific assumptions about the number of customers, number of units to be sold, the cost of the units, and your pricing strategy for the units. A new business will not go from zero sales to peak sales levels in its first month. It takes months, if not years, to build sales. Similarly, a seasonal business might actually be closed during parts of the year and would have no sales. In Michigan, we have two seasons: ten months of winter and two months of poor sledding. An ice cream parlor in Michigan is not going to have tremendous sales volumes during the winter months. Conversely, a snow plowing service had better not turn in projections that show even sales volumes throughout the year.

Your assumptions should be attached to the projections in the form of narrative memorandum. It does not suffice to tell your banker that your ice cream parlor will average sales of $3,000 per day during the busy season. That is a fairly useless figure until it is broken down into units sold. If you plan to sell ice cream cones for $1.50, that means you will have to sell 2,000 cones per day to meet your projected revenue figure. That might be a tall order in a town of 1,000 persons or might be a slam dunk in a town of 100,000 persons. If the Dairy Queen down the street sells cones for 90 cents, why would anyone buy your $1.50 cone in the first place? These are the types of questions a business owner needs to anticipate from her banker and to consider in building projections.

An ice cream parlor is a poor real life example to use. Most businesses will have more complex products or services with unique pricing and cost structure. A qualified CPA or other professional consultant can be of great assistance in creating meaningful projections. Entrepreneurs, especially those mulling over the start up of a new business, should not spare the expense of employing a professional in this matter. A few bucks spent at this juncture could save a lot of money and heartache later.

The final twist to estimating monthly income is to determine how much of your sales will be cash, check, and charge card and how much will be on accounts receivable. Since accounts receivable are collected later—as much as several months later—you cannot include those sales in your cash flow projection. Estimating how long the average account receivable will be outstanding will help you determine when (or where) to recognize the cash from sales on account. Lines 3 and 4 subtotal cash received and cash on hand.

Line 5 prompts you to write down all of your anticipated costs and expenses. Unless there is something very unusual about your business, most of those items are already labeled for you. Almost every one of these line items can be quantified prior to opening a business. A sign of poor management ability is to revisit these numbers several months down the road and find out that the actual numbers are significantly higher than expected. An entrepreneur I know once borrowed $200,000 to purchase agricultural chemical spraying equipment and to start a contract spraying business for hire by local farmers. Unfortunately, after making his big-ticket purchases, printing up business cards, filing corporate paperwork, and otherwise committing himself to debt, he discovered that liability insurance was prohibitively expensive. In fact, finding the necessary insurance at any cost was difficult. He liquidated the business before generating one dollar in revenue and lost his entire investment in a matter of two weeks.

For sole proprietors, it might be wise to build in all mandatory personal expenses, too. Include living expenses, house payments, car payments, medical expenses, and anything else that will have to be paid by draws from the business. Exclude these items only if you have an outside source of income that is sufficient to cover them.

All the expenses are totaled at line 6 and deducted from the total cash available at line 4. The difference is your cash position at the end of the month, which is carried to line 1 at the top of the next month's column. This is repeated until all twelve months have been completed and totaled in the last column. Just a note—the twelve-month period is the twelve months from the date you start your business and not necessarily a calendar year that commences with January.

Monthly cash flow projections help you and your banker determine your company's ability to repay a given loan and helps pinpoint months when additional capital might be required to replenish operating cash. Once the projection is completed, look for any month that has a negative number on line 7. If all goes according to plan, you will need to borrow at least that much money in that month to pay your bills. This is very helpful to the banker who can then establish lines of credit or build an appropriate amount of permanent working capital into the term loan.

ANNUAL PROJECTIONS

All well-run companies continually update projections for future periods ranging from one to five years down the road. Every business loan application should be accompanied by at least a two-year projection of income and expenses. Figure 5-2 is the format suggested by the U.S. Small Business Administration.

Figure 5-2 Projection of Income and Expense

PROFIT & LOSS - PROJECTIONS

INCOME STATEMENT:	Interim	%	Proforma 1	%	Proforma 2	%	Proforma 3	%	RMA %
STATEMENT DATE:									
NUMBER OF MONTHS:									
PERCENTAGE (%) CHANGE:									
Cash Sales		0%		0%		0%		0%	
Credit Sales		0%		0%		0%		0%	
Total Sales	0	0%	0	0%	0	0%	0	0%	
Less: Returns & Allowances		0%		0%		0%		0%	
Net Sales	0	0%	0	0%	0	0%	0	0%	
Cost of Goods Sold		0%		0%		0%		0%	
Gross Profit	0	0%	0	0%	0	0%	0	0%	
Compensation of Officers Salaries		0%		0%		0%		0%	
Salaries & Compensation		0%		0%		0%		0%	
Payroll Taxes		0%		0%		0%		0%	
Total Salaries & Compensation	0	0%	0	0%	0	0%	0	0%	
Repairs and Maintenance		0%		0%		0%		0%	
Bad Debts		0%		0%		0%		0%	
Rents		0%		0%		0%		0%	
Taxes and Licenses		0%		0%		0%		0%	
Depreciation & Amortization		0%		0%		0%		0%	
Advertising & Selling Expenses		0%		0%		0%		0%	
Pension, Profit Sharing, Etc. Plans		0%		0%		0%		0%	
Employee Benefit Programs		0%		0%		0%		0%	
Other:		0%		0%		0%		0%	
Other:		0%		0%		0%		0%	
Other:		0%		0%		0%		0%	
Other:		0%		0%		0%		0%	
Other:		0%		0%		0%		0%	
Other:		0%		0%		0%		0%	
Other:		0%		0%		0%		0%	
Total Other Operating Expenses	0	0%	0	0%	0	0%	0	0%	
Total Operating Expenses	0	0%	0	0%	0	0%	0	0%	
Total Operating Profit (Loss)	0	0%	0	0%	0	0%	0	0%	
Interest & Dividends		0%		0%		0%		0%	
Other Income:		0%		0%		0%		0%	
Total Other Income	0	0%	0	0%	0	0%	0	0%	
Interest Expense: SBA Loan		0%		0%		0%		0%	
Interest Expense:		0%		0%		0%		0%	
Interest Expense:		0%		0%		0%		0%	
Total Interest Expense	0	0%	0	0%	0	0%	0	0%	
Other Expense:		0%		0%		0%		0%	
Total Other Expense		0%		0%		0%		0%	
Net Other Income (Expense)	0	0%	0	0%	0	0%	0	0%	
Earnings (Losses) Before Taxes	0	0%	0	0%	0	0%	0	0%	
Income Taxes		0%		0%		0%		0%	
Profit (Loss) After Tax	0	0%	0	0%	0	0%	0	0%	
Dividends/Withdrawals		0%		0%		0%		0%	

This form is basically an estimate of what a business owner thinks his or her income statement will look like for the next two one-year periods. Owners of existing businesses can use historical numbers to forecast those results, particularly if the historical numbers reflect any stability or trend. Quite often, owners of existing businesses tweak the actual results for the last year ended by a fixed percentage, say 5 or 10 percent, more or less if historical trends point that way.

Owners of brand-new businesses can use the month-by-month projection to generate the first year projection and then assume a specified percentage of growth for the second year. If the new business happens to be a franchise, the entrepreneur is in luck. Franchisers include actual results of existing franchisees and usually categorize the results by type and size of market and time in business. Thus, someone who contemplates opening a particular franchise store in a town of 20,000 people can look at a franchiser's offering circular and pick out results for a similar store or average several similar stores together. Over the years, franchise owners with whom I have worked are consistently on-the-money with their projections.

The only caution I like to throw out regarding franchisers is to be wary about new ones to your area. This is not to castigate franchisers and to put them into the same class as the fly-by-night driveway-coating companies that pass through town every summer. I learned this lesson the hard way. I worked with a client once who wished to replicate a retail food franchise in my marketplace. He wanted to be the first to open a franchise that heretofore was found only in the midsouth part of the country. My borrower was a great candidate for a loan and had excellent credentials. He and I both did our homework. The budget was tight, but we sharpened our pencils and made a deal. When the store was just 50 percent built out, we discovered the unforeseen. The cost assumptions of opening the business had been developed by averaging the actual costs experienced previously by all the existing franchise locations. Unfortunately, we did not know that each of those stores was located in an area not dominated by labor unions. The labor costs in our market were as much as 60 percent greater, and we were faced with a large capital shortfall before the doors were even opened. The resulting problem was not that we had to scramble to find a way to loan more money to the customer, but that the customer now had to service a much higher debt load on income projected barely to service the original amount.

INVESTOR REAL ESTATE PROJECTIONS

Projected revenue and expenses for an investment real estate business is easy. Income is calculated by multiplying each unit by its corresponding rental rate. Expenses can be nailed down by using historical information or by using information widely available in the industry, like real estate listings of comparable properties or consultation by a real estate management firm that very likely manages several properties similar to the one in question.

For bank purposes, though, some additional standard expenses need to be considered. A bank will analyze investor real estate under the assumption that some day it will foreclose on the property and have to manage it until it is resold. Banks do not have the necessary staff to perform banking duties and to manage commercial real estate. Therefore, the bank assumes that it will have to pay someone else to perform most duties at the property. It will automatically reduce income by a vacancy rate factor of 5 to 10 percent. The vacancy rate depends on the capacity for number of tenants at a property. A 100-unit apartment building would be at the lower 5 percent rate; a 4-unit strip mall would be at the higher 10 percent rate. Right off the bat, projected income will be 5 to 10 percent less than the probable actual result.

The bank will build in a replacement reserve of 3 percent to help cover costs of updating the building. Good landlords and property management companies do this as a matter of practice, too. The bank also builds in a maintenance fee of 3 percent. An owner might perform his or her own maintenance, but a banker would rather pay someone else than dirty his or her own fingernails. Finally, no banker wants to receive phone calls at all hours from tenants, would-be tenants, or the police ("We just received an alarm from your building"). So, another 5 percent is deducted for a management fee with which the bank could hire a specialty firm to run the property.

Depending upon each case, the bank's assumptions could reduce the cash flow used for loan approval from 11 percent to 21 percent. It seems very conservative, but over the years, banks have gained accurate experience to justify those deductions.

CASH FLOW RULES OF THUMB

Your projections are the basis of your loan application. Good, well-thought-out projections provide a learning experience for the business owner. In retrospect, projections that prove to be true garner a great deal of admiration and respect for the business owner. Obviously, projections that turn out to be thoughtless and careless will, at least, cause an erosion of respect between banker and customer.

Capital

Capital encompasses all the assets owned by a company with which it produces its products or services. Capital may be either borrowed or owned by the business. The higher the percentage of capital in a business that is owned by the business, the better. The amount of capital that is owned by the business or its owners is called owner's equity. Capitalization is the term that describes the structure and ownership of a company's capital.

CAPITAL STRUCTURE

Proper capitalization should be a goal of both borrower and banker. Properly capitalized companies can, in theory, weather losses or other business calamities as long as owner's equity is positive. In my experience, the main reason most new businesses fail is poor capitalization, and this is just as much the fault of the banker as it is the business owner. Too many businesses open their doors and run out of cash to properly stock their shelves, to advertise, and to stick around long enough to develop a clientele. Unfortunately, a lot of eager entrepreneurs will lunge at any loan amount offered to them, despite the inadequacy of the amounts. A well-capitalized company can survive long ramp-up periods or prolonged sales droughts.

From a banker's perspective, the importance of proper capitalization lies in its psychological implications. The more money a person has invested in a business, the less likely he or she would be to throw in the towel and walk away from the business. There is no more hollow feeling than to be a banker and have a customer walk into your office, toss a ring of keys on your desk, and say, "I'm done. The business is all yours."

I have had numerous entrepreneurs sit before me and request 100 percent financing for their startup businesses. The word no smacks them like a sledgehammer. Then, with puppy eyes, they meekly explain, "I only came to the bank to borrow money because I didn't want to risk any of my own." Then, I explain the difference between bank loans and venture capital.

Bank loans are borrowed capital. Depositors lend their money to the bank in the expectation that they will be able to get every penny of it back. Banks, in turn, lend it to individuals and businesses. In order to meet the expectations of the depositors, banks try to make only those loans that it can be reasonably assured will be repaid. Any amount beyond that is venture capital. For most small businesses, the entrepreneurs are the source of the venture capital. It comes from savings accounts, retirement accounts, home equity, and liquidation of assets.

Many small loan requests are turned down because they include a large component of venture capital for which the bank is not willing to assume the increased risk. This means that those applicants would have to finance 50 to 80 percent of their business out of their own pockets in order to reduce the need for outside financing to an amount palatable to a bank. For this reason, bankers often hear "You will only lend money to people that already have money" from spurned business owners.

CAPITAL LEVERAGE

The price of a bank's stock is penalized if the return on their own equity is inadequate. Banks can tweak the return on equity by lowering credit standards to push more loans out the door, using capital to buy more banks (to achieve greater economies of scale) or pay increased dividends (thereby lowering equity that increases the return on equity ratio). They actually try to increase the leverage of their balance sheet in order to appease financial analysts. Too bad banks don't feel the same euphoria when their business customers increase their leverage.

Leverage is a very good name for the concept of using capital to lever debt. Imagine the owner's equity of a small business as being a weightlifter who has power lifted a large weight over his head. Every ounce that is added to the weights reduces his capacity to withstand more weight. Finally, as weight is added, the strongman collapses. This is what happens to businesses that have to clean and jerk more debt than their capital can support.

The time-tested formula that banks use to measure capital adequacy, or leverage, is the debt-to-worth ratio. This ratio is calculated by dividing a business's net worth into its total liabilities. Net worth, in this case, is usually further refined to tangible net worth. Tangible net worth is the net worth of the business less all intangible assets, including goodwill, noncompete agreements, loans receivable from company officers or shareholders, licenses, and other rights. The reason these assets are deducted is they are worthless once the company starts to go downhill. In a liquidation, they could not be sold to help repay a loan.

Until recently, banks would not loan money to companies with debt-to-worth ratios greater than 2.0:1.0 or to companies with negative net worth (accumulated losses). Competition and the need to deploy liquidity have forced banks to ignore the old standard. In fact, there is no set rule of thumb today. Companies with debt-to-worth ratios of 50 to 1 or with huge negative net worths are able to borrow money if other requirements established by the bank are met.

CAPITAL RULES OF THUMB

Generally, banks look for 20 to 30 percent owner's equity into any business. Anything less would be considered undercapitalized. In preparation of a loan application, business owners should try to put every available penny or asset into the business in lieu of borrowed dollars. Not only will this better prepare the business for the vagaries of economics, but will also impress the banker with the fact that you believe enough in your business to put yourself on the line.

Collateral

Banks do not approve loans based on collateral. Lack of sufficient collateral, though, could cause a loan to be declined. Collateral is the bank's back door out of a loan when a business does not generate enough cash flow to repay the debt. An applicant might have ten times the amount of collateral required to adequately cover a loan but, without cash flow, the loan will be turned down.

COLLATERAL VALUE

All collateral is not equal. Bankers speak about collateral value, that is, the value that a specific type or piece of collateral has in relation to the loan. All assets have a fair market value. Fair market value is the price that, given ample time on the market, a willing buyer would pay to a willing seller for an object. Bankers might assign a fair market value based on the asset's actual cost, its appraised value, or some other valuation method. The easier it is to obtain a security interest in an asset, the easier it is to maintain control of the assets and the easier it is to liquidate an asset, the more closely the collateral value is to the fair market value.

As an example, let us use residential real estate—our homes—since most people will be familiar with this asset. Banks normally will loan no more than 80 percent of the appraised value of a home. Why? First, how many people will walk away from a 20 percent equity stake in a home without pulling out all the stops to keep the payments current? Not many. Second, should the bank have to foreclose on your home, it will take at least one year for them to complete the process. The bank can lose at least one year's worth of interest payments on the loan and will rack up legal expenses in the process. Foreclosures are on the public record. Once the word is out that a home is under foreclosure, no one will make an offer for the appraised value. The bank will list the home with a local real estate salesperson to properly market the home. At closing, the salesperson will take a commission check equal to 7 to 10 percent of the sales price. All told, the bank will be lucky to net 80 percent of the original appraised value if they have to foreclose on a home. This is a firm number based on decades of home loan lending. (Yes, loans of 90 percent, 95 percent, and even 99 percent are available, but with costly mortgage insurance policies in place and much higher interest rates.)

The same analysis helps determine the collateral value of many asset categories. Again, the discount rate, the percent of the asset's fair market value that a bank recognizes as an asset's collateral value, is not plucked out of the air. The discount rates have been determined over years and years of lending experience to be very accurate measures of what a bank will realize from the liquidation of a given asset class. Table 5-1 shows a list of the standard discount rates used throughout the banking industry.

Table 5-1: Collateral Valuation

Asset Category	Discount Rate
Cash, CDs	100%
Accounts receivable	80%
Inventory	80%
Machinery and equipment	60%
Commercial real estate and buildings	75%
Residential real estate	80%
NYSE stocks	80%
NASDAQ stocks	60%
US Treasury bonds	90%
Corporate bonds	70%
Vehicles	50%
Collectibles	0%
Intangibles	0%

CASH AND CERTIFICATES OF DEPOSIT

This is money that is deposited at the bank and pledged to secure the loan. If the customer defaults on the loan, the bank simply takes the cash and pays off the loan and accrued interest. The value of cash is absolute and, when pledged, it is controlled by the bank. Since it is so easy to value, hold, and sell, it is given the highest value of any type of collateral. People use cash to secure loans in order to get lower interest rate concessions from the bank. Banks will typically charge a rate that is 2 percent higher than the rate being paid on the deposit account. That can carve down the cost of borrowing by one-quarter to one-third. Another frequent use of cash as collateral is when a guarantee from someone other than the borrower is secured by it. A mother may wish to help out a daughter, but not cash in a CD if at all possible. Instead, she pledges the CD, continues to take interest income from the account, and helps out her daughter.

ACCOUNTS RECEIVABLE

Accounts receivable are working capital assets that change in value daily because of sales and collections. Since most businesses maintain good, written records of accounts receivable and because the amounts owed to the business are usually collected within thirty days of the creation of the receivable, banks like to use this asset as collateral. Banks discount the book value of accounts receivable at a rate of 80 percent; this rate can and does change on a case-by-case basis.

Banks do not lend 100% of receivables for three reasons. First, in the normal course of business, some accounts receivable fail to pay up. Second, by the time a bank finds out its borrower is in trouble, the accounts receivable have been collected by the borrower and the funds deployed elsewhere. Last, once a bank takes over a portfolio of accounts receivable and contacts each customer, an endless game of "I don't owe that" begins. Years ago, I liquidated a lumber company. So many people argued that they had not yet received the materials for which they had been billed that I began to think the only way for a company to protect itself from nefarious customers was to videotape them leaving the premises with the goods! Even the customers who agreed that they owed money to the defunct company tried to whittle down the debts through negotiations.

INVENTORY

Inventory, similar to accounts receivable, is discounted by 80 percent in most cases. These assets can also disappear from the radar screen before the bank finds out that its borrower is in trouble. The saving grace for inventory is that its collateral value is based on cost and not the retail or resale value. Thus, in a liquidation scenario, a bank could actually sell inventory for more than its listed collateral value (but less than market prices in order to move it quickly). The amount of money a bank is willing to lend against any particular kind of inventory is based on the ease of valuation and control of the assets. Vehicles that are easy to value and track by their respective vehicle identification numbers are often allowed a discount rate of 95 percent. Gift shop inventory, composed of thousands of knickknacks, is not so easy to value or track; that type of asset might only warrant a discount rate of 50 percent.

Inventory collateral valuations have been a thorn in the side of the agricultural industry for years. Cows don't care whether the farmer is in charge or if the bank has foreclosed on the farm; they still have to be milked twice a day. Crops, out in the fields, are subject to perils like drought, flooding, infestation, hail, and frost. Crops in shiny storage bins are subject to mold, insects, and foreign markets. My old high school football coach, who was adverse to the forward pass, used to tell us, "There are three things that can happen when you pass the ball and two of them are bad." Agricultural inventory financing makes those odds look great.

Several years ago, at another bank, a hog-farming client skipped town, one step ahead of foreclosure and the law. My boss dispatched one of my colleagues to go out to the farm to feed and water the hogs. My co-worker discovered that the hogs had been shut in a barn for nearly one week. He had no choice but to go in and take care of business. Prior to leaving, he noticed that his suit was impregnated with the nauseating smell of methane and ammonia, which emanated from the hog barn. Stripping down to his skivvies, he simply discarded the suit in the farm trash bin. Fortunately, he stopped home for a shower and new clothes before returning to the bank.

Another subcategory of inventory is work in process. This category is a standard classification for a manufacturing company. Raw materials are excellent inventory collateral since they can be readily marketed to other manufacturers. Once that raw material has been altered, it becomes work in process and remains so until it is completed as the final product. In order for a bank to sell work in process, it would have to "run" the company long enough to complete all the work. Most bankers do not have the necessary experience or inclination to run a manufacturing company; therefore, they do not allow any collateral value for work in process.

MACHINERY AND EQUIPMENT

This category is very diverse and ranges from staplers to monster-size machines that stamp out half a car at a time. Naturally, machines that have the longest useful life are the most difficult to move, and those that are most technologically up to date will carry higher discount rates. In general, banks allow 60 percent of book value of machinery and equipment as collateral value. Too many entrepreneurs hope to borrow 90 percent of the cost of outfitting their home offices with office equipment; that is the kind of equipment bankers normally consign to "supplies" expense rather than assets.

Some industrial equipment not only holds its value, but also increases value over time. Quality printing presses and plastic injection mold machines are two categories that come to mind. In fact, some manufacturers are so confident in their products that they will guarantee to buy the equipment back from a bank—if necessary—for a specified amount that usually equates to the balance of any loan used to purchase the equipment originally.

The reason for the lower discount rate on equipment than on accounts receivable or inventory is the expected cost of preparing the equipment for sale. When a bank encounters a liquidation that involves equipment, it normally will have to spend considerable sums to clean up, repair, and move the assets. Most larger pieces of machinery require the services of electricians or plumbers to make them ready for resale.

COMMERCIAL REAL ESTATE AND BUILDINGS

Previously, we discussed the advance rate on residential real estate as an example to which everyone can relate. Commercial real estate is different due to liability laws and government regulation. Prior to foreclosing on a commercial parcel, a bank must perform environmental due diligence surveys to ensure that they will not assume major environmental expenses. It may also be required to maintain higher cost liability insurance or flood insurance on the property. Property tax rates are often higher for commercial properties than residential properties, too. The market for commercial real estate is not the same as for residential real estate. Look at any commercial building in your vicinity and imagine that it is vacated, for whatever reason, overnight. How long and far would one have to look to find a suitable buyer at a fair price for that building?

Applicants often ask for loans with which to purchase vacant land or try to pledge vacant land as collateral for a loan. At best, banks will use a discount rate of 50 percent of the cost of the land. Not only does vacant land carry all the regulatory baggage as does developed commercial real estate, but it also holds speculative risks. There are an infinite number of suckers in America who will buy bare ground in the belief that "the railroad is coming through." Much of the purchase price of vacant land is based on an assumption of the intended use of the property. Granted, in Michigan, we have people who buy tracts of land up north for the express purpose of owning a vacant piece of ground on which to hunt or fish. Typically, though, buyers pay more than a piece of property is worth under the assumption that the land value will go up once they have completed their "development." That is of no value to a lender who, if foreclosure occurs, will not pursue the debtor's dream development use.

RESIDENTIAL REAL ESTATE AND DWELLINGS

This category was discussed earlier in the book. Suffice it to say that residential real estate is much easier to appraise, and the market is much more stable than that of commercial real estate.

MARKETABLE SECURITIES—STOCKS AND BONDS

Marketable securities make for excellent collateral because they are easy to value, easy to control, and easy to liquidate. The difference between the discount rates for the subcategories of New York Stock Exchange (NYSE), National Association of Securities Dealers Automated Quoting (NASDAQ) system, government bonds, and corporate bonds is the perceived size of the available market for each. It has long been presumed that NYSE stocks are easier to sell than NASDAQ stocks because investors typically would rather own the stock of well-known companies than that of smaller companies. This is not necessarily true today, but banks still allow higher advances against NYSE securities. The same holds for government bonds and corporate bonds. Investors will typically take a bond backed by the full faith and credit of the U.S. government before a bond simply backed by a corporation.

Closely held securities like stock in nonpublic corporations are not readily marketable and do make for good collateral. Banks often do take closely held stock for collateral for reasons other than value. Banks can convert the ownership of the stock to the bank and have immediate control of a company when difficulties arise.

VEHICLES

As mentioned earlier, once a vehicle leaves the dealer's lot, half its value evaporates. Enough said.

COLLECTIBLES

Over the years, I have been asked to use guns, stamps, coins, Hummel figurines, Christmas ornaments, antiques, military memorabilia, baseball cards, and like collectibles for collateral. Unfortunately, these assets fail to meet the three-way test of acceptable, valuable collateral because they are difficult to value, control, and liquidate. The applicant that sits down with me and says, "I am selling off my collection of antique pottery in order to lower the amount of money I need to borrow," is the applicant that stands a great chance of getting a loan from me.

The value of collectibles is consists of rarity and buyer sentimentality—neither of which a banker can adequately judge. Bank vaults are designed to hold files, not stacks of Civil War artillery. Banks cannot afford the time or effort to search for the best buyer for a collection, either. Auctions are the norm, and that means prices will be set by the local market, which might not be the best market at the time. It is best to not offer to pledge collectibles or to report them on your personal financial statement unless you are willing to sell the collection in whole or part in order to raise money. No banker will allow any discount factor whatsoever on collectibles.

INTANGIBLES

The largest intangible asset that appears on business balance sheets is goodwill. Goodwill is the amount paid above asset value to buy a business. The concept of goodwill assumes that the business's reputation alone will account for a minimum amount of trade. This is perfectly legitimate. Unfortunately, by the time a bank gets around to liquidating a company, any goodwill that did exist is gone—forever. Banks do not assign any collateral value to goodwill. Many banks will require the entire amount of goodwill that is included in a purchase price to be paid out of owner's cash or to be financed by the seller.

The second most prevalent intangible asset owned by small businesses is franchise or licensing fees. These are fees paid up front to a third party to secure the right to transact business under an already established system or name. Unfortunately, the franchiser or licensing agency holds the rights to resell its business concept; the bank cannot "foreclose" on the franchise rights and find a new franchisee without the express approval of the third party. For this reason, banks seldom allow any collateral value for these rights.

Professionals often run into collateral problems due to the asset makeup of their businesses. The major asset owned by doctors, lawyers, dentists, and others is their client files. These are of value only to a succeeding practitioner. The success of the succeeding professional will depend upon his or her acceptance by the clients on the existing roll. If they do not like the new person, they will seek out someone else, which renders the files worthless.

Trademarks, patents, and copyrights are intangibles that may or may not hold value. One positive example was a radio station client of mine. The station operated with the call letters WSTR. Another station, well outside this customer's market, developed a sales program that evolved around the slogan, "Star Radio." It looked at various call letter combinations that were available and decided to make my client an offer to purchase his call letters. It was an offer he could not refuse; the letters did not have any special significance to him or his market. Sadly, a bank cannot anticipate that value. The Internet craze has even spawned a whole industry that speculates on business names that end in ".com." Add that to any phrase, name, or word you come across; can you peg a dollar value for that combination? Probably not.

Patents usually are of some collateral value, but it takes a specialist to determine for how long the patent will be of value due to competition, expiration of patents, or changing technology.

Capacity

Capacity is a legal concept that refers to contract law. Commercial loans are contracts. Individuals must be at least 18 years old and of sound mind to enter into a valid contract. Partnerships, corporations, sole proprietorships, and limited liability companies also have legal capacity to enter into contracts if they are properly registered in their respective states and counties.

Obviously, those nonperson entities listed cannot function without human beings acting on their behalf. Thus, partners, officers, proprietors, or members can legally bind those entities. A person who signs on behalf of one of those entities must also have legal capacity. That is, documentation must be presented to the bank to prove that a person is properly authorized to transact business on behalf of the subject company. This is a vital piece of the puzzle for the bank.

Frequently, a company will authorize several individuals to act on its behalf but require that more than one, if not all, must sign documents. This is a wise check and balance for the business owners. It can cause nightmares for a careless banker who issues a loan to a company based on insufficient signatures. If problems with the business or between the owners crop up, the banker might as well kiss that money good-bye. I once granted a line of credit to a husband-and-wife partnership that bought and rehabilitated real estate for use as rental properties. The husband came in one day and asked me to advance the remaining funds available on the line of credit. In one of the greatest, bone-headed moves of my career, I cut the check for several tens of thousand dollars and gave it to the gentleman. A few days later, quite to my surprise, the wife appeared in my office to let me know that her husband had packed up and left her several days earlier. She wanted to make sure that I would not lend any more money to him. Gulp! I turned the palest shade of ashen gray.

The varying business structures and resultant requirements to prove capacity are best left to the advice of professionals like attorneys or certified public accountants.

Conditions

This is a subjective category that may trip up many applicants and may, at times, seem like the banker keeps moving the target. It is a make-or-break topic of which an applicant must be cognizant or risk exposing important management weaknesses to the banker.

CONDITION OF APPLICANT

The bank will analyze the financial condition of the company to determine whether it can absorb the new debt from both balance sheet and income statement perspectives. It will seek to determine whether the business has the required staffing to meet the new challenges or to differentiate it from its competition. The bank, above all, will subjectively guess if the company has the mythical staying power that it looks for in its customers. I use the term *guess* specifically to emphasize the fact that no one can look into the future and that surprises abound in this business.

This is the one place that a well-researched business plan can head off problems or delays at the bank. The business plan should be written in your own words and should represent your interpretation of market data and information. Please do not kill off two or three trees just to include copies of all remotely pertinent demographic or market data that you find on the Internet. Reference any key information from those sources in the body of your business plan. The business plan should lead the banker, or other investors, by the nose down the path that leads to one inescapable conclusion: All the stars are aligned exactly right for your business.

CONDITION OF MARKET

The bank will analyze the market in which the borrower does business. Specifically, what advantages does the applicant have over its competitors in the market, and what are the demands of the local market. Demographic analysis, though rarely formalized, is done almost subconsciously by the bank loan officer.

CONDITION OF THE ECONOMY

National and international economies impact the smallest businesses everywhere in America. Bankers are aware of conditions around the country and keenly follow leading economic indicators. I have seen mom-and-pop logging operations closed down by dips in Asian lumber demand. Who would have thought that building trends in Japan would affect a small business in Michigan that logs off only a few dozen acres each year?

The evolving composition of our economy is also important. We are truly in an electronic/information age now. Even the Rust Belt states now are hardly dependent upon those old industries that gave them that horrid nickname.

The topic of conditions is a free-for-all exercise in thought. Applicants really need to think about the impact of existing and anticipated conditions to successfully advocate their loan requests at a bank. Worst-case scenarios must be explored and tested within a business's projections and breakeven analysis. Bankers are much more interested in worst case than in optimal case. Develop a worst-case war plan and include it in your loan application.

Bank on It

+ Bankers use the six C's of credit as the measuring stick to decision loan requests.
+ Character is the most important of the C's.
+ Sufficient cash flow, either historical or projected, must be present in order for a bank to approve a loan.
+ More than adequate collateral does not replace a lack of cash flow.
+ Owner's capital helps cushion a business from losses and catastrophes.
+ Business loan applicants must argue why current conditions are right for their companies.

six

The
Loan Proposal

Now, we will fashion a loan proposal by using the six C's of credit as building blocks. Once completed, the importance and interrelationship of each will be obvious to you. Top salespeople master the ability to make conceptual sales, that is, state their case in a nutshell. For example, a banker might call on a prospective customer and ask, "What would you say if I could save your business $30,000 of loan interest each year?" That tells the prospect that there might be a benefit for him to listen to the banker's full sales pitch. It is also an open-ended question designed to pull the prospect into a meaningful dialogue. Make no mistake about it, a business owner must also be a salesperson when it comes time to sell the loan request to a bank. Thus, the loan proposal must be a conceptual sales tool—short and to the point.

A properly written loan proposal is a lot like a resume. In just a few pages, you cannot possibly convey all the background and history that have gone into you. Your job is to outline for the prospective employer who you are, what you want, and why you deserve it. Think of a loan proposal as a resume for your business.

Too many people use voluminous business plans with reams of data that are disguised as loan proposals. Only the largest deals seen by any given bank warrant that kind of production. Remember, though a $50,000 loan might be incredibly large to you, it is a drop in the bucket to most banks. A 3-inch thick loan proposal in support of a small business loan is another sign that an applicant is unrealistic and impractical.

This chapter will show you how to construct a clear, concise loan proposal. The format is modeled on the internal loan approval forms used by three major banks. This conceptual style is consistent with bank practices and will make for a quick read by the bank loan officer. Bankers despise loan applications that omit important information or that are so overly complicated as to make deciphering them next to impossible.

Figure 6-1 is a sample of a winning loan proposal for an existing business. Figure 6-2 is an example of a loan proposal for a startup business.

Figure 6-1: Loan Proposal for an Existing Business

LOAN PROPOSAL

BORROWER:

Name:	Jones Construction, Inc.
Address:	1234 Main Street
City, State, Zip:	Jones, MI 49112
Phone:	616-555-1000
Fax:	616-555-1001
E-Mail:	jones@jonesbuildsit.com
Tax Identification Number:	38-123456789

PRINCIPALS:

#1   Name: Jackson H. Lasher
       Address: 1109 Omena Drive
       City, State, Zip: Sturgis, MI 49091
       Phone: 616-555-9898
       Social Security Number: 384-11-9999
       % Ownership: 75%
       Position: President and Treasurer

#2   Name: Scarlett Bergeron
       Address: 707 North Adams Street
       City, State, Zip: Jones, MI 49112
       Phone: 616-555-4427
       Social Security Number: 369-10-8989
       % Ownership: 25%
       Position: Vice President and Secretary

REQUESTED LOANS:
1) $500,000 five-year term loan
2) $100,000 line of credit

SOURCES:		USES:	
Cash On Hand	$225,000	Buy Gravel Plant	$725,000
Term Loan	500,000		
TOTAL:	$725,000	**TOTAL:**	$725,000

CASH FLOW:

	Historic Year 1	Historic Year 2	Historic Year 3	Interim	Projected Year 1	Projected Year 2
Date	12-31-97	12-31-98	12-31-99	4-30-00	12-31-00	12-31-01
Sales (000's)	$580	$750	$1,100	$525	$1,400	$1,750
Net Profit	85	105	145	101	205	280
Depreciation	30	30	35	14	50	50
Interest	15	12	11	4	45	42
Total Cash Flow	$130	$147	$191	$119	$300	$372
Debt Service	125	125	125	42	125	125
Coverage	1.04x	1.17x	1.52x	2.83x	2.40x	2.97x

*Payments based on 5 years amortization and 9% interest rate.

COLLATERAL:

Asset (000's)	Market Value	Discount %	Collateral Value
Cash		100%	
Accounts Rec.	$80	80%	$64
Inventory	$125	80%	$100
Machinery	$1,100	50%	$550
Real Estate:			
Commercial		75%	
Residential		80%	
Less Prior Liens			
_____			
_____			
Total Value:	$1,305		$714
Loans:			
#1	500		500
#2	100		100
Surplus	$705		$114
Collateral Coverage	217%		119%

Sources of Values:

All_____	Net Book Value
_____	Cost
_____	Appraisals, dated _____.
_____	Other _____.

SUMMARY:

Based on our historic results, we have sufficient cash flow to more than pay for this loan. The proceeds will allow us to purchase the equipment required to meet our new contract with the state's Department of Transportation for road construction. Our projections are based on maintaining the current level of business and adding the revenues from the state contract (see attached contract).

ATTACHMENTS:

Balance Sheet and Income Statements for 1997, 1998, and 1999.
Federal Tax Returns for same periods.
Interim Balance Sheet and Income Statement for 4/30/00.
Projected Income Statements for year-end 2000 and 2001.
Copy of Contract with state.
Sales Proposal from equipment manufacturer.
Personal Financial Statements for principals.
Federal Tax Returns for each principal for the years of 1998 and 1999.
Certificate of Incorporation

The undersigned certifies that all of the information contained in this document is true and accurate.

Borrower Name: Jones Construction, Inc.

Representative: Jackson H. Lasher, President
                           Name   Title

Date: May 31, 2000

Figure 6-2: Loan Proposal for a Startup Business

LOAN PROPOSAL

BORROWER:

Name:	Theresa A. Lasher d/b/a Anna's Antiques
Address:	707 North Main Street
City, State, Zip:	Fowler, IN 48836
Phone:	765-555-0121
Fax:	765-555-0122
E-Mail:	tal@anna-tiques.com
Tax Identification Number:	To be determined

PRINCIPALS:

#1

Name:	Theresa A. Lasher
Address:	707 North Main Street
City, State, Zip:	Fowler, IN 48836
Phone:	765-555-1234
Social Security Number:	369-62-0918
% Ownership:	100%
Position:	Sole Proprietor

REQUESTED LOANS:

1) $50,000 term loan to buy base inventory of antiques

SOURCES:		USES:	
My Cash	$25,000	Buy Antiques	$75,000
Bank Loan	50,000		
TOTAL:	$75,000	**TOTAL:**	$75,000

CASH FLOW:

	Historic Year 1	Historic Year 2	Historic Year 3	Interim	Projected Year 1	Projected Year 2
Date					12-31-01	12-31-02
Sales (000's)					$210	$265
Net Profit					35	42
Depreciation					7	6
Interest					6	5
Total Cash Flow					$48	$53
Debt Service					12	12
Coverage					400%	441%

*Payments based on 5 years amortization and 9% interest rate.

COLLATERAL:

Asset	Market Value	Discount %	Collateral Value
Cash		100%	
Accounts Rec.		80%	
Inventory	75,000	80%	$60,000
Machinery		50%	
Real Estate:			
Commercial	90,000	75%	67,500
Residential		80%	
Less Prior Liens			
Land Contract	(60,000)		(60,000)
Total Value:	$105,000		$67,500
Loans:			
#1	50,000		50,000
Surplus	$ 65,000		$17,500
Collateral Coverage	210%		135%

Sources of Values:

_____	Net Book Value
XXX	Cost
_____	Appraisals, dated _____.
_____	Other _____.

SUMMARY:

Collateral is provided by the inventory to be purchased and equity in a building that I am buying on land contract. Cash flow is realistic based on similar antique stores in other communities in our county and based on my experience in the estate auction business in this area for the last ten years.

I have an outside source of income to pay my personal expenses. Additionally, I live in one of four apartments above the antique store location (rent free). The other three apartments provide more than enough cash flow to service the land contract and cover any unexpected maintenance on the building.

ATTACHMENTS:

1. Personal financial statement and last three years' tax returns
2. Copy of land contract
3. Business plan (projections and assumptions on page 16)
4. Letters of intent from three area estate/trust attorneys to recommend to their clients use of my store for consignment sales
5. Lists of antiques sold at most recent auctions held at Lafayette Antique Depot (to provide idea of cost of inventory)
6. My resume
7. Assumed Name Certificate

The undersigned certifies that all of the information contained in this document is true and accurate.

Borrower Name: _Theresa A. Lasher d/b/a Anna's Antiques_

Representative: _____

Theresa A. Lasher   Proprietor

Date:_____

Identification of Borrower and Loan Request

Unbelievably, many applicants fail to tell bankers who they are, where they may be contacted, or what they want from the bank. This section leads off the loan proposal and must be clear. When a loan officer sorts through the piles on his desk, the easy-to-understand applications will get priority attention. Why not? They are the easiest ones to process and clear off the desk. A fuzzy and ambiguous proposal might sprout roots on the desk by the time the loan officer feels up to tackling it.

The information in this section of your proposal allows the bank to assess the character and capacity "C's." Names, addresses, and tax identification numbers are needed to generate third-party credit reports like those sold by TRW and Dun and Bradstreet. Credit reports will objectively portray a company's or an individual's character in regard to how debt has been handled historically and the applicant's respect for commitments. Credit investigation may not end with these basic reports, either. Banks will often call an applicant's suppliers, creditors, and customers to research how the applicant handles its business affairs. The bank might even call its own customers, who may be competitors, suppliers, or customers of the applicant, without divulging any financial or competitive information, to inquire about the applicant's reputation.

IDENTIFICATION OF BORROWER

The first section of any loan proposal must clearly identify who or what is the applicant. If the business is a partnership, corporation, limited liability corporation, or professional corporation, its legal name must be included in full. An individual's name should appear here only if the business is a sole proprietorship. If the applicant uses a trade name other than the name of the legal entity, that name should be stated on the second line. Here are several examples:

Example 1
General Sales, Inc.
d/b/a Mega Widgets

Example 2
Big Eleven, A Michigan Partnership
d/b/a Pigskin Souvenirs

Example 3
Lisa J. Smith
d/b/a Smith Investments

The initials d/b/a stand for "doing business as." When a business uses any other name than that of its legal entity, it must file an Assumed Name Certificate in the counties in which it operates.

Note that the first example uses the standard abbreviation for the word *Incorporated*. Companies can be registered using abbreviations like Inc. or Corp. or the complete words for which the abbreviations substitute. Do not write General Sales, Incorporated if you filed the corporation name using just the abbreviation. Any deviation can cause delays in the bank's due diligence or, later, in documenting a loan.

It is common for married couples to make loan applications under both names of the individuals. It is not correct to do so. If the business is a sole proprietorship, then list only the individual in whose name the business is registered. If both individuals in the marriage share ownership in a business, then, legally, the business is a partnership. We send couples away every day with marching orders to file a Certificate of Co-Partnership with their local county clerk. Most banks will require the couple to formalize a partnership agreement, too.

The next section after the proper legal name of the applicant is the correct current address and telephone numbers for the business. A street address is mandatory, but include a post office box number if you have one. The street address will help the bank in its analysis if location is a key issue and to process certain due diligence functions. Omission of a street address connotes a fly-by-night or shoestring operation. Telephone numbers should include the business's facsimile machine line if available.

The last line of the company identification section should be its federal tax identification number. If the business is new or a startup and no number has yet been received, it is permissible to write "To be determined" or "Applied for."

Next, the principals, or owners, of the business must be identified. Every shareholder or partner should be listed along with his or her percent of company ownership, home address, telephone number, and social security number. The titles and roles played at the business for each shareholder should also be included. If there are key managers at the business who do not own any of the business, they should also be listed in the same manner as shareholders with the percent of owner-ship listed as "0." If the applicant happens to be an individual, replica-tion of information from the company identification section is recommended.

IDENTIFICATION OF LOAN REQUEST

It sure seems this would be a no-brainer, but so many applicants get it wrong. The purpose of this brief statement is tell the bank how much money you need to borrow, how long you need it for, and what you plan to do with the money. Every application I receive that asks for "whatever you will lend to me" or a "line of credit to open my new business" immediately is returned to the applicant with a brief note urging the person to visit a business consultant.

This is basic information that will be used by the banker as he or she works through the loan application to analyze how the applicant stacks up against the cash flow, capital, collateral, and conditions tests. Examples of clear requests are:

Example 1
$250,000 15-year term loan to expand present building.

Example 2
$75,000 5-year term loan to purchase equipment for pizza shop.

Frequently, a business will have more than one requested loan. This is addressed in the following manner:

Example
1) $100,000 15-year term loan to purchase building for second location.
2) $50,000 1-year term line of credit to purchase inventory for second location.

Do not include an interest rate in your request unless you already have a legal commitment from another bank and you simply are trying to test the waters to see if a lower rate is available. Most rates requested in loan proposals are amazingly unrealistic and, at best, provide hints to the banker that any relationship that arises from the application might become cumbersome. This is especially true for startup entrepreneurs who believe they should get the same interest rate as their buddies who have been in business, and successfully at that, for many years. That signals to the bank only that the applicant's thought process might be haywired.

This completes the introduction section of your loan proposal to a bank. It is simple and straightforward. The bank loan officer will know exactly who made the request and what has been requested. You have the lender's attention and have started him or her down the right path to understand your needs and abilities.

Sources and Uses of Finances

For many reasons, some of which have been covered earlier in the book, banks do not lend 100 percent of the cost of purchases or against the value of pledged collateral. Banks need to know from where every dollar into a project will come. Of particular importance is how much money the business or its owner will inject into the project. This is the applicant's chance to highlight the owner's capital (one of the six C's) that will be invested into the business or project. Here are a few examples of clear sources and uses sections.

Example 1 Purchase of an asset by an existing business

Sources:		Uses:	
Business cash	$25,000	Purchase Heidelberg 6 Color Printing Press	$100,000
Bank loan	$75,000		
Totals:	$100,000		$100,000

Example 2 Purchase of a business

Sources:		Uses:	
Cash on hand	$15,000	Buy Smith Machine, Inc.	$350,000
Seller's note	$85,000		
Bank loan	$250,000		
Totals:	$350,000		$350,000

Example 3 Opening a franchise business

Sources:		Uses:	
Cash from sale of stocks	$50,000	Franchise fee	$10,000
Loan from Uncle Bob	$50,000	Equipment	$160,000
Grant from city	$5,000	Supplies, inventory	$15,000
Bank loan	$95,000	Pre-opening expenses	$10,000
		Wages first two weeks	$5,000
Totals:	$200,000		$200,000

There are three important points on which to focus in constructing a sources and uses table. First, be very specific on the sources of your cash. The amount of cash on your personal financial statement or business financial statement should match or exceed the amount that you show here. Otherwise, the banker will think that you are using smoke and mirrors to hide the fact that you will have to borrow the down payment elsewhere or that the actual uses will be less than shown here (that is, once you take out the loan you believe the bank will never be the wiser and the bank will be into the deal at a higher than intended loan-to-value ratio). If you will supplement cash in your checking account by selling marketable securities, borrowing against the cash value of a life insurance policy, taking out a home equity loan, or from some other source, you must explain the sources and any terms of obtaining the needed cash.

The second important item is to provide as much detail as possible on the uses of all financing, not just the loan proceeds. Detail is important to the banker, who will use the information in structuring the loan. It will provide the banker clues to the proper term of the loan and alert him or her to new assets that might be used for collateral. One use that should never appear on a loan application is to use the proceeds to pay debts owed to shareholders or officers of the business. Banks abhor making loans only to see the borrower or its principals frolicking about town with toys purchased with the loan proceeds. In the banker's mind, the company principals are always last in line.

The last factor is a simple one: Make sure that the total sources equals total uses. It is an obvious sign that you don't know what you are doing when the two columns don't equal the same amount. It also leaves unanswered holes in your application such as, "Where is he going to spend all this cash?" or "Is she aware she does not have enough money to accomplish this deal?" Any question that arises from the sources and uses table also implies doubts about your management ability, attention to detail, and forthrightness. Since simple math can prevent this problem, it should never occur.

Cash Flow

This section is the meat of your application. Without proven historical cash flow or substantiated projected cash flow, all the character and collateral in the world will not help you to get a loan. Use the formula from Chapter 5 to construct the spreadsheet shown in Table 6-1 of historical and projected cash flows. Be sure to include total sales in the first line of data to set the stage.

Table 6-1: Cash Flow (000's)

	Historical Results			Interim Results	Projected Results	
	12/98	12/99	12/00	6/30/01	12/01	12/02
Sales	$490	$510	$550	$305	$625	$700
Net profit	62	71	85	42	90	105
Depreciation	14	12	10	8	18	17
Interest	19	17	14	5	21	19
Total	$95	$100	$109	$55	$129	$141
Proposed P & I*	19	19	19	9	19	19
Coverage	5.00	5.26	5.73	6.11	6.78	7.42

*Payments based on $75,000 loan with a five-year amortization at 9%.

There are several nuances to a cash flow table that need to be understood in order to put one together correctly. List up to three historical year-end periods if your business has been in existence that long. Always include the most recent interim results; if possible, include the interim results from the same period one year ago right next to this year's interim period. Projections for the next two years should be included as shown.

This example shows a company with a nice trend of increasing sales and profitability. The projections do not seem out of line with the past performances given the upward trend. Be forewarned—if your projections anticipate large increases in sales or profitability, you should include your key assumptions as footnotes. A significant increase in my mind is anything more than 10 percent over the previous year's results. Your assumptions are the factors that make you believe that those results will come true. Keep the footnotes brief—do not replicate a business plan here.

I did not include any one-time expenses as add-backs to cash flow in this example. Valid, nonrecurring expenses are rare. If your business has sufficient cash flow without adding quirky expenses back in, avoid doing so. The example also assumes that there will be no other loans outstanding after the proposed loan is made. If there will be other loans that require principal and interest payments, deduct those payments from total cash flow first to arrive at an available cash flow number. Deduct the proposed loan payments from that amount.

The proposed principal and interest payments must be based on some assumptions as to length of the loan and interest rate. When banks calculate these payments, they use an artificially high rate of interest; normally, it is 2 percent over the actual or expected rate. For an applicant's purposes, I would use a rate equivalent to the current national prime rate plus 2 percent. The national prime rate may be found in the *Wall Street Journal* every day. You may need to consult amortization tables, which are available at most libraries or in many popular software programs. Or ask a friend who owns a financial calculator if you are not familiar with calculation of amortization and payments. Footnote your payment assumptions at the bottom of the table.

Note that the payments are annualized and compared to historical, interim, and projected results. If historical cash flow is sufficient to cover the new payments, you more than likely are going to be approved for the loan. In the interim results, the principal and interest payments have been adjusted to reflect the payments that would be required during a similar period—in this case, six months.

A key ratio that bankers love to use is cash flow coverage. This is the last numeric line of the cash flow table. Simply divide the annual principal and interest payments into the annual cash flow for each period. The result is the coverage ratio. Banks typically look for a minimum coverage of 1.20. The minimum would be higher for startup concerns because it is calculated from unproven and, hence, unreliable projections.

Collateral

Another one of the six C's, collateral, also warrants a special section in your loan proposal. The purpose of a collateral summary is to demonstrate to the bank that, if required, it could liquidate the pledged assets to generate cash with which to pay off the loan balance. You will need to play with this concept; tweak it until you find the right combination of collateral that yields 100 percent coverage, on a discounted basis, of the proposed loan.

If business assets are sufficient to cover the loan amount, do not pencil in "Personal residence" because the bank will gladly take you at your word and slap a mortgage on your home. Conversely, you must be realistic. If you crunch the numbers and still end up with a large collateral shortfall, you must find other assets for the bank (like your home) or cut back on your loan request. Remember, your loan proposal is not a "wish list" or a way to advertise your "pie-in-the-sky" dreams. Unrealistic proposals paint negative pictures of the management talent behind the proposals.

Table 6-2 shows a sample collateral summary.

Table 6-2 Collateral Summary

Asset	Market Value	Discount %	Collateral Value
1) Machinery	$300,000	60%	$180,000
2) Real estate/bldg.	$750,000	75%	$562,500
3) Personal residence	$150,000	80%	$120,000
Less: 1st mortgage	($55,000)		($55,000)
TOTAL VALUE	$1,145,000		$807,500
LOANS:			
CREM	$345,000		$345,000
New request	200,000		$200,000
TOTAL LOANS	$545,000		$545,000
SURPLUS	$600,000		$262,500
COVERAGE	190%		148%

1) Net book value

2) Appraisal, date 11/12/95

3) Tax valuation

Table 6-2 is constructed by listing the available assets in one column. The fair market value of the asset is listed in the next column. Normally, these values are based on book value or an appraisal. Footnote the source of the values at the bottom of the table. The next column is where the discount rates are shown. Refer to Chapter 5 for industry standard discount rates and stick with them. Only vary from those rates if you know of a detrimental factor that would lower the amount realized from the liquidation of any asset. For example, a manufacturer may have several pieces of dormant equipment in its shop. The company's balance sheet reports a value for those pieces of equipment even though it might take a sum of money to hook up or update the machines for use. A honest manager will lower the overall book value to reflect true conditions.

The final column is the discounted value of the assets. The figures in this column are what a bank could hope to realize from the forced sale of the assets. If a particular asset has a purchase money loan outstanding against it, you must deduct the present balance of the loan. In the example, there are two loans that are handled in different manners. In order for the bank to realize any proceeds from the sale of a personal residence, it would have to first pay off any senior mortgages; thus, outstanding home loans are deducted immediately after the asset is listed in the summary. The acronym CREM is an abbreviation for commercial real estate mortgage. In this case, the commercial mortgage loan was made to the customer by the bank that is considering the new business loan. The loan, therefore, is deducted in a different place along with the proposed loan and any other outstanding loans at the subject bank. The reason for this is that most banks will cross-collateralize business loans with all business assets. In other words, when the bank makes a loan to a business, it generally puts its arms around all the company's assets. Any future loans can be secured by the same arms' load of collateral.

The sum of all business loans, existing and proposed, is deducted from the total collateral amounts—both fair market value and collateral value columns. Any collateral value remaining is called surplus collateral value. Division of the total collateral amounts by the amount of the loans yields the collateral coverage ratio. The collateral coverage ratio is a key measure that banks use for a quick glance at a loan package. The key number in the whole collateral section is the coverage ratio result under the last column. This number needs to be 100 percent or greater to satisfy most bankers. A coverage ratio of 100 percent means that the liquidated value of collateral should completely pay off the outstanding loans. Any number less than 100 percent means the bank might face a loan loss in a liquidation scenario.

Why even show fair market value if it is not used in the credit analysis? Good question. Most borrowers when faced with a workout situation cooperate with the bank in order to obtain maximum value for the sale of collateral assets. There are three reasons why a business owner would cooperate with the bank in a liquidation. First, the customer is wise enough to know that continuance of the business is only going to dig a deeper financial hole for him or her. Second, the customer knows that by cooperating, his or her character reputation at the bank and in the community will be preserved. Third, by squeezing as much as possible out of business assets, the customer will not have to reach as deeply into his or her own pocket. Unfortunately, bankers must plan for the worst-case scenario, so we use the discounted collateral value. The fair market value provides a benchmark that we can use in discussions with a client during workout negotiations.

Summary

This final section of the loan proposal is the catchall. If you have a business plan, pull the salient points from it and list them here, but do not replicate it. Existing businesses should keep comments short and sweet. The two topics that must be covered are the benefits of the loan to your business and your business's repayment ability.

"This loan will allow me to achieve my lifelong dream" is not a benefit! If we were all entitled to our dreams, I would be teeing it up at St. Andrews or hiking in the Tetons every Saturday. Benefits need to be objective and easy to understand. This is easiest for existing companies. Here are some examples of statements of benefits for existing companies.

Example 1

"The new equipment will allow us to increase production by 15 percent in order to meet current overdemand for our products."

Example 2

"We have been offered a contract by the Regional Airport Authority, which will require us to dedicate two new pieces of snow removal equipment to that site. Approval of this loan will allow us to accept the contract. The financial benefits have been built into the projections above."

Example 3

"Our existing facility was built in 1915 and costs us a fortune to heat and cool. Production efficiency is about 40 percent of our average competitor's. The loan will allow us to build a new, multipurpose building, which will put our production efficiency at 135 percent of our average competitor. This translates to an improvement of $65,000 to our net profit, based on last year's results."

Example 4

"We have experienced rapid growth and profitability. This has caused us to tie up our working capital in higher levels of inventory and accounts receivable. This loan will enable us to continue to meet payroll and to earn terms from our suppliers."

Startup business owners will find it difficult to make a simple statement without sounding starry-eyed. Yet, they should resist the temptation to replicate the extraneous information contained in the business plan. Good statements for startup entrepreneurs might be:

Example 1
"Based on conclusions in my business plan, this is the minimum loan amount required to get the business started on proper footing. The equipment to be purchased with the loan will generate up to $300,000 in annual sales and $35,000 in net profit, according to the plan."

Example 2
"The loan will allow me to purchase the existing business known as Main Street Electric with average annual sales of $600,000 and profit/owner's compensation of $85,000."

Example 3
"I have practiced my profession at my existing firm for five years. This loan will allow me to establish my own practice in a location better suited to my clientele and to provide them with more personalized service."

At least one sentence should start with these words, "Repayment of the loan will come from. . . ." If the applicant is an existing business and the cash flow table included in the proposal shows historical loan coverage in excess of 1.2, the conclusion of the statement is fairly easy, "by proven cash flow."

Applicants that do not have a proven history of sufficient cash flow will have to work harder to finish the statement. For many companies, the benefits of the loan may be expanded to show that the loan will actually help increase cash flow. Examples include:

Example 1
"Repayment of the loan will come from revenue generated by increased production."

Example 2
"Repayment of the loan will come from revenue from the new contract."

Startup companies will need to refer to business plans or other data like franchise offering circulars.

> Example 1
> "Repayment of the loan will come from revenue generated by gaining 1 percent of the local market. Refer to business plan, page 17, for details."

> Example 2
> "Repayment of the loan will come from revenue from the store. The average Hockey Puck Burger Joint franchise has annual cash flow of $65,000 in the first year of operations. Refer to business plan for more details."

If there is no justification that the business will be able to earn the required cash flow—and we see plenty of applications like that—the applicant should move on to what bankers call back doors.

> Example 1
> "Repayment of the loan will come from profits of the business. Since this is a new business and the ability to earn the minimum amount necessary to repay the loan is speculative, secondary repayment sources will be available from my spouse's salary, which is $125,000 per year, and net rental income from our duplex, which is $16,000 per year."

> Example 2
> "Repayment of the loan will come from expected business earnings per the business plan. Should the expected earnings not materialize, collateral is substantive enough to retire the entire loan upon liquidation."

As these examples illustrate, this is not the place to create a smoke screen for your loan officer. If the banker notes any hint of the scent of smoke in the air, he or she will probably not bother to look at any supporting information you have attached to the loan proposal. Be concise and critical of the data contained in the loan proposal. Your honest assessment that it might be a struggle for the business to cover the loan payments will be better received than any amount of obfuscation.

Attachments

At this point, your loan proposal has piqued the interest of the banker who is now willing to roll up his or her sleeves and do some real work to determine whether he or she will grant the loan. Anticipation of the information that your banker will require will reflect positively on you as a well-prepared applicant and will save days or weeks in the process. All too often, bankers have to track an applicant down to request more information in support of an application. Once the banker sets the original application down on his or her desk, it goes to the bottom of the pile. If everything necessary is already attached to the loan proposal, the banker faces a simple task of thumbing through it right away and making a recommendation.

Figure 6-3 is a master checklist of materials that should be attached to a loan proposal. Not every item applies to every loan or situation. Some may apply but not be available or completed at the time of the application. Include as much as you can. Unlike the fluff that appears in business plans, these items are all meat; let the banker pick and choose what he or she wants to use.

Financial statements are a given. Include up to five years of historical year-end financial statements or for every year the business has been in existence if fewer than five years are available. The comparable federal tax returns should be included, too. Long gone is the era when the banker would look the other way when presented two sets of books ("one for the bank, one for Uncle Sam") The most recent interim financial statements are mandatory, and they should be dated within ninety days of the application. Do not give a banker a one-month statement ended January 31 for an application dated September 1. Inclusion of the interim statement for the same period one year earlier will allow the banker to compare this year's results to last year's easier. Projections with good assumptions can be compared to previous years for viability and accuracy. If the source of any required cash equity is

Figure 6-3

LOAN PROPOSAL CHECKLIST

Subject Business:

Last three years' federal tax returns.

Last three years' balance sheets and income statements.

Interim balance sheet and income statement dated less than ninety days old.

Accounts receivable and payable agings if applying for working capital.

Schedule of collateral.

Schedule of existing term debt.

Projected income statements for next two years.

Projected cash flow statement for next twelve months if request is for working capital or for a new business.

Affiliated Businesses:

Last three years' federal tax returns.

Last three years' balance sheets and income statements.

Interim balance sheet and income statement dated less than ninety days old.

Statement detailing relationship to applicant.

Principals:

Last two years' federal tax returns.

Personal financial statement dated less than ninety days old.

Resume.

Transaction (if pertinent, provide copies of the following):

Invoices

Purchase agreements

Appraisals

Surveys

Contracts

Leases

Business plan

Other

unclear, include bank or brokerage statements or some other identification of its source and value.

Accounts receivable and accounts payable agings are very helpful to the banker. From them, they can tell a lot about your business, including whether you have a risky concentration of sales to one client, the value of your receivables, your relationship with your suppliers, and so on. A schedule of all term debt owed by the business now or anticipated to be owed at the time of the loan closing should include source of debt, original and current balance, payment terms, maturity date, interest rate, and any collateral pledged to secure the loan.

A complete set of financial statements should be provided to the bank for any affiliated businesses that are owned wholly or in part by the applicant company or its principals. This information, though not directly pertinent to the application in hand, tells the bank plenty, too. The banker can determine whether money flows back and forth between the companies and whether this loan is actually a loan to another, substandard company. They can further clue in the bank about the management ability of the applicant company's owners. Finally, the statements can bolster arguments for repayment ability, particularly when the businesses are identical (like franchise locations) or alike in some other facet.

A current personal financial statement (see Figure 6-4) should be included for every owner of the business and any key managers who have financial decision-making authority for the company. Copies of the last two years of federal income tax returns should accompany each personal financial statement. Although federal law prohibits banks from requiring financial information on spouses, it is a good idea to include spousal assets and income on the personal financial statements. This can only help the proposal. If you are determined to not bring your spouse into the fray or if your spouse refuses to go along with your new venture, the personal financial statement should list only assets that are owned solely by you. Unfortunately, you will need to list all debts jointly payable by your spouse and you since you are legally liable for the whole amount. You get the picture; without inclusion of the spouse, most personal financial statements deteriorate rapidly.

Collateral information should include a list of all available collateral of significant value. Please do not itemize staplers, supplies, and the contents of your janitorial closet. Figure 6-5 is the SBA's standard form for listing collateral. An option for many companies is to attach a depreciation schedule to the loan proposal. A depreciation schedule is kept by accountants and provides a breakdown of the current book value of all capitalized assets. Remember to include personal residences only if necessary to show enough collateral value to cover the loan.

If you will be buying assets with the loan proceeds, it is helpful to include copies of invoices or quotes for those assets from bona fide suppliers. If the purchase is contract based, include a copy of the contract, especially in real estate or business purchase transactions. If you are buying an existing business, a written statement from the sellers explaining why they are selling the business would be welcomed ("because Wal-Mart is moving in across the street and will blow me out of business if I don't sell fast" might not be a good statement to turn in with your application). In real estate transactions, where real estate is being purchased or will be pledged as collateral, include any available paperwork like appraisals, surveys, title insurance policies, flood insurance certificates, hazard insurance binders, environmental surveys, or listing agreements. Copies of leases either with the business as tenant or landlord help the banker's analysis.

If any loan proceeds will be used to pay off an existing debt like a bank loan or land contract, include a copy of those debt instruments along with an amortization schedule if available. For bank loans, a copy of the last invoice or the payment book coupon is helpful.

Resumes for each shareholder in the business and all key managers are extremely important. The resumes speak to management ability and help to flesh out the character traits of the individuals, too.

For franchises, include copies of the proposed franchise agreement and the franchise's offering circular. For all other businesses, include a copy of a business plan if one is available and it is consistent with the loan proposal. Many business plans are written in a vacuum and prior to implementation become obsolete because of changed assumptions or realities. As you can see from this list, the banker will have enough reading to do without having to wade through hundreds of pages of

Figure 6-4 Personal Financial Statement

PERSONAL FINANCIAL STATEMENT

U.S. SMALL BUSINESS ADMINISTRATION

As of _____ , 19 ___

Complete this form for: (1) each proprietor, or (2) each limited partner who owns 20% or more interest and each general partner, or (3) each stockholder owning 20% or more of voting stock, or (4) any person or entity providing a guaranty on the loan.

Name	Business Phone

Residence Address	Residence Phone

City, State, & Zip Code

Business Name of Applicant/Borrower

ASSETS	(Omit Cents)	LIABILITIES	(Omit Cents)
Cash on hands & in Banks	$	Accounts Payable	$
Savings Accounts	$	Notes Payable to Banks and Others	$
IRA or Other Retirement Account	$	(Describe in Section 2)	
Accounts & Notes Receivable	$	Installment Account (Auto)	$
Life Insurance-Cash Surrender Value Only (Complete Section 8)	$	Mo. Payments $	
		Installment Account (Other)	$
Stocks and Bonds (Describe in Section 3)	$	Mo. Payments $	
		Loan on Life Insurance	$
Real Estate (Describe in Section 4)	$	Mortgages on Real Estate (Describe in Section 4)	$
Automobile-Present Value	$	Unpaid Taxes	$
Other Personal Property (Describe in Section 5)	$	(Describe in Section 6)	
		Other Liabilities	$
Other Assets (Describe in Section 5)	$	(Describe in Section 7)	
		Total Liabilities	$
		Net Worth	$
Total	$	Total	$

Section 1. Source of Income		Contingent Liabilities	
Salary	$	As Endorser or Co-Maker	$
Net Investment Income	$	Legal Claims & Judgments	$
Real Estate Income	$	Provision for Federal Income Tax	$
Other Income (Describe below)*	$	Other Special Debt	$

Description of Other Income in Section 1.

*Alimony or child support payments need not be disclosed in "Other Income" unless it is desired to have such payments counted toward total income.

Section 2.   Notes Payable to Bank and Others.   (Use attachments if necessary. Each attachment must be identified as a part of this statement and signed.)

Name and Address of Noteholder(s)	Original Balance	Current Balance	Payment Amount	Frequency (monthly, etc.)	How Secured or Endorsed Type of Collateral

SBA Form 413 (2-94) Use 5-91 Edition until stock is exhausted. Ref: SOP 50-10 and 50-30   (tumble)

Figure 6-4 Personal Financial Statement

Section 3.

Number of Shares	Name of Securities	Cost	Market Value Quotation/Exchange	Date of Quotation/Exchange	Total Value

Section 4. (List each parcel separately. Use attachment if necessary. Each attachment must be identified as a part of this statement and signed.)

	Property A	Property B	Property C
Type of Property			
Address			
Date Purchased			
Original Cost			
Present Market Value			
Name & Address of Mortgage Holder			
Mortgage Account Number			
Mortgage Balance			
Amount of Payment per Month/Year			
Status of Mortgage			

Section 5. (Describe, and if any is pledged as security, state name and address of lien holder, amount of lien, terms of payment and if delinquent, describe delinquency)

Section 6. Unpaid Taxes. (Describe in detail, as to type, to whom payable, when due, amount, and to what property, if any, a tax lien attaches.)

Section 7. Other Liabilities. (Describe in detail.)

Section 8. Life Insurance Held. (Give face amount and cash surrender value of policies - name of insurance company and beneficiaries)

I authorize SBA/Lender to make inquiries as necessary to verify the accuracy of the statements made and to determine my creditworthiness. I certify the above and the statements contained in the attachments are true and accurate as of the stated date(s). These statements are made for the purpose of either obtaining a loan or guaranteeing a loan. I understand FALSE statements may result in forfeiture of benefits and possible prosecution by the U.S. Attorney General (Reference 18 U.S.C. 1001).

Signature: Date: Social Security Number:

Signature: Date: Social Security Number:

Figure 6-5 Standard SBA Form for Listing Collateral

UNITED STATES SMALL BUSINESS ADMINISTRATION

SCHEDULE OF COLLATERAL

Exhibit A

Applicant		
Street Address		
City	State	Zip Code

LIST ALL COLLATERAL TO BE USED AS SECURITY FOR THIS LOAN

Section I-- REAL ESTATE

Attach a copy of the deed(s) containing a full legal description of the land and show the location (street address) and city where the deed(s) is recorded. Following the address below, give a brief description of the improvements, such as size, type of construction, use, number of stories, and present condition (use additional sheet if more space is required).

LIST PARCELS OF REAL ESTATE					
Address	Year Acquired	Original Cost	Market Value	Amount of Lien	Name of Lienholder

Description(s):

Figure 6-5

SECTION II-- PERSONAL PROPERTY

All items listed herein must show manufacturer or make, model, year, and serial number. Items with no serial number must be clearly identified (use additional sheet if more space is required).

Description - Show Manufacturer, Model, Serial No.	Year Acquired	Original Cost	Market Value	Current Lien Balance	Name of Lienholder

All information contained herein is TRUE and CORRECT to the best of my knowledge. I understand that FALSE statements may result in forfeiture of benefits and possible fine and prosecution by the U.S. Attorney General (Ref. 18 U.S.C. 100).

_____   Date _____

_____   Date _____

SBA Form 4 Schedule A (8-91) Use 4-87 edition until exhausted.

meaningless statistics and multicolor graphs. A business plan is not mandatory for a loan application.

Once you have packaged the loan proposal with all the required attachments, you are set to meet with the bankers. The more organized businessperson will bind the proposal in a three-ring binder complete with tabs. Don't worry if you are not up to it; bankers expect business owners are busy enough without the worries of self-publishing a loan proposal!

Bank on It

◆ The loan proposal is a conceptual sales tool.
◆ Do not duplicate your business plan in the loan proposal.
◆ Focus on the six C's of business credit. Prove that your business meets the requirements of each category.
◆ Projected cash flow must be based on sound, verifiable assumptions.

Target the Right Bank
for Your Business

Now that your loan proposal is complete, you must select a bank or banks to approach with it. Proper selection of a bank is nearly as important as any other factor in the loan application process. This chapter will help you find the bank that is most likely to do business with you and to avoid costly errors. Poor planning at this stage may hamper your spirit, causing you to give up or lose faith, or unfairly stack the deck against yourself. By the end of the chapter, you will also find that it is not so much the bank that counts as it is the individual banker.

The Shotgun Approach

Many businesspeople who have a loan proposal in hand will simply make a dozen copies of it and drop off one copy to each bank in town. This is the shotgun approach: Shoot a wide enough pattern and you are bound to hit something. To bankers, this is akin to throwing crap against the wall to see what sticks. Bankers do not like to view themselves as the wall in this case. Strike one against the applicant.

The shotgun method is another sign that the business's management is careless, thoughtless, or impatient. I have received many loan applications over the years that have been elaborately bound in velum and are addressed to a competitor bank in town. First, if your loan application is addressed to any bank other than the one where it rests, it is not a legal application. Second, it makes the banker feel like a poor cousin or the last resort for a desperate businessperson.

The mere fact that an applicant has delivered the application to a bank with no regard to which banker lays eyes upon it is enough for me to pass it up. Indeed, at most banks, the anonymous loan application will be handed off to the rookie loan officer whose lack of experience might prevent him or her from taking risks or might make his or her superiors much more conservative in rubber-stamping the rookie's recommendations. When any banker stares down at one of these mass-produced anonymous applications, his or her mind is already predisposed to decline the loan. Unless the application is stellar, it is all too easy to find every credit weakness and mail an equally anonymous declination letter. Strike two against the applicant.

The banking industry is a fraternity. Every banker in a given town knows all the other bankers. They likely worked together in the past or served together in some charitable or benevolent capacity. They see each other at breakfasts, lunches, and golf fundraisers. They say things like, "Hey, did you get a copy of the application floating around town for that jungle theme park?" And they find fun in ridiculing each other for taking any such application seriously. This is not collusion. They do not get together and decide to turn down any application. Once it is known, though, that an application is floating around to all the banks in town, the shadow of death will settle in and hover over the application. Strike three against the applicant.

An applicant might very well visit every bank in a given town after prioritizing each and working down the list. Applying to banks by default is the last resort in selecting a bank to which to make your application. The best way to get a loan approved is to target a specific loan officer who might be sympathetic to you. Let's look at some of these preferred methods.

The Power Referral

Referrals are a strange psychological lever in human society. People who are asked to make referrals subconsciously hear, "I value your opinion and expertise." Their status in the order of things (as they perceive it) is immediately elevated. If the referral is successful, the person who made the referral receives the "thanks" of two different parties: the person who was referred and the person to whom that person was referred. Talk about two birds with one stone!

People are naturally complimented when they are referred to someone by someone else. Why would anyone recommend me to anyone else if I were not worthy of it? It feels plain good to have someone think that highly of you. Similarly, if you are at the receiving end of a referral, you are complimented by the fact that someone thinks highly enough of you to entrust one of their friends or associates to you. A referral is a win–win–win situation. The referrer, the referred, and the referee all come out feeling good about themselves. It stands to reason then that any goal is best pursued, first, via a referral network. This is very true in commercial lending. All things being equal, the applicant that has been referred to me has the edge.

Personal Referrals

A personal referral is a referral based on personal relationships. Make a mental inventory of the pool of personal relationships you have established in your community. Start by thinking of sets of relationships rather than individuals. Sets include your neighborhood, church, hobby groups, parent groups, and the like. Now, focus on each set to find a banker. The banker does not have to be a loan officer. It could be a computer operator, a teller, or a secretary.

Here's a dirty little secret that will help your confidence in approaching any bank employee you might know—even if your acquaintance is slim. Nearly every bank rewards its employees with some form of incentive in exchange for referring prospective customers to the bank. It gets better. When you ask a bank employee to refer you to someone at his or her bank, you actually are giving the employee an opportunity to put money in his or her pocket! They will be glad that you asked. So ask! Also, banks with referral incentive programs have pretty remarkable tracking methods to make sure that the referral is handled in a timely and friendly manner.

If you wrack your brain and come up empty in the banker-for-friends category, that is all right. Search your social circles for someone who has a connection to a bank or banker. A member of a bank's board of directors would be a fantastic person to refer you to a bank. A board member referral is powerful. It usually enters the bank through the chief executive's office and filters down to the appropriate person. Normally, the person who handles the referral is required to report to the chief executive with details of the decision. The lender will make sure no stone is left unturned prior to making that call!

The absolute best person to ask for a referral, though, is the spouse of a banker. If I drop the ball or give short-shrift to anyone else's referral, I only have to put up with questioning and harassment at the office. If I blow off a referral made by my spouse, I hear about it twenty-four hours a day. Nobody, absolutely nobody, wants to let down their spouse or to make their spouse look bad. It is a simple gift for a spouse to make the spouse look good in the eyes of one of his or her acquaintances. Consequently, you will need to extend your probe into the social circles of your own spouse. If your spouse socializes with a spouse of a banker, let your better half ask for the referral. A spouse-on-spouse referral multiplies the angst at the banker's end of the referral.

Business Referrals

Businesses are a good source of referrals for applicants and banks. These include run-of-the-mill businesses, CPAs, attorneys, and commercial real estate brokers.

An existing customer of a bank can make a very powerful referral. Whenever one of our good clients calls in with a referral, we waste no time or effort in meeting and working with the applicant. If we can make the loan work, we have cemented our relationship with the existing client and started a new one with the applicant. The bank stands to lose two clients if it cannot make the new application work.

CPAs, attorneys, and commercial real estate brokers are traditional referral sources to which bankers cater. Every client of a CPA is a potential bank customer. Nearly every client of a commercial law attorney is a potential customer of a bank. Every transaction created by a commercial real estate broker is an opportunity for a bank to get two new clients (buyer and seller). If you have a relationship with any of these professionals, visit with them about referring you to a banker. Statistics suggest that each CPA refers about twenty-seven clients to a bank in a given year; attorneys refer about seventeen persons each. Because of the importance to a bank's business, any referral made by one of these professionals will be worked hard toward an approval. You can also ask a friend or another business owner for a referral to one of these professionals who, in turn, might refer you to a banker.

Your suppliers can also provide great referrals. They have a vested interest in seeing that you are successful in obtaining a financing package (continuing or growing sales). Bankers are likely to view the supplier as a form of guarantor for any loan made to you, too. In dire straits, the supplier can offer the bank advice on liquidation of the referred business or help to find a buyer for the business among its other customers.

Your customers are not a good referral source. Imagine a retailer who posts the following sign next to his or her cash register: "Needed: New bank to finance this business. Please let us know if you can help!" To ask a customer to introduce you to a bank is akin to wearing that sign around your neck. If I am that customer, I would look for a new source of product immediately.

Community Contacts

The first two sources of referrals are largely dependent upon personal knowledge of other people or businesses. Sometimes it simply is not possible for an entrepreneur to line up solid referrals from individuals or businesses. Thankfully, every community has a pool of individuals who are very happy to make referrals and whose referrals mean something at a bank.

Local clergy can be of immense help, especially if you are new to town. I have received numerous referrals from local ministers and rabbis over the years. There is something sacred about these referrals that grabs a lender's attention. Dropping the ball on a referral made by a spouse is horrific enough, but imagine screwing up a referral from God!

Politicians are good to approach. Congress members, mayors, city commissioners, state representatives, and county officials make high-profile referrals that are not easily ignored by banks. Try to avoid any politician with a radical reputation to jump on any bandwagon for publicity. Salt-of-the-earth types come to mind as the description of the sort of politician whose referrals are taken in earnest.

The very best referral sources in a community are those individuals who spend their days working to better the business community. This includes chamber of commerce officials, economic development group members, local Small Business Development Company (SBDC) and Service Corps of Retired Executives (SCORE) staffers, and service club members (Rotary, Optimists, AMBUCS, and the like). These people maintain strong channels of communication with all the banks in their respective communities. They sponsor workshops and seminars specifically designed to help small businesses form the capital required that will grow jobs in the community.

An applicant needs no prior personal knowledge of any of these groups. It is a simple matter of stopping in at a chamber of commerce to ask for a list of such groups. Many full-time chambers of commerce have at least one person dedicated to be a small business ombudsman. An added bonus is that most of the groups mentioned will provide free consulting or other services to a fledgling business to help it get off the ground successfully.

Prioritizing Targets

Let's assume that you are not able to generate any referrals or that you have several referrals to different bankers. How do you prioritize which banks or bankers you will approach? First, you must research the various banks to determine which one might be most receptive to your loan application. Second, you must dig up some intelligence on the loan officer with whom you will meet.

Prioritizing Banks

There are three things to do in order to prioritize the banks you will visit with your loan application. First, you need to categorize the banks and match them with your needs. Second, you need to review the banks' own annual reports. Last, you need to seek out advice from local sources on the best bank for your type of enterprise.

In Chapter 2, we discussed the different types of banks and the types of business for which they are generally known. In Chapter 3, we also discussed the ways in which banks approve loan applications. In general, existing businesses with good track records will probably be best served at larger, multibranch banks with quicker turnaround times and a wider expanse of products. Very small businesses, startups, and businesses owned by individuals with little financial savvy will generally be better served by smaller community banks that function almost as much as consultant as bank. These are generalities and certainly will not pertain categorically to every bank and every region of the country. This will, however, help to refine your list of banks to approach.

Remember to balance the bank size issue with the fact that larger banks typically invest larger individual loan authorities in its loan officers who, consequently, don't sweat the small stuff. In other words, smaller loans do not get the same degree of analysis and are more likely to be approved with less trouble. These issues are very important factors when you finally call to make an appointment with a bank officer. Try not to spin your wheels by making a presentation to someone who cannot approve your loan request. If you are up against a deadline, large banks can also provide fast turnaround on loan requests; smaller banks, where loan committees are still the rule, may take much longer.

From the preceding generalities, make a list of likely banks to target in your community. This is your starting point from which we will make adjustments based on two other factors.

Every bank issues an annual report. Usually, a person can pop into a branch office lobby and find a stack of the reports sitting on an out-of-the-way end table. If not, ask the branch manager for a copy. Grab a copy from every bank in town and go find a quiet place to sit down and read through them.

Publicly traded banks usually include an extensive narrative in the reports. The narrative is a great source of information about the bank. Frequently, management will state unequivocally its focus on small, minority, and women-owned business lending and how the bank is structured to meet the needs of its small business customers. Other clues about a bank's appetite for small business lending may or may not be as obvious.

If mortgage lending, corporate banking, or international finance absorb the lion's share of discussion, it is likely the bank does not emphasize small business lending. Often a bank will discuss massive restructuring or past loan losses that key the reader to the possibility that the bank may not be interested in lending money at all. In general, look for something that jumps off the page at you.

A review of the bank's financial reports can help you target a bank, too. On the balance sheet, look to see if any detail is provided about the types of loans on the bank's books. Many banks break down this asset category into specific types of loans, including small business loans. If small business loans appear as a subcategory, that is a good sign. Most banks will segregate agricultural loans, too. If your business is farm related, look for an indication that the bank makes agricultural loans.

Also on the balance sheet, look for the total loans amount and the total deposits amount (the first is an asset, the second a liability). Divide the first number by the second to arrive at the bank's loan-to-deposit ratio. If loans are 80 percent or more of deposits, the bank is considered fully loaned up; that is, any more loan volume might imperil necessary liquidity required by regulators. Look for banks with lower loan-to-deposit ratios since those banks might be hungrier to better deploy their capital.

On the income statement, look for the loan loss reserve charge or bad loan charge, an expense item. This line item is known by many names, so be careful to review the income statement line by line. This is the amount of loans charged off by the bank during the past year. If a bank has charged off a large chunk of loans, its appetite for new loans will be weak. Those banks will spend considerable time in review of existing loans to make sure the mistakes that caused the hefty losses were not duplicated elsewhere in the portfolio rather than to make new loans. To determine the relative size of the charged off loans, divide the loan loss expense by the total loans number from the balance sheet. If the resulting number is 1.5 percent or higher, chances are the bank in question will rein in its new business development program in favor of cleaning house. Any number lower than 1.5 percent points to a bank that is on cruise control and ready to make new loans.

After you sift through all the available annual reports, you will find a few bank names have bubbled to the top of your list for one reason or another. Prioritize them on a list with the best bets on top and the worst at the bottom.

The next step to finalize your list of banks is to find tangible, local evidence that the banks provide the type of financing that you need. You can call the chamber of commerce, Small Business Development Center, Service Corps of Retired Executives (SCORE), or any other "in-the-know" organization. Tell them you would like their opinion on which bank in town to approach with your loan application. Explain to them your business concept and your experience. Then listen. They will, in all likelihood, give you the names of several banks that currently make loans like the one you need. The word *current* is important. Banks shift policies and procedures all the time. Today, most banks run temporary blitzes aimed at specific market segments (for example, small businesses). The local experts have their fingers on the pulse of the local banking scene and can provide valuable advice.

Next, contact a few business owners who operate businesses that are close in size and industry to your own. Be careful not to contact companies that are or will be competitors. Ask the owners with which institution they bank. You may wish to call businesses very similar, if not identical, to your own in other towns outside your own market. The owners of these businesses may give you the name of a bank that has a branch in your town. This is particularly helpful for franchise businesses. Franchise owners are a fraternity unto themselves and are very glad to help out.

A sneaky way of finding out which banks work with a specific company short of making a phone call is to obtain a check from the company's account. You might come across a check in the normal course of business or find out from an employee upon which bank its paychecks are drawn. At a minimum, you will know that a specific bank is familiar with the industry.

Cross-reference the names given to you in the course of this research with your list compiled after reading the various bank financial statements. By now, a few names should clearly be heads and shoulders above all others. These few are your top priorities. It is now time to call and make an appointment.

Profiling the Banker

Let's hope you have more than one bank on your list to call for appointments. Key in on any bank that pays incentive compensation or commissions on loans. Naturally, anyone paid on a commission basis is going to work harder to make a deal work than someone who collects a flat salary. Annual reports might speak to compensation and sales initiatives at banks. Word on the street might clue you in to which banks pay incentive compensation. Inquiries at bank branches might offer information about pay structure, too.

You will either call a specific person to whom you have been referred or a general business loan department. The bank or banker will try to screen your phone call to make sure that your request fits the department or officer. Eventually, you will end up with an individual on the phone who will agree to set up an appointment with you. Now that you have the name of a specific banker, you need to do some fast, last-minute homework.

Your job now is to turn your loan request into a leg loan for that particular lender. To do this, you need to find out what industries, if any, the loan officer specializes in. You need to find out the banker's interests, hobbies, and background. You need to find a bridge of common interest between you and the banker.

If the loan officer is acting on a referral from someone you know, you have an easier job of this. Contact the referring individual to pick his or her brain about the loan officer. If you got to the banker by calling a central switchboard and know absolutely nothing about him or her, your road will be tougher. Prior to hanging up the telephone with the banker during the initial phone call, ask the loan officer for references. I probably have had three people in my entire career ask this of me.

Most applicants are shy and believe that they are negotiating from a position of weakness. You will take every loan officer by surprise with that question, but after chewing on it, the loan officer will gladly give you a couple of names of good clients. Loan officers, after all, are proud of their part in the success of their clients. Since a loan officer is likely to give you the names of only a few of his or her closest clients, they will be names of people who know the loan officer best. Do not hesitate to call these people. Tell them that so-and-so at the bank gave you their names as references. They will be just as surprised to get your call as the banker was to get your question. Most customers will download a complete file from the top of their heads about their loan officer. Listen for anything that will tip you off to an interest, hobby, or specialty.

Your banker's hot button might be a business just like yours (doubtful!), gourmet restaurants, geranium propagation, horse racing, Cistercian studies, or adventure travel. Preferably, single out one or two topics you are also interested in or you have some minimum knowledge of. If your business pertains to any of these, so much the better. If not, do not be afraid, during the course of your appointment, to state, "I hear you are interested in pheasant hunting." Bankers deal with numbers all day long. Once in a while, it is great fun to talk with someone about a topic of mutual interest. Anything that promotes a higher frequency of such conversions (like making a loan to that person) is not beneath us! Seriously, the personal bridge that you build with a loan officer can make all the difference in the loan application process. Once you have struck a chord and built a bridge, your application is automatically elevated to a status above other applications on the desk.

Transaction Versus Relationship

The last consideration in targeting a bank is the decision whether you simply want a transaction financed or a relationship built. Using many of the same processes already discussed, you can quickly formulate which banks are best at funding transactions and which are best at building relationships.

In this day, many fast-flying, successful companies simply want transactions completed. They do not need any more friends, particularly meddlesome bankers. Smaller businesses typically need the support offered by banks in a relationship. Individual bankers can have reputations that differ from that of their employers; be sure to consider the reputation of each.

A relationship is most important during tough times, which we have not seen for many years. In tough times, a relationship with a bank will help small business owners through crisis periods. A banker with whom you have only completed transactions feels no loyalty or debt of gratitude toward you or your business. Although times might be great right now, a prudent business owner might look ahead to rough spots in the road and consider the importance of a strong banking relationship.

Meeting the Banker

The most important advice that I can give anyone about face-to-face meetings with bankers is to be yourself. Do not affect airs or costumes. If you run a garage, come on in dressed in greasy clothes and shake my hand with your grimy paw. If you work out of your home, do not show up in my office dressed in a three-piece suit—you will pop the bubble of my dream of what it is like to work at home. Nothing is worse than to have an applicant sitting across from me, trussed up in a very dated suit with a tie and collar constricting blood flow to his head. I spend more time worrying about whether I remember the proper sequence and techniques for cardiopulmonary resuscitation (CPR) than listening to the prospect.

Every banker has had sales training, personality training, communication training, and negotiation training. We see through every just-learned ploy a person trots out on us. Just be yourself. That is the best form of honesty there is.

Bank on It

+ Larger banks are generally quicker to act on loan requests.
+ Small banks often take a more consultative approach with loan applicants, which can be an enormous benefit to owners of startup or young companies.
+ A power referral enhances the chances that a loan application will be approved.
+ Banks with bad, local reputations might have an individual banker on staff who had a great reputation and vice versa.
+ Homework on both the bank and banker is a must.

eight

If the
Bank Says Yes

Upon bank approval of a loan request, many applicants drop their guard and roll over for the bank. "Hey, I've got my money. I don't care about anything else" is not a wise attitude. Now is the time to be on your toes and use caution. Business owners should not allow a banker to lead them by the nose through the postapproval process. This chapter outlines the most common documents that banks use to close commercial loans.

The Commitment Letter

The bank should deliver to you a commitment letter that spells out exactly what they have approved to offer to you. Until you have a letter in hand, you do not have a legal commitment from the bank. This is crucial.

I have seen many small businesspeople get into trouble by taking a soft approval, informal discussion, or proposal for discussion purposes as a firm commitment. Only after making financial commitments of their own do they find out that the bank has not made a commitment or that the actual loan commitment is not what they expected. Suddenly, the business owner is in financial and legal trouble. Do not assume anything until you have a commitment letter in hand. The commitment letter is an offer from the bank to you. Figure 8-1 shows an example of a commitment letter.

The addressee of the letter should be verified. Make sure the bank has addressed the letter to the proper entity and/or individuals. If any other names appear here, the bank is probably requiring other guarantors or cosigners on which you did not plan. The bank may have misunderstood your proposal or what you were willing to do.

The body of the letter details the terms the bank has offered to you. The important lines or paragraphs include amount of the loan, interest rate, term, payment amount and frequency, fees, required collateral, required insurance coverages, required guarantors, and required due diligence. Review each line to make sure that it jives with your own thought process. Call the banker about any item that is a surprise to you and might be unacceptable to you. Ask why it appears in the letter and ask why your plan or idea is unacceptable. Do not be afraid to call anything in question. Honest misunderstandings happen, and honest disagreement is part of business.

Pay special attention to any due diligence, contingencies, or other categories. The bank may have approved the loan subject to obtaining an SBA guarantee on your loan. That means you will not have a true commitment until the SBA approves your loan. The due diligence might include things like appraisals, environmental studies, or other requirements that you must first meet in order to get the loan. Occasionally, these requirements are such that an applicant cannot possibly meet them either in principal or within the time frame of the commitment's expiration date. Make a list of anything you find questionable and ask your banker about them.

Do not tell the banker where he or she can put his commitment letter unless it's amended to your satisfaction or threaten to walk on the offer—unless you have another bona fide offer on the table. Bankers will call your bluff; when you come back with your tail between your legs, they have you wrapped around their finger.

The letter, usually in the closing, includes a drop-dead date when the offer expires if not accepted by you. You accept the letter by signing an acknowledgment included in the letter and delivering it to the bank.

Figure 8-1: A Commitment Letter

OLD FAITHFUL NATIONAL BANK
ONE GEYSER SQUARE
YELLOWSTONE, WY 43209

August 1, 2001

Ms. Myrtle Hodapp, President
Hodapp's Flowers, Inc.
936 West Bridge Street
Plainwell, WY 43206

Dear Ms. Hodapp:

It is our pleasure to offer you the following loan commitment. This commitment may be revoked at any time by the bank prior to acceptance by you.

Purpose:	Purchase new building located at 725 West Bridge Street, Plainwell, WY 43206.
Amount:	$150,000.00.
Term:	Five years.
Amortization:	Fifteen years.
Interest Rate:	Wall Street Journal prime rate plus 1.5%, variable.
Collateral:	1st mortgage on subject real estate; 2nd mortgage on 936 West Bridge Street, Plainwell, WY; 1st lien on all assets of corporation.
Guarantee:	Unsecured, unlimited guarantee of Myrtle Hodapp.
Commitment Fee:	1% or $1,500.

Hodapp's, p.2.

Other: Loan is subject to receipt and satisfactory approval by bank of appraisals, surveys, environmental transaction screens, flood certifications, and title insurance commitments for each real estate parcel. Borrower will be responsible for all closing costs and out-of-pocket expenses incurred by the bank.

If this commitment is acceptable to you, please acknowledge by signing where indicated below. Please return the original copy of this letter to the bank prior to August 15, 2001. This commitment expires at the close of business on that date.

Sincerely,

John Q. Smith
Vice President

Accepted by Hodapp's Flowers, Inc.

By:_____
    Myrtle Hodapp, President

Date:_____

Documentation

Once you accept the bank's offer of a loan, it will commence documentation and due diligence. This period may take as little as one day or as long as several months, depending upon the complexity of the loan. It is not common, but does occur either through bank error or through poor practices, that sometimes documents totally unrelated to the commitment letter appear in closings. For example, your loan commitment called for a specific lien on one large piece of equipment, yet the bank, at closing, has a blanket lien for you to sign. Another example is the inclusion of a spouse on a personal guarantee when the spouse was not named in the commitment letter.

A working knowledge of the various components of documentation and due diligence is a simple way to prevent overcommitting your resources or assets. This section lists major items that any small business owner might find at a closing or in the documentation process.

PROMISSORY NOTE

This is the guiding contract of every loan relationship. The promissory note sets into stone the principal amount, interest rate, payment amounts and periods, maturity date, and obligors. The note may establish the rules for how money may be borrowed from lines of credit or revolving lines of credit. The fine print lists all the reasons and ways a bank may demand immediate repayment of the loan principal. The note might also mention the bank's right of offset—the ability to tap any of the obligor's deposit accounts to make payments or to pay off the loan.

The most frightening language on promissory notes is the vague, ambiguous wording that gives the bank the right to demand immediate repayment at any time if it feels repayment of the loan is questionable or if any default of loan terms and conditions occurs. This rarely occurs without absolutely, solid legal reason since to do so injudiciously can raise severe liability problems for the bank.

Be aware that most bank documents are generated from canned software or preprinted forms. The language is almost always boilerplate or standard verbiage. You will not typically be able to change any of the language.

LOAN AGREEMENT

The loan agreement establishes the boundaries of your relationship with the bank. The agreement will contain a great deal of redundant fine print that will also appear in the promissory note and other documents. There are three important sections to a loan agreement with which you must be familiar.

The first section lists the financial reporting requirements to which you will have to adhere. Normally, you will be required to provide your year-end financial statements and tax returns to the bank within ninety days of the end of your fiscal year. The bank will require either management prepared or CPA prepared financial statements. This is important to you if only due to the increased expense of higher levels of financial reporting requirements. The loan agreement will also spell out the frequency and level of any interim financial reporting. You might also be required to provide periodic accounts receivable and accounts payable agings. If the loan is guaranteed by individuals or other businesses, the frequency of the financial reports from the guarantors will also be listed.

The second section contains affirmative covenants. Affirmative covenants are things that you agree to do. These may include maintaining current management, outside employment, proper insurance coverage, plant and equipment in good condition, current contracts, and so on. If you fail to do any of the things that you promise to do in the loan agreement, the bank may claim that you have defaulted and call the loan due and payable immediately. Financial covenants also appear in this section. The bank will establish baseline measurements at the time the loan is closed based on your current financial condition or on your own projections. Annually, the bank will compare actual results and measurements to those required in the loan agreement. If any of the measurements have deteriorated below the standard set in the loan agreement, you might be in default. Standard measurements include tangible net worth as stated in whole dollars, debt-to-tangible net worth ratio, current ratio, cash flow coverage of debt service ratio, and working capital as stated in whole dollars.

The third section of the loan agreement contains negative covenants. This is a list of things you promise not to do. This list might include not pledging any unencumbered collateral, not selling or buying any assets, not opening new locations, not paying dividends or bonuses, not increasing owner's wages, and so on. Again, if you break any of these promises, the bank may claim that you are in default.

SECURITY AGREEMENTS

The security agreement connects the loan with the collateral the bank takes to secure the loan. The security agreement may place a blanket lien on all the borrower's assets; just a category of assets, like inventory; or specific assets. This document gives the bank the legal right to take possession and to dispose of the pledged assets in order to generate funds to repay your loan. In order to perfect a lien (that is, to make it legally enforceable), it must be filed with the appropriate government department. Because security agreements are sometimes rather lengthy and because the bulk of the agreements are boilerplate language, the law allows banks a shortcut. Rather than sending in the entire security agreement, the bank may file a UCC-1 or UCC-1a with either the county or state administration or with both of them. UCC stands for Uniform Commercial Code, a body of law adopted by nearly every state to help govern interstate commerce. Form 1 covers all asset categories, and Form 1a covers fixtures. It is necessary to have a separate form for fixtures since these assets are generally considered part of the real estate and building, and liens against them must be filed with the local county's register of deeds. The UCC form simply provides public notice that you have borrowed money from a specific lender and what collateral has been pledged. The public notice does not list any financial information—not even the amount of the loan. This action is intended to prevent borrowers from defrauding lenders by pledging a piece of collateral to more than one lender.

ASSIGNMENT OF LIFE INSURANCE

One of the greatest risks to a small business is the death of one of its owners or key managers. Prudent small business owners maintain life insurance coverage to insure the continued viability of the business and for estate planning purposes. In many cases, the death of a key owner or manager also signals the death of the business. For this reason, banks often require that life insurance be carried on those individuals and that it be pledged to the bank. In the event of an untimely death, the life insurance proceeds can pay off the loan. Even if policy proceeds cannot pay off the entire loan, the loan can often be reduced to a level sustainable by the company under new management. Life insurance proceeds can also offer surviving owners or family members enough time to sell the business for a fair price.

The assignment of life insurance must be acknowledged by the borrower, the life insurance policy owner and beneficiary, and the home office of the insurance company. This eliminates any later claims by beneficiaries who lose out on insurance proceeds and prevents mistaken payments to the beneficiaries by the insurance company.

ASSIGNMENT OF DISABILITY INSURANCE

Banks often require that a borrower maintain disability insurance and an assignment of that policy to the bank. These assignments are prevalent in businesses where the hands or mind of the business owner generates revenue. Examples include craftspeople, doctors, lawyers, and dentists. The amount of disability insurance required normally equates to the loan payment amount. This insures that if something unfortunate happens to the borrower, the loan payments can still be made.

REAL ESTATE MORTGAGE

The mortgage is one of the better known and most despised collateral documents. Mortgage-burning celebrations are a part of the American landscape. This document ties a piece of real estate and any improvements on that real estate, like a house or factory, to the loan. It is recorded at county offices to provide public notice of the loan and pledged collateral. Again, the public notice prevents fraudulent behavior on the borrower's part and honest mistakes on everyone's part.

The mortgage itself will list all the conditions under which the bank may foreclose and sell the property. A borrower may default and find himself or herself in foreclosure for inaction as innocuous as not paying property taxes, not keeping the property properly maintained, and not keeping appropriate insurance coverage in place. Technically, a bank could foreclose on a perfectly healthy business that has made every loan payment on time and has cash in the bank if it believes the value of the real estate collateral has been jeopardized for any reason.

Most mortgages contain a brief blurb of sneaky language called the "all other indebtedness clause." This clause could allow the bank to use the pledged real estate to secure other loans made to the company, its affiliates, or principals. I have witnessed this clause catch people two different ways.

Every year, a number of business owners decide to walk away from a losing venture in the belief that the bank will satisfy itself with whatever money it can generate by liquidating business assets. The owner simply goes on with life with a hard lesson learned. If that business owner is also a home mortgage loan customer of the same bank, he or she could be in for a real shock. The home mortgage, which may have been closed years before the business even opened, might contain the all other indebtedness clause, which would allow the bank to foreclose on the home to further reduce any business indebtedness.

Even worse is the common situation when an old, established company finally hits the end of its business life and goes out of business. The decision to terminate the business may have been forced by creditors or might simply be a strategic decision by the business's owners. The calculation to close the business might hinge on the thought that the bank will liquidate whatever accounts receivable, inventory, and equipment is available and write off whatever loan balance is left over. At the time the business closes its doors, it might not have any real estate debt outstanding; however, if it ever borrowed commercial mortgage money or pledged the real estate for loans, the mortgage might still be in the bank's files. As you have already guessed, the bank can use the old and paid off mortgage to foreclose on the real estate to collect on seemingly unrelated debts.

The lessons drawn from these horror stories are to always ask that the all other indebtedness clause be struck from the mortgage document and to always hold a mortgage-burning party when a mortgage-backed loan is paid off. Follow up with your local county register of deeds to make sure that the mortgage has been discharged, too.

ASSIGNMENTS OF RENTS AND LEASES

This assignment is often included as a clause or paragraph in a commercial mortgage, but standard practices would also have the bank ask you to sign a separate form. This form is important if you collect rents or lease space to anyone, including related companies. Simply, if you default on your loan, the bank can legally notify your tenants and have all rent payments sent directly to the bank. The income is then used to make payments on your loan. It seems silly for banks to require this document when the real estate is owner occupied, but should the business fail, the bank can lease the real estate out to generate income with which to make the required loan payments.

ASSIGNMENT OF LEASE AND LANDLORD CONSENT

This form is always required when the borrower business operates in leased space. It is vital to the bank's interest for two reasons. First, the bank cannot legally access the premises (in the event of a bankruptcy or business closure) to take possession of collateral or records. Entering the property without the landlord's consent might constitute illegal entry or trespassing. In some states, landlords have the right to sell any assets left in a vacated space to satisfy unpaid rent and expenses. By signing the consent, the landlord subordinates that right to the secured lender. The second reason is that the bank might desire a certain period of time in order to hold an orderly liquidation of assets or to find a buyer for the going concern. The consideration from the bank to the landlord in these cases is the promise to bring and keep rent current and to abide by other terms of the lease.

ASSIGNMENT OF PURCHASER'S INTEREST IN LAND CONTRACT

Many business transactions are financed with land contracts. This means that the seller acts as the bank and holds a lien against the real estate. Payments are made to the seller per the terms of the land contract. A bank may seek to place a lien against any equity in a real estate parcel that is being acquired on land contract. Rather than placing a mortgage on the property, it takes this assignment.

Land contract sellers have special rights that mortgage lenders do not hold. The primary one is ease of foreclosure. Should the buyer miss or be late on a payment, the seller can repossess the property immediately. Because of these special perks, banks will require that the seller acknowledge the assignment and agree to notify the bank of any default on the contract and to give the bank a specified period to rectify the default.

ASSIGNMENT OF SELLER'S INTEREST IN LAND CONTRACT

Similar to the previous document, this one assigns the right to the payment stream and all other rights of the land contract seller to the bank. The bank will pay close attention to the principal yet to be collected on the land contract sale. If necessary, the land contract could be sold by the bank, at a discounted value, to quickly raise proceeds with which to make payment on the loan in question. People treat the seller's interest in land contracts like a negotiable monetary instrument.

ASSIGNMENT OF DEPOSIT

If a bank account or certificate of deposit will be a part of the collateral for a loan, it will be necessary to complete this form. It simply states that in the event of a default, the bank may take the deposits to make loan payments.

ASSIGNMENT OF MARKETABLE SECURITIES

This is an assignment that lists the specific securities that have been pledged as collateral. Traditionally, the bank must also have physical possession of the actual certificates in order to perfect its lien. The person or entity that pledges the marketable securities will receive a collateral receipt from the bank to record the delivery of the certificates.

STOCK POWER

Transfer of ownership of marketable securities is accomplished by the signature of the registered owner on the back of the certificates. If the bank had certificate owners sign the actual certificates, the certificates become bearer instruments and could be transferred at will by anyone who got his or her hands on them. So, that is not done for the protection of both the bank and client. Yet, if no mechanism existed to transfer ownership of the certificates to the bank when the bank needs to do just that (in a liquidation), the pledged assets would be worthless as collateral. After all, who in his or her right mind would pop into the bank after being notified that the bank was liquidating his or her business to jolly-well sign off on the marketable securities? No one would, of course. Thus, an instrument called a stock power was invented. It is a simple form that is similar to a power of attorney that gives the bank the authority to sign the certificates on behalf of the owner.

REGULATION U, FORM U-1

This form is mandated by federal law so that the government may keep tabs on risky lending practices. One of the major problems during the Great Depression was widespread bank failures caused by banks lending too much money against publicly traded stocks. When the market crashed, the collateral supporting the loans evaporated. Banks were wiped out by now unsecured loans that went bad.

TITLED ASSETS

Vehicles, boats, airplanes, and specialized equipment are examples of titled assets. States issue titles or registrations for these big-ticket assets in order to track ownership for law enforcement and tax purposes. In order to perfect a lien against this class of equipment, a bank must put its name on the title of the specific equipment as secured lien holder. The Federal Aviation Authority maintains the records on aircraft, and the U.S. Coast Guard maintains records on larger watercraft.

ASSIGNMENT OF LIQUOR LICENSES

Many types of businesses must have a liquor license in order to operate. These include grocery stores, restaurants, convenience stores, and taverns. Because a license is required to operate these businesses and because liquor licenses are heavily regulated by government agencies, they are, in effect, a barrier to entry. Further, because of the relative scarcity of licenses or limitations on the number of licenses available in any one area, they have a monetary value. Banks will take assignments of liquor licenses for two reasons. First, it would allow the bank to try to sell the connected business as a going concern to realize top dollar. Second, it could sell the liquor license independent of the other business assets to generate funds. The bank cannot sell the business as a going concern or the liquor license alone without the approval of the transfer by the governing body in the specific state.

GUARANTEE

Often, banks will require that its loan be guaranteed by an individual or entity outside the subject business. Any or all owners of the business may be required to guarantee a loan. Related or affiliated companies might be required to guarantee the loan. It all depends on the level of comfort the bank achieves during its credit analysis.

A personal guarantee is signed by an individual. If the business fails to honor its obligation, the bank can demand that the guarantor pay off the loan or make the required payments to bring the loan current. The bank can make this demand before it tries to liquidate other collateral or go after other guarantors.

A partnership or corporate guaranty is the same thing except the guarantor is an entity rather than an individual. I recommend that anyone who is requested to sign a guaranty on behalf of any entity first have legal counsel review the document and its implications. Liability can extend, unwittingly, to individual partners or shareholders in some cases.

A limited guaranty limits the signer's liability should the bank demand payment from the guarantor. An unlimited guaranty is the standard form and does not place any limitations on the amount of money a bank may seek from an individual guarantor. Pro rata guarantees are used when several owners of a business sign guarantees but limit their individual liability to a percentage of the debt equal to their percentage of ownership in a business. If I own 40 percent of Smith Company and am a pro rata guarantor of a $100,000 loan to the company, my contingent liability would be $40,000. As the principal balance is paid down over time, my whole dollar liability is reduced, but the percentage of the outstanding debt for which I am liable stands at 40 percent.

Do not take false comfort in the fact that you may share guarantee honors with several other guarantors. The bank, at its discretion, may seek to collect from the deepest or closest pocket. That might mean one guarantor ends up being sued to pay off the entire debt. Unless the guarantors had some sort of formal agreement between them to address just such an issue, the stuck guarantor cannot seek redress from the fellow guarantors.

Due Diligence Documentation

Even though you have a loan commitment in hand, the bank may have stipulated one or more contingencies that must first be answered to the bank's satisfaction. Many of these contingencies pertain to validating the value of collateral. The time line from point of loan approval to closing can be stretched out several weeks or months due to these contingencies.

REAL ESTATE SURVEY

A survey maps out a legal description of real estate. There are two kinds of surveys: a stake survey and a mortgage survey. The stake survey requires the surveyor to place stakes along all boundaries of a parcel of land. This can be an expensive proposition, especially for large tracts of land like farms or manufacturing sites. Bankers normally visit the site of collateral real estate, but what they see is not necessarily what they get when it comes to collateral. The stake survey will identify any encroachments or potential ownership disputes. Problems are frequently found due to a variety of reasons.

In fact, I once owned a small farm complete with a 100-year-old hay barn. The neighbor to my north decided to subdivide the parcel of land adjacent to my barn. Wasn't I surprised to come home from work one day to find that his surveyors had the property line going right through the middle of my barn! The problem was quickly discovered to be a miscalculation of an angle and the property line was once again where it belonged. We have all heard horrible stories about neighbors who feud for years over innocuous things like hedgerows, trees, or picket fences that encroach 6 inches over one person's property line. Imagine the lawsuits that go back and forth when a fast-food franchise is built on the wrong property or a driveway to a business is laid out on top of a property line. A proper survey before any loan proceeds go out the door can save the bank a lot of headaches in money and court appearances. This is why banks are very careful to review surveys whenever commercial property is part of the collateral package. It can also do wondrous favors for the customer, too.

A mortgage survey only requires the surveyor to mark the corners of a property along the street frontage. The surveyor then draws an approximation of what the plot looks like on paper. This type is inexpensive and used primarily for residential home loans because most homes are built on subdivided lots that are well marked out or otherwise identified.

FLOOD CERTIFICATION

Federal law requires banks to verify whether any of its collateral, real estate or personal property, lies within a designated flood plain. The Army Corps of Engineers has mapped out most of the country and identified areas where floods are likely to occur at least once every 100 years. Any borrower who has collateral assets located in one of these flood plains must purchase insurance from the national flood insurance program that is administered by the Federal Emergency Management Administration (FEMA). These insurance policies are very expensive.

If a customer refuses to purchase the insurance, the bank may either pay for the coverage and charge the costs to the customer or pass on the loan. If the bank fails to notify the customer that the customer's property is located in a flood plain or insure that the insurance coverage is obtained, it may be liable for any losses caused by floods and subject to punitive damages. Because of the seriousness of the hazard and the teeth in the law, most banks use a third-party service provider to check records, issue Flood Certificates, and monitor flood insurance policies. Naturally, all these costs are passed on to the borrower. The Flood Certificate will state one of three things: assets are in a flood plain, assets are not in a flood plain, or no map is available for the specific location.

TITLE INSURANCE, COMMITMENTS, AND SEARCHES

Real estate ownership and transactions are very complicated. Until the early 1980s, banks would hire an attorney to review the Abstract of Title on a real estate parcel and to issue an opinion letter as to the legal ownership of that parcel. The Abstract of Title is basically the list or copies of every document ever recorded that pertains, at least in part, to the subject real estate parcel. Nearly every piece of real estate can be traced back to an original grant of title from the U.S. government to some homesteader or speculator.

You can imagine that over the course of two centuries the ownership of any parcel of land may have changed many times even if only passed down from one generation to the next in the same family. The simple matter of recording deeds, easements, wills, court orders, divorce decrees, and tax liens can cloud the title to a piece of property. There is always the risk that unrecorded documents exist and will surface someday. It is possible ol' granddad had a floozy on the side and that he gave her a letter granting her ownership to the back forty upon his death. Decades later, the floozy's descendants might come across that letter in an attic and decide to test its validity in court. There is also the chance that someone could completely make up a false claim to a real estate parcel. The owner of record has just one choice: litigate the claim in court.

Banks formerly only rested reasonably assured that their borrowers had clean title if the attorney issued that opinion in the letter. Losses did occur, though, as banks were forced to defend against spurious or legitimate claims to the property that had previously been unknown. A better system took root and became the rule in the mid-1980s. It was title insurance.

Insurance companies developed statistics that allowed the underwriters to review the abstracts and issue insurance to cover either the owner or the bank should any unknown claims to the property's title arise. Premiums were charged accordingly. Generally, the owner can obtain a policy that would reimburse him or her for the purchase price of the real estate should a superior claim to the title arise and the bank can obtain a policy to cover the outstanding principal of a loan secured by the property.

The insurance company receives a request from the bank on a specific parcel of land that identifies the amount of coverage needed. The insurance company reviews the abstract of title and issues a title insurance commitment. The commitment is not an insurance policy. The commitment will list any tasks that need to be completed in order to satisfy the insurance company that the ownership of the property is or will be as requested by the bank. The list might include paying any outstanding tax liens, addressing any property line disputes, discharging any old, paid-off mortgages, or filing deeds to remove deceased owners or divorced spouses. It is unlikely, particularly on larger parcels of real estate, that every cloud on the title can be cured. For example, utility companies often have rights-of-way over private property granted or leased to them for indefinite or long periods of time. The title companies will issue a commitment for a policy with exceptions. The exceptions are listed, like a utility easement, and any problems or losses that occur due to that exception will not be covered. If a landowner builds a new building that overlaps a utility easement, the utility can bulldoze the building to protect its power or gas lines or to put new ones in.

On smaller dollar amount deals or renewals of existing debt, banks might only request a title search. A search creates no liability for the title insurance company. It simply gives the bank a list of all recorded and in-force documents on a given parcel. It is up to the bank to determine the risks of using the property for collateral.

APPRAISALS

An appraisal is an expert assertion of the value of a specific asset. The purpose of an appraisal is to give the bank an idea of its collateral value on a fair market basis and on a liquidation basis. Fair market value is the appraiser's best idea of what price an asset would sell given the following conditions: Both seller and buyer must be willing participants under no duress, and the asset can be marketed properly for a reasonable time period. Liquidation value is the appraiser's opinion of what price an asset would sell in an auction.

Appraisers use three methods to calculate these values. The first is the market comparison approach. The subject asset is compared to assets that have been recently sold and are similar in size, use, and condition and are in the same general location. The prices of the comparable assets are used as a baseline value for the subject asset. Dollars are subtracted or added based on notable differences between the subject and comparable assets to arrive at a suggested value for the subject.

The cost approach requires the appraiser to calculate how much it would cost to replicate the asset today. That figure is reduced based on the physical depreciation or functional obsolescence of the subject asset to arrive at a final cost valuation.

The income approach requires the appraiser to assign a value to the asset based on the income that it generates. This would normally be used for investment real estate assets. This valuation technique all but ignores the actual cost of the asset and treats it more like a cash machine that spews out a defined stream of money for the owner.

Complete appraisals will employ all three methods and average the three out to arrive at a fair market valuation. These appraisals will also contain reams of pages that discuss the location, region, and economy where the subject asset is located.

Liquidation appraisals are more nebulous in that the accuracy depends on the experience of the appraiser in actual liquidations. For this reason, auctioneers often do double duty as appraisers—especially for equipment assets.

ENVIRONMENTAL CERTIFICATE AND QUESTIONNAIRE

Environmental contamination liability hit banks hard during the 1980s and 1990s. Even though banks did not own or manage real estate that had been pledged for collateral, they were held liable (as the deep pocket) and forced to clean up many locations by the government. If the bank was lucky enough to escape initial liability, it put its profitability or life on the line when it foreclosed on a contaminated parcel of real estate. As the new owner of a piece of property, the bank was liable for any pollution problems.

Banks quickly discovered that to adequately protect themselves, they needed to know more about potential collateral before it was pledged to the bank. A whole new industry sprouted up: environmental survey. Nearly every commercial customer of any bank is now required to fill out an environmental certificate and questionnaire regardless of whether real estate is part of the collateral package or not.

These two documents do three things. First, they survey you to find out whether the property is already contaminated or not. Second, they survey you to find out if anything you do in your business might be a potential source of contamination. And, third, they extract a promise from you that you will not contaminate the property and that, should contamination be discovered, you will clean it up on your own tab.

ENVIRONMENTAL SURVEYS

Dependent upon the size and complexity of the loan, the bank might require a Phase I environmental survey. This is performed by a third-party environmental engineer who performs a check of public records and visits the property to look for any signs of potential environmental problems. Examples of potential problems might be the fact that the parcel was once used as a gas station fifty years ago or that spots on the driveway look suspiciously like motor oil that has leaked into the ground.

If any potential problem is noted, the engineer will recommend a Phase II environment study. If the bank ignores this recommendation, makes the loan, and later has to fight off liability created by a contamination problem, it will have a tough go of it in court. For this reason, banks will give applicants the choice to drop the loan request or to pay for the Phase II study. Phase I studies can cost anywhere from $500 to $4,000; Phase II studies can run into the $10,000 and up range.

Phase II studies require an engineer to do actual physical testing such as drilling wells, taking air and water samples, and other technical work. If any indication is found that purports a contamination problem, the engineer will recommend remediation or further testing. At this point, most banks would walk away from a business loan application because the increasing expense would negatively affect the applicant's ability to repay any loan.

Bank on It

+ The commitment letter is the bank's loan proposal to you. Read every word carefully.
+ Never let any point go unclarified.
+ Do not hesitate to question any term or condition that seems unreasonable.
+ Your third-grade teacher was correct—the only dumb question is the one not asked.
+ Have a lawyer preview all documents before you sign them.

nine

Your Banking Relationship

Some of my customers have turned into some of my best friends during the last two decades. It is an amazing feeling to gain the trust of someone who will confide both personal and financial details to you that he or she would not even share with a spouse. Times have changed. Bankers run hard now and rarely have the time to devote to building these kinds of close relationships. The burden is more likely to fall on the shoulders of the commercial loan customer. A strong, close relationship is something for which every businessperson should strive.

I once inherited a loan customer who coincidentally was a longtime friend of the family. His company ran into deep financial problems. We discussed the fact that things might get sticky between him and the bank in the very near future. I asked if he would rather have some other officer handle his account from that point forward. After all, if he needed to vent anger or frustrations, he might be more likely to empty both barrels at an anonymous banker than he would at me. He told me no and that given the choice, he would rather have a lender whom he could trust. I was flattered, but scared of choices that would have to be made soon. Fortunately, we were able to keep the business going long enough to find a qualified buyer to bail the customer out of debt.

The days of plying your banker with fifths of booze and swanky trips to build relationships are long gone. The key to building strong relationships is communication. Business owners who maintain frequent communication with their banker, even to the point of forcing the issue, will win over most bankers. Besides forwarding periodic financial information to your loan officer, a businessperson should also pass along good and bad news as it occurs. It is great to hear about a big, new contract or a favorable article in a publication. It is also wonderful to hear about personnel changes or additions. Although it is not so wonderful to hear about lawsuits, loss of key people, or contracts, it is much worse to read about it in the newspaper or learn about it long after the impact causes irreparable harm.

Your banker can also be a source of business for your own company. Does the bank use the products and services that you sell? How about the bank's other customers? A commercial loan officer can be a bottomless well of referrals for many types of businesses. Suggest to your banker that he or she sponsor a "meet and greet" for business customers that allows all of his or her customers to network with each other.

Bankers occupy a unique position in a community. They are aware of business trends, openings, closings, developments, and competition well before anyone else. Ask your banker any form of question that begins, "If you were in my position. . . ." This may yield particularly useful information about where to locate a business, what kind of business might work, and so on.

Bank loan officers will never be wealthy in a financial sense. We do find tremendous rewards, though, in helping small business owners achieve the American Dream. Your relationship with your own banker should play to that pride. This chapter discusses several key components of an ongoing bank relationship.

Negotiating with the Bank in Good Times

Every other person with whom I meet appears to have read the most recent self-empowerment book on negotiating. It is great sport to play the game with them. Negotiation is at the heart of a banker's daily regimen; so most bankers are experts at it. It is often hilarious to listen to a prospective client, particularly someone who is starting up a business on a shoestring and prayer, make demands of me. These points of demand range from loan pricing below that which we provide to our best and biggest clients, collateral that will not be pledged, guarantees that will not be offered, and people over my head who will get an earful if I do not comply.

Unless a business owner has a proposal or commitment letter in hand from another bank or a track record of good performance at the current bank, there rarely is any room for negotiation on the front end of a loan. If an entrepreneur runs from bank to bank with commitment letters trying to better each successive offer, many bankers will choose simply not to do business with that customer. Why should a bank expend any effort when the prospective customer would be willing to jump ship for an eighth of a point in interest savings? The smart banker will let the business go to another bank. Sooner or later, the business owner will give other banks a chance to underbid the original bank. At that point, the business will have a better track record and will be more likely to stay put at one bank for a longer period of time. Most bankers, when they smell a shopper, will be hesitant to even issue a written proposal or commitment letter. Experience tells us that the last bank visited by a business owner gets the business—after all, it gets the last shot at beating the deal of the moment.

Existing businesses with a proven track record can build a case to negotiate on almost any loan term. The universal caution is not to burn any bridges in the process. I have firsthand experience of customers playing too hard at negotiating changes only to have the bank advise them to look elsewhere for banking services. These are cases of major league bluffs being called. The business owners may find themselves high and dry and forced to reapproach the bank with their tails between their legs.

Six months or one year do not make a track record. Many businesses jump off to great starts only to experience a leveling of growth several months out. This is very true in hospitality businesses like entertainment, restaurants, bars, and hotels. In those industries, whatever is new is hot. Certainly, if a business's financial results match or surpass the projections or business plan that was presented to the banker at the outset, a good argument can be made for the bank to revisit the original terms of the deal.

One fact that is used often by business owners to support requests for better pricing or structure on loans is the amount of money that the business runs through its deposit accounts. I have heard about the "millions of dollars my business deposits in your bank every year" from dozens of clients over the years. Unfortunately, most of those businesses also write checks for amounts equal to or greater than the deposits every year. The bottom line is that the actual balance in the accounts never amounts to anything. The stable balances are what matter most to bankers. Banks cannot use money that flows into an account on one day and out the next day. The money that stays in an account more or less permanently is the money that banks use to make the loans from which their revenues are derived.

There are three basic things for which customers negotiate: lower interest rates, release of collateral or guarantees, and more money. Loan pricing is based on the risk associated with any given loan. Almost by definition, the more seasoned a loan becomes, the lower the risk. A seasoned loan is a banker's term for a loan that has been outstanding for a period and has been handled as agreed by the customer. A customer is always within his or her rights to request an interest rate reduction during the life of a loan. If the banker claims that the request is too early in the life of the loan, the customer always has the option to shop the loan at another bank. Bankers salivate at the opportunity to steal business from other banks, especially when they can make the other bank look rigid in comparison. The threat of a competitor entering the picture keeps banks honest in their pricing discipline.

The release of collateral and/or guarantors is the second most negotiated item. Often, it is a matter of the customers' pride in that they want to tell peers that they borrow based only on their signature or that their company borrows on an unsecured basis. This is irrelevant for small businesses since collateral and personal guarantees are almost universally required by banks. Business owners should put pencil to paper, using the collateral valuations provided earlier in this book, to determine the proper amount of collateral the company should have pledged to secure loans. It is a simple process to show a banker figures, based on standards of the banking industry, and say, "You have more collateral than you need. Release the appropriate amount of assets if only for housekeeping purposes."

The last point that is often negotiated by borrowers is an increase in their loan amounts. Normally, the requests are for increases in lines of credit. Again, many of the requests for increased lines are simply a matter of pride to the borrowers. It seems that "line envy" is infectious. Clients should remember that any line of credit that a bank commits to customers costs the bank money due to federal regulations and accounting practices. Ideally, lines of credit should be set at amounts no higher than what a customer will actually use. Any amount set aside higher than that actually costs the bank money. Understandably, pegging the exact high watermark of a line of credit is not practical, and most lines of credit have a buffer amount of availability built into them. Negotiating for window dressing in lines of credit is not worth anyone's time.

Negotiating with the Bank in Bad Times

Unbelievably, the best time to negotiate with a bank is when things look bleakest. When a loan appears to be in jeopardy, bankers are quick to make concessions that will lead to preservation of the loan principal or eventual collection of the loan—wholly or in part.

Even if the end is not in sight and the business is only suffering from a cyclical trough, it is wise to ask the bank for concessions. Interest rate reductions, extension of terms, and postponement of payments all have positive implications for current cash flow. Money that might be spent on debt payments could be used to promote new markets, add more productive assets, including employees, and other positive uses.

If the continued viability of the business is in question, it is time to negotiate tougher issues like release of guarantees, collateral, or offer a compromise. If the owner of a failing or underperforming business is key to the bank's ability to maximize collection of its loan to the business, the bank might be willing to exchange the release of a guarantee or a mortgage on the owner's home for the owner's continued cooperation and assistance in closing out the loan. If the owner has other sources of financing, the bank might accept a lump sum payment of some amount less than what is actually owed as payment in full (called an offer and compromise). These types of negotiations happen every day.

Many businesspeople, thrust into a financial crisis, might not think of these possibilities. Therefore, when a loan enters a workout phase at a bank, it is wise, if not mandatory, for the business owner to engage a commercial law attorney. The attorney will be aware of all possibilities and, from an objective viewpoint, will be able to recommend actions in the best interests of the small business owner.

When the Going Gets Tough

Given that four out of five new businesses fail within five years of startup due to any number of reasons, it is surprising to learn that the biggest mistake entrepreneurs make is the failure to keep their bankers informed. Bankers have lived through dozens of bad loan situations and witnessed hundreds of others within their own bank. They have learned from these experiences. There is no one better qualified to offer advice to business owners who find themselves in trouble than a banker.

It never pays to hide information from your banker. Even if a problem resolves itself and your business comes out smelling like a rose, once the banker does find out about the past difficulty that you did not feel compelled to call him or her about, he or she may have lost trust in you. Because of their vast individual and collective experience, bankers can recognize many red flags that will clue them into possible troubles at your business. Hiding any bad news is a temporary avoidance of the inevitable. Face up to any situation and get your banker involved early.

RED FLAGS

Here is a list of the common red flags, as seen by bankers, that business owners may cure before they are raised up the flagpole:

1. *Lack of timely financial information.* Reasons for delaying or not sending financial information to your banker could include that you are just too busy to fuss with them. Your banker, though, will assume that you do not want the bank to know about bad financial performance or that you do not have enough money with which to pay your accountant.

2. *Sudden or excessive borrowing.* If you suddenly start borrowing out of character for your company, it could mean that you are suffering negative cash flow.

3. *Declining deposit balances.* Again, if declining balances are out of character for the customer or season, the banker might wonder why you are draining your cash.

4. *Another bank enters the picture.* If another bank loans you money, your primary bank will find out through periodic lien searches or when it is contacted by the other bank during that lender's routine credit check on you. This could be indicative of fraud, at worst, or deteriorating cash flow. At best, your banker will wonder why you did not call him or her first. Maybe something has happened that you do not want your banker to know about.

5. *Rash of credit checks by suppliers.* Banks provide credit references on their clients every day. If a rash of credit checks or unusual credit checks arrive at the bank, it could signal that you have worn out your welcome at old suppliers or that you have not paid existing creditors per their terms.

6. *Short-term loans are not paid off.* When a customer cannot pay off seasonal or short-term borrowings, it could indicate one good thing: growth. More than likely, it points to poor performance or poor management of funds.

7. *Cancellation of insurance policies.* When banks take collateral, they require that your insurance reflect the bank as loss payee or mortgagee. If a loss occurs, the insurance company cuts payment directly to the bank to cover the loan. If your policies are canceled due to late or nonpayment of premiums, notices are also sent to the bank. This could signal profitability problems at your company.

8. *Tax liens filed against business or individuals.* Every day, a business owner somewhere decides not to send his or her payroll taxes to the IRS because he or she needs the money more than Uncle Sam. The owner thinks that he or she will make it up in a few days and will be able to catch up. Many never do. When the government slaps a tax lien on a business's assets, secured lenders have thirty days to protect their

own liens. That means the bank has to start liquidation procedures immediately. The only safety valve for the business owner is to find enough cash to satisfy the government taxes and the penalties before the bank takes final action. Many entrepreneurs are not aware of the fact that even if the taxes are owed by their corporation, tax laws can pierce the corporate veil to make the individual stockholders personally liable for taxes and penalties (which may be monetary or prison sentences). Let's just avoid this red flag altogether: Never convert tax funds for business use.

9. *Loan payment delinquencies.* This is an obvious problem. If a business cannot keep payments current on secured credit, then it is logical that all its liabilities are out of control. Many business owners will claim that business is so good that they used their cash to grow the business or some other excuse with a positive spin. Entrepreneurs would be far ahead to call the banker to discuss a new loan to help fuel the growth. Past due payments are etched into a bank's computer system. Your next loan officer at the bank or credit officers who review your next loan request will see your payment history in the most negative light.

10. *Loss of key customers and accounts.* The loss of a large piece of business will affect sales and profitability. That is the primary concern when a bank gets wind of fleeing customers. Of secondary concern will be the underlying reasons why the accounts left you. Has your company lost its competitive advantages? Are you properly staffed? Have your business practices slipped so customers cannot trust you to deliver the required product with integrity and support? There are dozens of reasons why a major account might leave one business for another. Most do not reflect well upon the former.

11. *Deferred maintenance of assets.* Nothing throws more fear into a banker than to visit a customer's plant and find buckets placed around the floor to collect raindrops from a roof that could collapse at any moment. Failure to keep up the plant and equipment will catch up to a business sooner

or later. At the first sign of poor or neglected maintenance, your banker will start looking under the hood for more signs of decreased viability.

12. *Lavish spending.* Yes, this is a contradiction to the previous red flag. It seems that every small business owner that feels compelled to build a Taj Mahal plant as a permanent memorial to himself or herself ends up bankrupt. Also, many businesspeople believe if they look highly successful, they will convince more people to do business with them. Consequently, there are nickel millionaires who buy or lease Mercedes, BMWs, Jaguars, or Porsches in order to look the part. These people also usually end up bankrupt after they have spent every penny dressing up rather than building businesses. Practicality is a characteristic bankers love in their customers.

13. *Stale or obsolete inventory.* A common mistake made by business owners can be corrected easily enough by a good accountant. I have toured many places of business and seen unbelievable quantities of inventory that could never be sold. A small business might report a high level of inventory on its financial statements. Upon closer inspection, though, much of the inventory is outdated or obsolete. Instead of having value to the company, it will actually cost the business money to pay someone to haul it away. Sure, bell-bottom jeans came back into vogue twenty-five years after their first run of popularity; but I am not holding my breath while waiting for vacuum tubes to become a popular component in electronics again.

14. *Poor employee morale or attitudes.* During plant or office tours, bankers can quickly tune into the atmosphere among employees. Granted, every employee has a bad day now and then. On occasion, though, a banker will happen into a pit of viperous people who seem on the verge of tar and feathering the boss at the drop of a hat. Angry employees will never translate into happy customers. Unhappy customers take their business elsewhere. Disgruntled employees could signal wage or benefit cuts, delayed payrolls, stressed

out management, and other things that signal to the banker that she should take a closer look at what is going on with the customer.

15. *Changes in behavior of key managers or owners.* Some changes are laughable. The president of my own (former) bank and two of my old customers are perfect examples. When a middle-aged man shows up with a stiffly coifed new hairdo, you know something is up. In all three of the aforementioned cases, within a short period after the new look appeared, the men were seen sporting trophy women (not their own wives) on their arms. Divorces soon followed. The two customers were forced to take on huge loads of debt in order to satisfy the divorce decrees; in one of the cases, it was too much for the business to handle and the company folded. As for my old boss, he slipped off into retirement shortly thereafter. Bankers are just like spouses. They will notice changes in appearance and attitude, liquor on your breath, and nervous tics before anyone else. This red flag will flap furiously in the wind like a bad comb-over until the banker finds the cause for the change.

16. *Changes in management.* Prior to extending a loan to a company, the banker will analyze a business's management talent. Naturally, if a key manager leaves the customer, concerns will be raised simply about the ability of any replacement. Other concerns will include the direction of the company and whether the owners of the company are in a state of conflict.

17. *Litigation.* Lawsuits are never a good sign. Jury trials can go either way and can have radical penal components. There is no way to adequately prepare for the outcome of a trial except to plan for the worst case. If lawsuits outside the normal course of your business are filed, your banker will be very nervous and interested in an exercise in contingency planning.

18. *Bad publicity.* This is the kiss of death for some businesses—restaurants, for example. Newspaper editors love to print the results of Department of Health inspections of restaurants and particularly those that fail the inspection. Who in their right mind is going to patronize a restaurant that fails a health department inspection. Those restaurant owners might as well shutter the store right now. Bad publicity can extend to owners or employees of the business. If your company owns vehicles, the last thing you want is a photograph of your delivery truck delivering a dose of road rage to a parking lot full of cars. When bankers see something derogatory about a client in the public arena, they will keep a finger on the company's pulse until they are satisfied that the bad notice has not affected the company's finances.

19. *Failure to return phone calls.* This is my pet peeve. My experience tells me that if a customer does not return my phone calls, something is wrong. It might be personal or it might be business. Whatever it is, my stomach acid content will be at an increased level until I find out why the customer has not returned my calls. And if the situation ends up dire, the customer might not be treated to the same level of cooperation he would have received had he or she cooperated up front.

20. *Declining sales or profits.* This is a no-brainer that should raise red flags for the business owner, too.

21. *Increases in returns and allowances.* This might signal a reduction in quality due to any number of reasons. It also might signal that a customer is using smoke and mirrors to pad sales levels. That is, the business owner ships product to customers who did not order the goods but records the transaction as a sale in one accounting period. The customers return the goods since they did not want them in the first place, but this transaction is accounted for in a later period. The bank customer uses the financial statements from the earlier period to borrow more money or to keep bankers at bay. Red flags always awake the most devious thought in a banker's mind.

22. *Increased bad debts.* How many bad debt losses can a company sustain and stay in business? If bad debts are increasing, what is the quality of the rest of your accounts receivable? Are you struggling to generate a minimum level of sales that you have compromised your credit standards to sell to unworthy credit risks?

23. *Increasing accounts receivable and payable.* These rising numbers could signal many problems with the most common being a cash crisis. The range of other problems could be difficulty in providing good customer service to being flat broke.

Understanding why certain issues raise red flags is critical to small business owners. If a banker sees a red flag, a seed of mistrust will be planted in the banker's mind. In fact, any red flag signals another problem: poor communication. If a banker learns about potential problems from any source other than the mouth of the business owner, it signals a breakdown of communication between the two. The likely scenario from that point forward is that the banker will protect his or her own interests unilaterally. That means mutually beneficial actions are no longer a concern to the banker—the business owner has figuratively burned his or her bridge.

There is absolutely no shame in calling a banker with bad news or problems. You will further cement the degree of trust you have established with the bank. You may also gain insight into curing the difficulty from the banker's own experiences with hundreds of other companies. Timely communication from the business owner to the banker prevents any red flag from being raised up the flagpole.

Loan Workout Situations

Let us assume that your business is on the ropes. You have met with your banker and bared your soul. Your banker will pursue one of three strategies. The first is to do nothing, leave you to your own devices, and hope for a turnaround. The second is to implement controls and increase the bank's oversight of your business. The third is to plan for the liquidation of the business.

It is a nightmare for bankers to pull the plug on a business and shut it down. During my first year in banking, I was assigned the job of liquidating a local lumberyard that had been an institution in my city. My first task was to help the owners break the news to the two dozen employees who had gathered in the main office of the business. My suit was absolutely drenched in sweat despite cool November temperatures. The employees were equally divided between full-blown tears and teeth-gnashing glares. Several years later, I worked with a client who owned a string of specialty clothing stores. The business's trends were increasing losses and decreasing sales for several years. I counseled them to pull the plug themselves and to cut their personal losses. Yet, they believed that they could buck the trends and return to their earlier glory. Unfortunately, they played it out to the bitter end and not only lost the entire business but also most of their personal wealth. Sometimes, it really is best for all concerned to close up and go on with life.

If your banker decides to sit on the sidelines and let you try to fix the situation, plan to provide periodic updates to the banker. You may wish to provide immediate updates anytime something positive happens, daily accountings, or weekly summaries. But, above all, keep the banker informed.

The second option of implementation of controls might range from simple daily business reports to cash collateral accounts. The bank may wish to update appraisals or environmental work in preparation for a possible liquidation. It may take control of your checkbook with a cash collateral account. Cash collateral accounts require all incoming payments to your business to be sent to the bank. The bank deposits them into a special account. You will be able to issue checks only with prior consent of the bank. This way the bank can make sure that you do not pay unsecured creditors or otherwise waste cash that might be needed to pay off your loan. This setup can also provide a great deal of relief to a business owner who may be inundated with phone calls from creditors who seek payments. The business owner can simply state, "You'll have to take it up with my bank. They took over my checking account," and deflect that pressure.

It is only natural for a business owner to become contentious upon hearing that the bank is going to implement new controls on the business's finances. Business owners should fight that urge at all costs. It may only alienate the banker and force him or her to further entrench himself. If the entrepreneur finds any of the suggested controls unappealing, a good lawyer should be contacted immediately. The business owner should let the attorney make enemies with the bank.

Bankers must toe a fine line in workout situations. Any miscue on their parts could be cause for a legal action known as lender liability. Many banks have been forced by courts to pay fortunes in fines and penalties to business owners who proved that banks acted inappropriately in workout situations. Lender liability issues prevent bankers from being belligerent, oppressive, and careless. Bankers, in fact, bend over backwards to be fair in these cases simply to avoid liability claims.

If you are lucky, you may treated to a banker version of good cop, bad cop. This is when two bankers show up at your office. One reads you the riot act and tells you how bad things are for you. The other buffers the first and tells you that things could work out fine for you, if only you would cooperate with them. The conversation might go back and forth driving your emotions from anger to complacency and back to anger. Since this ploy is rather obvious and easy to recognize, you can turn the tables on the bankers by inviting your lawyer to sit in to perform your own rendition of good cop, bad cop.

It is crucial to understand that a business owner's cooperation is vital in a bad loan situation. No one knows the business, the employees, and the customers better than the business owner. No one knows the competition—potential buyers of the business—better than the owner. No one knows where all the skeletons are hidden and where all the records are maintained better than the owner. Cooperation is the biggest bargaining chip that a business owner holds.

Without the owner's cooperation, a bank has few options other than to simply liquidate a business via an auction. An auction will never produce as much cash as a sale of the business as a going concern or as an orderly liquidation. Bankers often find themselves willing to give up something in exchange for the owner's cooperation. An owner might trade cooperation for the release of any collateral that secures his or her personal guarantee. The bank may limit personal liability or even offer to pay the owner a consulting fee for his or her help. By all means, have an attorney perform this bargaining for you.

The manner in which a bank handles a liquidation or problem loan differs from bank to bank. Generally, larger banks have special departments that assume responsibility from the account officer. At smaller banks, your loan officer will probably handle the matter. Some banks hire outside firms or even sell the loan to specialized companies at a discounted value. The most important money a business owner can spend is to hire a good attorney or certified public accountant who has experience with troubled businesses. Not only will that person act as a buffer between the business and the workout people, but he or she will also provide wise counsel to the business owner. Since most business-people in this situation will be experiencing it for the first time, the advice of someone who has seen it all before will be invaluable. As card sharks say, "You have to know when to hold them and know when to fold them."

Bank on It

+ The key to strong banking relationships is communication.
+ Negotiating better terms is better accomplished after a track record has been established.
+ Negotiating during bad times may be productive as the bank tries to garner your cooperation.
+ Red flags signal the banker that something is amiss at your business; it is better to call the banker and deliver bad news yourself.

ten 10

When the Bank Says No

Many, if not most, unprepared small business loan applicants will have their applications declined by banks. The reactions of spurned applicants vary from timidity to anger. I have had more than my fair share of saliva-spewed diatribes delivered, point-blank, by ticked-off business owners. Anger is an understandable emotion in these situations. At the other end of the spectrum, many applicants tuck tail and back out of the banker's office, all the while bowing to the almighty banker. Neither reaction is wise. The first will further entrench the banker in his or her obstinance; the second emboldens the banker to decline more deals.

No matter what course a person's emotions take upon hearing bad news from a banker, the last thing an applicant should do is to beat a hasty exit from the banker's office. Now is not the time to give up on your dreams or yourself.

Educate Yourself

The first thing to say to a banker is, "Thank you for considering my application. I appreciate the effort that you put into it on my behalf." These two sentences accomplish several things. First, it puts the banker off balance. He or she was not prepared to be thanked for turning the businessperson down. The banker will try to stammer a response, but there exists no good, reasonable response to those statements. Second, if the banker did not put any time or effort into the review of the application, you will instill a measure of guilt into the banker's mind. Third, the banker's mind will be racing with thoughts like, "Gosh, this person is a good person. I wish I could help her out."

The next words out of the applicant's mouth should be, "If you were in my shoes, what would you do to make this work?" The banker can answer that question in three different directions. Preferably, the banker will tell you what needs to be done to make the application bankable. Indeed, most banks contain provisions in their loan policy that require it to counsel any applicants who have had loan requests denied in order to make those requests bankable. In the real world, though, bankers do not have time to be unpaid consultants. Good, old-fashioned bankers will have tried to mold an application into something that they could approve prior to issuing a cold declination. That old-fashioned sensibility has its costs, though.

Too many times I have seen a banker restructure an application to make it work for the bank only to offend the applicant. Two things can happen in this situation. The applicant makes the rounds of all the other banks in town which, each in turn, make the same suggestions. The applicant ends up taking the offer from the last bank approached, not because it is the best bank for that particular business, but because the reality of the situation has finally seeped into the brain of the applicant. The first banker, who had the courage and savvy to offer constructive advice, loses out on the deal because the applicant is too embarrassed to go back to that bank. The other thing that happens is that another bank approves the application as it stands. If the bank is hungry for business or if the banker is overmatched by the applicant, the applicant can end up paying for his or her imprudence when cash flow tightens up or markets fail to materialize. Believe me, I have seen many business owners go out of business because they would not swallow their pride and listen to the banker. They opted to do businesses with bankers that preferred not to make waves, and it cost them dearly in the end.

Federal regulations require the bank to give declined applicants a written explanation of the reasons for the declination. With this letter in hand, the applicant has a checklist of problems to address. Any banker worth his or her salt will verbalize these reasons when the declination is communicated whether it be in person, over the telephone, or in a letter. Ask the banker to suggest ways to address each of those points. After each item has been discussed, the applicant should ask the banker, "If I cure every one of these points, will you make the loan?"

This puts the banker in an uneasy position. To say yes would be a verbal commitment that could be legally enforceable. To say no could alienate the applicant and certainly indicates that there is another unspoken reason why the loan was declined. Probably, the banker will invite the applicant to bring a new, retooled application back in once it has been overhauled. The applicant, with no apparent new ground gained, might be justified in feeling exasperated at this point. But, not so.

Let's hope the applicant has learned much from the process and can now fine-tune the application. The new and improved application can be resubmitted to the original loan officer. A cover letter should accompany the new application and should be very clear in pointing out that the weaknesses identified in the first application have been addressed according to his or her advice. The voice of the letter should assume that the loan is all but a done deal now. This will pressure the loan officer into honoring his or her word. If the loan is again declined, the applicant has every right to ask for an appointment with the loan officer's supervisor, the local executive officer, or the community relations officer for the bank.

The squeaky wheel often gets the grease. The simple act of contacting a management-level officer at the bank should translate into one last, very detailed look at your loan application. At best, the senior officer will try to circumvent any potential meeting and conflict by instructing the subordinate loan officer to find some place in the bank to place the requested loan. In my experience, very few customers press for meetings with supervisors. The ones who do typically claim some form of discrimination. The basis might be gender, race, creed, or lack of wealth. For what it is worth, I have never seen a case of discrimination at any of the banks where I have worked. Indeed, every banker with whom I have worked has tried valiantly to bend over backwards to help women- and minority-owned businesses. Prior to making claims that are no more than gasping at straws, applicants need to be brutally honest with themselves and their applications.

Some business owners may be able to enlist the help of local influential people like members of the clergy, neighborhood association executives, and other civic leaders. These highly visible people, who would not know a good loan if it bit them on the nose, can exact pressure on banks. This pressure appeals to the bank's involvement in a community and to the bank's need to accrue brownie points for the next government audit of its investment in the local area.

Frequently, banks will make loans that it recognizes are bad right from the start only to satisfy the requirements of the Community Reinvestment Act. Smile, maybe your loan can be one of those! Actually, it is a sad commentary on how our government does business. It demands that banks prove that they serve the needs of everyone in their respective markets. The best way, according to the government auditors, is to make loans to disadvantaged applicants. Unfortunately, a high percentage of those loans become uncollectible. In order to make up those losses, the bank then has to charge higher rates and fees to other customers and might even rein in its credit-granting standards. Consumers get this invisible tax passed onto them in the higher costs, and banks become even more reluctant to make loans to poor credit situations. If left alone, banks might increase their profitability and invest some of those increased profits in disadvantaged markets. Instead, the government all but mandates more lending to poor credit risks. It is a vicious circle.

The trick to take advantage of these loans, which bankers call CRA loans after the Community Reinvestment Act that mandates involvement in more risky loans, is to show how a loan to your business would benefit the community. The aforementioned community activists can trumpet those reasons for you in a public and political way. These reasons might include the fact that the loan will allow you to renovate a dilapidated building, create jobs, provide a missing and needed service, or increase the visibility of a role model in a neighborhood.

The number of applicants who can validly take advantage of the CRA ploy is very limited. Applicants need to revisit the six C's of credit and make sure that their application stacks up against those requirements. If the business owner is still convinced that the request is bankable, it is time to visit alternate banks in town. If not, it is time to look outside the box that confines banks.

Looking Outside the Box

To acknowledge that one's business is not bankable is a quantum leap in attitude. It also might be a sign of good judgment! It is no reason to give up or quit on a dream. Bank loans fill one niche in small business finance. It's just that banks are the easiest niche to find. Now is the time to get creative and pull out all the stops.

The first thing to do is to ask your banker to point you in the right direction. Quite often, the banker will have a good idea how your business can get the required financing and will be able to match the business with available sources. The first thing not to do is to sign any contract with anyone who promises to get the money for you. We will discuss this later; for now, trust me.

If you have not yet availed yourself of other local resources, now is the time to swallow your pride and make some appointments. The following is a list of places that every business owner should contact in the quest for financing. Each will be discussed more completely in later chapters.

LOCAL CHAMBER OF COMMERCE

Chambers exist to promote business activity within their respective communities. At the very least, chamber executives can set an entrepreneur up with an appointment with an aggressive banker or other source of money in the local community. Chambers of commerce in even modest-sized towns often have a business development arm that is dedicated solely to help startups or new businesses in the town. Chamber executives will be attuned to any special local programs or groups that may be able to help. For example, in my town, there is an independent Downtown Development Authority that has a small fund from which it grants money to businesses that are located in the authority's geographic area.

SMALL BUSINESS DEVELOPMENT CENTERS (SBDCS)

Small Business Development Centers are located throughout America and are largely funded by the U.S. Small Business Administration (SBA). For the most part, SBDCs are housed within colleges, universities, and chambers of commerce. These offices act as business consultants to small businesses and entrepreneurs. The development of loan applications and referrals to sources of money are key services provided by SBDCs.

SERVICE CORPS OF RETIRED EXECUTIVES (SCORE)

This is another organization with offices scattered throughout that country that is also funded by the SBA. The organization provides expert advice to entrepreneurs across a broad range of topics. The staff members are retired business executives with decades of management experience and long lists of local contacts.

LOCAL COLLEGES AND UNIVERSITIES

Nearly every college and university of moderate size offers some form of assistance to owners of small businesses. Some colleges exchange free services for use of the specific business as a case study for one of the academic courses offered by the schools. A small business owner contacts the school and puts a specific problem or goal on the table. One or more students tackle the case as a learning experience. The business owner gains valuable assistance, and the students gain valuable knowledge. I have reviewed many business plans and loan requests formulated by students from our local college. The quality is high because of oversight by professors or advisors.

Many campuses house business incubators or entrepreneurial institutes, too. Fledgling business owners would be wise to telephone a nearby university simply to inquire about any available assistance.

Caveat Emptor

Once a businessperson wanders outside the conservative cocoon of the banking world, caution must be exercised. Customers are relatively protected while inside the box by a tangle of government rules and regulations. Outside the box, though, it can be a jungle where the only rule is survival of the fittest. Loan sharks and hustlers exist in real life and not just in cable television movies. Every day we read stories about people who have been taken advantage of by some swindler who duped them with phony investments. And those were people who were not looking to give their money to anyone. One can imagine the success swindlers have with people who come begging for a deal!

A common trick employed by lender-swindlers is to promise to find the required money for the business but require an up-front deposit toward expenses and commissions. Of course, the swindler takes the money and disappears or later claims to have used up the deposit in the search for the promised money. Another trick is to actually loan the money to the business owner and paper-up the transaction with onerous documentation. The hustler makes a loan with terms that cannot possibly be met. The result is that the hustler legally forecloses on the collateral assets (which are worth much more than the loan amount), trumps up expenses of foreclosure, and liquidates the collateral. This nets the swindler a huge return on the original investment and leaves the borrower flat broke and homeless. Loan brokers operate on the fringe of regular banking and other service professions. Unfortunately, many of the types of problems highlighted here emanate from dubious loan brokers. For this reason, Chapter 11 on alternative sources of capital includes a discussion of loan brokers.

Each of the following chapters will highlight nonbank sources of money or capital for small businesses. Included in every chapter will be a description of each alternative source, a discussion of its products or services, recommendations on how to work with the provider, and where to find such a provider.

Bank on It

+ Use any bank declination as an opportunity to fine-tune your loan proposal.
+ Try the bank again after amending your loan proposal.
+ The squeaky wheel does get money more often than the meek mouse.
+ Go outside the box for advice.
+ Watch out for so-called finance professionals who make money by preying on desperate business owners. Never sign any agreement with someone who promises to find you money without an attorney's counsel.

eleven

Loan Brokers and Financial Advisors

Because the first inclination of many business owners after failing to locate bank financing is to sign up with a loan broker, they will be the topic of the first chapter on alternatives to banks.

Loan Brokers

It has been my pleasure to work with two fantastic individuals who are loan brokers. They perform excellent services for their clients and do so for less than stellar remuneration. Unfortunately, I have worked with dozens of other individuals who call themselves loan brokers whom I would just as soon see locked up. The ideal description of a loan broker is to imagine a freelance commercial loan officer who is free to place his or her customer's loan at whichever bank or other entity provides the best bang for the buck. The broker works hard to portray the client in the best possible light and to sell the financing request to the appropriate source of such financing. In payment for these services, the loan broker earns a commission based on the amount of financing obtained for the customer.

Most reputable loan brokers with whom I have worked in the past charge a flat commission rate of 1/2 to 2 percent of the financing amount. On the other hand, I recently came across a loan request that had been submitted to us by a broker from a major metropolitan city that called for a commission of 6 percent. It was a case of an unscrupulous shark feeding on the desires of a very motivated would-be entrepreneur. In the past, I have seen commission rates as high as 10 percent. That is outrageous. Frankly, any businessperson who would agree to pay a figure that high would not be someone to whom I would want to make a bank loan.

It is too bad that many clients of loan brokers adopt an apathetic attitude toward the frequently hefty commissions. The thought is, "I don't care what the commission is as long as I get the money I need." That is desperate logic. It also shortchanges the client. After all, had the business owner located the third-party source of financing, that extra few percent could have been invested in the business. Businesses are lost on tenths of percentage points.

Another less common method that compensates loan brokers is the payment of finder's or referral fees by the third-party source of financing. The bank, finance company, or other lender pays a fee, usually 1 or 2 percent of the financing amount, to the loan broker for bringing the deal to it. This appears fairly painless to the small business owner; the fee is coming out of someone else's pocket. Sorry, faulty logic there, too. The lender probably has offered a higher interest rate, financing charge, or fees to the client from which it will compensate the loan broker. Thus, the client pays for it in the end. Again, had the business owner located the source of financing by himself or herself, unaided by a loan broker, the financing might have been negotiated at a lower rate or cost to the borrower.

Many brokered financing packages end up being sold to secondary market investors. These investors will pay more than the face value of the debt and still net a higher-than-average interest rate return. The entity that sells the financing package earns an immediate, attractive premium. The broker pockets a commission. And the small business owner pays more than he or she should so everyone else in the food chain can live fat and happy. The point is that business owners should employ a loan broker only after every other possible source of money or information about sources of money have been exhausted.

THE CONTRACT

When the services of a loan broker are engaged, the broker will require that the client sign a contract. The contract is similar to a real estate listing agreement that requires the selling homeowner to pay a commission to the broker if a buyer is found who is willing to pay the contract terms for the real estate. The basic clause in a loan broker contract states the amount of money to be found for the client and the commission to be paid to the loan broker.

Prior to signing any business contract, I recommend that a qualified commercial law attorney review it. Understandably, there will be people who believe that such contracts are insignificant in the scope of the world of finance, who are pressed for time, or who do not trust attorneys. These next few lines are for those people.

Never sign a loan broker's contract that does not specifically identify for what the broker will be paid. A few years ago, I made a loan to a large church for construction of a new, multipurpose church building. The church had been referred to me by one of its members. Months after construction started, the bank discovered that a lien had been filed on the church's building. The lien had been filed by a loan broker with whom the church had entered a contract more than one year earlier. The contract called for the church to pay the broker a commission of 2 percent of the total financing if and when financing was located. The contract did not limit the commission to financing found and placed by the loan broker or within a certain time period. We were able to recommend a particularly tenacious attorney to the church who eventually whittled the loan broker's commission to less than 1 percent.

The contract needs to be as specific as humanly possible. The amount of principal, interest rate, payment amounts and frequency, term, amortization, and collateral should be specified. This will protect the client from paying onerous fees even if the financing found or delivered by the broker is unacceptable to the client. Why pay a 2 percent commission for a loan structured to the detriment of the client? Since most business plans are time sensitive, a deadline for delivery of the needed financing should also be stated in the contract. Note that the trigger is delivery, not location, of financing.

If a loan broker refuses to individualize a contract, the client should seek another broker. Good loan brokers gain reputations within banking and financial circles because they look out for the best interest of their clients. That would include limiting the circumstances for which they get paid to precise, measurable goals.

Financial Advisors

Financial advisors include accountants, attorneys, investment brokers, certified financial planners, business consultants, commercial real estate or business brokers, and others. Loan brokering is one of the arrows in their quiver of services. Finding a professional who can help the small business in areas in addition to placing the financing is a great boon to entrepreneurs. In many instances, the small business receives greater value for the buck.

A professional who has intimate knowledge of the subject business, the business owner, or, at a minimum, the transaction has a head start over anyone else who could be brought in to help find money. That knowledge makes it exponentially easier to sell a loan to an investor than without it. The quest for financing is but one piece of any individual's or business's puzzle; the professional advisor can consider the entire puzzle and what would best fit into the open space. Issues that might go hand-in-hand with financing include liability protection, estate planning, succession planning, tax planning, contract law, and accounting. Any member of one of the mainstream professions would add value to basic loan brokering.

One caution about using a professional advisor is to be wary of conflicts of interest. Most of the professions have national umbrella organizations that espouse codes of conduct for their respective members. Standard in all codes is the requirement to do what is right and best for the client. Thankfully, it is very rare to come across a circumstance where a professional violates that part of their code. To be safe, prospective clients should demand and expect to compensate professionals based on an hourly rate. Contingency fees, like those paid to attorneys in personal injury lawsuits, should not be paid for successful referrals to investors. Planning, advice, and referrals should be part of the normal advisory services offered by the respective service provider.

As soon as a commission is introduced to the equation, the potential for conflict of interest becomes a reality. The presence of a contract means that the professional now wears two hats: trusted advisor and contract vendor. By definition, the advisor should perform for the client's best interest. Conversely, a contract vendor must look out for its best interest. This delicate balance can be successfully handled by many professionals, but it opens the doors to later problems.

This type of conflict of interest is most common where the professional has the opportunity to earn commission income at both ends of a transaction. Business brokers (not necessarily real estate brokers or salespeople) have more opportunities and incentive to double-dip than most other professions. A business broker will be paid a commission by the seller of a business when the broker closes the sale of that business. If an entrepreneur is working with a broker to find a business to buy, the broker should be looking for a business opportunity that best fits the client's abilities and desires. If the same broker acts as loan broker, a major conflict of interest exists. Whose best interests are served by finding the first and fastest source of financing? It's the loan broker's, for he or she stands to earn two quick commissions. The double-dipping of commissions is not the problem. The real problem is that the first and fastest source of financing may not be, and in all likelihood is not, the best available package for the client.

Another caveat is to be wary of any professional who offers to exchange services for part ownership of a client's business. I have come across more than one attorney and accountant who are rumored to own pieces of every business in their respective towns. Struggling business owners and would-be entrepreneurs find these offers to be irresistible because it costs them no cash at a time when they can least afford to spend any money. This type of offer should provide the business owner a clue that the business does have value—and probably more than he or she realizes.

Whenever possible, business owners should seek out professional advisors who do double duty as loan brokers. Simply queries of law and CPA firms will yield the names of any individuals who are up to the task in any given town. It is understandable that many entrepreneurs are extremely anxious to find the required money and open the doors to their businesses. A modicum of caution and prudence at this juncture can save money, time, and heartache over the long haul and actually be a positive factor in prolonging the life of the business venture.

Bank on It

- ✦ Loan brokers and other professionals who can shop your loan proposal are best found via referrals from attorneys, CPAs, and other trusted individuals.
- ✦ Always ask for references from the prospective loan broker.
- ✦ Never sign a loan broker's contract without a lawyer's help.
- ✦ Often, a CPA or lawyer can provide loan broker services along with the other services he or she provides.

12

Your
Own Pocket

An adage bantered about by some highly successful business-people is, "Good businesspeople make money on their money. Geniuses make money on other people's money." Quite!

Many unsuccessful loan applicants over the years have told me that they do not want to use any of their own money because if the business failed they would lose it. That's why they came to the bank . . . to use our money instead of their own. Losing one's money is a valid concern that should be weighed carefully prior to opening or expanding a business. The bank certainly considers that point before it makes a loan decision! If an entrepreneur believes that the likeli-hood of losing the money invested into a business is strong, it prob-ably would be a good idea to skip entrepreneurialship and opt for a 9 to 5 job until a better idea comes around. If the entrepreneur believes, however, that the business idea is sound and the bank still will not lend any money, the entrepreneur may have to look no fur-ther than home to get the necessary money. Even if a bank agrees to make a loan for the needed cash, some business owners might be wise to look to personal resources for the cash. Personal resources might provide fewer strings attached, lower interest rates, and tax advantages. This chapter discusses many places to find money at home.

Home Equity

I really know that an applicant believes in the subject business when the loan application or business plan offers a pledge of the applicant's home equity to secure any loan. Regardless of whether it is offered or not, home equity is the first asset that banks look to when an application has shortcomings. Today, it is not uncommon for people to receive several blind home equity loan offers from distant banks in a week's mail. These loans typically offer long-term paybacks, up to fifteen years, and attractive interest rates. Some banks offer ridiculously low introductory interest rates with which to lure new customers. Why not take advantage of such offers if the bank is going to require the pledge of the home anyway? Any funds raised from a home equity loan reduce the amount of a bank loan that may be needed. The funds are equity into the business, which improves the overall picture for the bank. And since the home is or would presumably be completely loaned up, the bank cannot take it to secure other or larger debts.

Some specialty companies offer loans up to 125 percent of the value of the equity in a home. That is far more than any commercial banker would allow. The tradeoff on most of those "no-equity" loans is higher costs to the borrower. Even a noncommittal banker will gladly refer an applicant to the bank's home equity department since, in today's cross-selling environment, the banker is likely to receive some form of incentive compensation for the referral.

Home equity is the single largest source of savings the common person owns. When an entrepreneur really believes in the opportunity, it is an easy source of cash. Home equity loans are approved by lenders by proprietary formulas that take into account an applicant's personal income, other outstanding debts, and home valuation. Entrepreneurs would be wise to line up a home equity loan prior to quitting a day job for the glories of business ownership since a lender cannot give any credence to self-employment income without a solid track record. Suffice it to say, the more income a person has that is not dedicated to making credit card, car, and department store account payments, the higher home equity loan amount that would be available.

Personal Savings and Investments

Many people segregate personal savings from the available pool of funds for use in a business. Unless there is a strong reason for maintaining a large savings balance, entrepreneurs should look to use most, if not all, of those savings in their businesses. Common reasons for keeping a substantial sum of cash on hand are college tuition (real and expected), health needs, and retirement. The idea that a rainy-day fund is needed for no particular reason is admirable and good financial planning, but bankers would rather see that money invested in the business prior to its lending other people's savings to the business.

Many people start businesses today with funds withdrawn from qualified retirement plans like individual retirement accounts (IRAs), 401ks, and pension plans. These are expensive sources of startup capital in several senses. First, the government frowns upon the early withdrawal of money intended for retirement so much that the owner will have to pay hefty taxes and penalties on any money taken from those investments. Second, the owner will have to be very successful in the new venture to make up the lost retirement money and the potential capital gains that may have been realized had the money been left to accumulate until retirement. Banks are barred, by law, from using these assets for collateral. The liquidation of them by their owners for the purpose of starting or feeding a business should be a last resort.

Many people, today, own investments outside of retirement plans. The two prominent investments are real estate and marketable securities. Investment real estate may include rental houses, duplexes, apartment buildings, or commercial buildings. Any equity in those pieces of real estate can be tapped to generate funds. A lender will base the amount of a loan upon the fair market value of the equity and the cash flow generated by rents paid by the tenants. Since investment real estate is a business in itself, this is a great way to raise money to expand the owner's business empire.

Marketable securities also are a store of potential capital. Naturally, the investments could be sold to transform the current market value into cash. A better solution for many people is to margin the stocks. To margin stocks means to borrow against the value of the stocks. Banks can make loans to people based on marketable securities for collateral.

Brokerage firms offer customers margin accounts that are highly convenient and practical. Generally, the brokerage will lend the account holder up to 50 percent of the market value of the account, at attractive interest rates and repayment plans. There are no applications or other strings attached to the loan. Most brokerages provide margin account customers a checkbook with which to write their own loans.

The one caveat with margin loans is the potential for a margin call. A margin call is when the loan to value of the stocks goes above 50 percent. The brokerage contacts, or calls, the customer to request the deposit of additional securities or the repayment of enough principal to reduce the loan to value to 50 percent or less. Margin calls share much of the blame for the Great Depression. When the market crashed in 1929, investors were forced to sell their investments at increasingly large losses to meet margin calls. Of course, as the market continued to fall, accounts continued to fall out of margin, forcing further fire sales of already depressed stocks. The vast loss of wealth and the subsequent inability for capitalists to invest in businesses caused job losses and stagnation for many years. It was not until Franklin Roosevelt embarked on his enormous public spending spree that the economy returned from the abyss. The market has never dipped by 50 percent since then, and it is believed to be a relatively safe loan advance rate; thus, it is the rule of thumb at most brokerages.

Insurance Policies

Some insurance policies contain a savings component that grows over time. These policies are called whole life or permanent insurance contracts. The policies have two values: face value and cash value. Face value is the amount of money that would be paid to beneficiaries in the event the policyholder dies. Cash value is the amount of money in the savings component of the contract that would be given to the policyholder immediately upon cancellation or surrender of the policy. The cash value can also be borrowed by the policyholder; some policy contracts allow 100 percent of the cash value to be borrowed.

Life insurance is notoriously complicated. Life insurance agents enjoy a sleazy reputation built more on their collective inability to make policies clearly understandable to their clients than on any dishonesty. When in doubt, a good accountant or independent financial advisor can help policyholders determine what type of policy is owned and what cash value might be available. Cash value loans from insurance companies are also quick and easy and come with just two strings attached. If the borrower dies or fails to keep up premiums, there are consequences. In the event that the borrower dies before repaying the loan, the proceeds from the life insurance policy would first go to pay back the loan before any is paid out to beneficiaries. If premiums are not paid, the insurance company can tap the policy's cash value to cover the payments. If there is no cash value available, the policy can be canceled and the policyholder loses the insurance benefits (including a preferential premium rate).

Other Assets

Hungry entrepreneurs need to review every asset that they own. Anything of marketable value must be considered a source of funding for the business. The choice to sell any specific item must be weighed against the choice of not going into business. Which would the entrepreneur rather do without? The most common "other" asset that banks are asked to use for collateral by applicants are collections. Art, gun, card, figurine, car, and antique collections are meaningless to 99 percent of the banks in America. An entrepreneur must decide what is more important, funding the business or fondling the collection. The collection might hold sentimental value that exceeds any value that might be created by a business. The businessperson might feel that he or she is really just a caretaker for a collection that will eventually be passed along to other family members. That is all well and good. Don't start the business then. If the collection is purely an investment, the time is as good as any to cash it in and reinvest the proceeds elsewhere.

Bank on It

+ Banks look upon applicants who maximize reliance on personal assets in a business startup with great favor.

+ Because of potential tax or contractual issues, people should consult with a good accountant prior to selling investments to raise cash.

+ Disclose all of your assets on your personal financial statement.

+ If you are a collector, ask yourself why you are collecting. If it is for sentimental reasons, don't sell your collection. If it is for investment purposes, the sale of the collection must be considered as a source of funding.

Friends and Family

A sage in my family has told me hundreds of times, "Friends are friends. Business is business. Friends and business is horseshit." The grammatical structure is intentionally folksy, I am sure, since the source of this wisdom spent his entire career, quite successfully, in public education. How someone who never set foot in the arena of private enterprise could be so dead-on is beyond me. More times than not, involvement of friends and family in a business enterprise creates complexities and heartache beyond belief. When those friends or family members are involved as investors or lenders, the chances for grief rise proportionally.

Remarkably, many new businesses are started with investments, gifts, or loans of money by friends or family members to the entrepreneur. Those transactions that have happy endings have one common trait. In all successful marriages (pardon the pun) of business and family or friends, the one common characteristic is a high level of communication between all parties prior to the injection of the investment. This chapter will discuss many ways that friends and family can help launch a small business, the pitfalls that commonly occur, and steps to take to ensure successful endings to these relationships.

The No-Money Assist

There are a few ways that friends and family members can help a fledgling business owner without writing a check. Bankers often see sound business plans backed by an entrepreneur with good, if not strong, management capability. They are forced to decline the applications because of the lack of financial wherewithal. Many of these projects could be saved, as is, and approved with a nod from an existing bank customer or an influential member of the community. A simple referral from someone bolsters the bank's view of the character of the applicant. Potential applicants need to wrack their brains for key friends or family members who might make one phone call to the bank.

In another common situation, we see parents who wish to help children establish themselves in a business. The parents have one financial advantage over their children and that is time to accumulate wealth. Usually this is limited to a high percentage of equity in the parent's home, a vacation home, or small inheritances from older generations. In general, the personal financial statements of the parents will be in much better shape than those of the children. Quite often, just the unsecured guarantee of a parent or parents will be enough to salvage a loan application. There must be something unique in the bond of bloodlines because we seldom see nonrelated friends offer to personally guarantee a loan! Naturally, the guarantee offered by a family member sometimes needs to have assets pledged to secure it in order to make a deal work. This collateral might take the form of a second lien on a home, pledge of marketable securities or certificates of deposit, or other acceptable assets.

Yes, in my career, I have found it necessary to foreclose on homes owned by parent-guarantors. It is not a fun aspect of a banker's job. I have also witnessed many successful transactions that involved parents as guarantors. In one such case, a retired gentleman pledged several hundred shares of a mutual fund to back a loan for his son's startup retail business. The business flourished, and the father's mutual fund more than tripled in value during the duration of the five-year loan. When he stopped in to pick up his mutual fund certificates after the loan had been paid off, he winked at me and said, "Had I not pledged these things to you, I would have sold 'em once they'd gone up 10 percent! My boy's loan tripled my investments by forcing me to hold on to 'em." I only wish I could have taken credit for the favorable investment returns.

If a business already has a loan on its books from a friendly party, the debt might be subordinated to new or existing bank debt. A subordinated debt is paid off after the debt to which it is subordinate. The bank may ask that the friendly debt be entirely subordinated, which means that payments of principal and/or interest may not be made without the bank's permission. The bank may require the debt to be subordinated as to nonscheduled principal and interest payments—this allows regularly scheduled payments to be made to the debt holder. That is important especially when the debtor, such as a retired parent, relies on the payments for living expenses. Banks treat subordinated debt as equity in the business. Like the business owner's own investment, subordinated debt cannot be taken back out of the business until the bank's loans are satisfied.

Cash Investments and Loans

The major difference between a friend or family member and a banker is the friend or family member already accepts (we hope) the applicant as an excellent character risk. That provides a big head start in the process of selling a business plan to someone. Friendly money may be just enough to raise the owner's equity in a business to an acceptable level for bank consideration or may finance most, if not all, of a business's needs. If a banker has not already advised the applicant, the applicant should ask if additional cash equity would help the loan application. This will determine how much money the entrepreneur will need to try to raise from friends and family. Cash provided by friends and family members may take the form of a loan to the business or the business owner or as equity in the business. Loans may be secured or unsecured.

Business owners should be professional in the request for investment from friends and family members. The mere opportunity to ask a nonbank source for money is the singular advantage of these connections. Big problems arise when sentimentality and emotional games are used to grab money. It is far better to work for someone else from 9 to 5 than to go into business by burdening oneself and one's investors with emotional baggage.

Investment of Assets

This method is growing in popularity because of the peace of mind it offers both borrower and lender. Rather than forking over cash, the friend or family member loans or leases an asset. The asset might be office space, manufacturing space in a pole barn, a piece of machinery or equipment, or telecommunication equipment. Unlike cash, the asset can be felt and seen every day by the investor. At worst, the asset can be returned to the investor who can otherwise employ it or sell it. When a person invests cash, all sorts of questions and thoughts race through his or her mind. I wonder if the business is making money? I wonder how much money the business is losing? Why is the owner driving a new Mercedes? Did my investment just pay for the remodeling of the guy's kitchen? Gosh, I'm going to be rich off this investment. I hope my other kids don't find out about this because then they will want their share now, too.

It is much easier for an entrepreneur to convince someone to lend, lease, or invest a tangible asset than cash. If a person is asked to decide between loaning a car or $100 to a friend, the likely decision will be to loan a car even though it is worth far more than the cash. An old customer of mine, a man endowed with a heart bigger than a basketball, decided to help out an individual who had faced tough odds in his life. My customer set the man up in a business similar to the customer's own business. My customer borrowed money to buy the key and expensive equipment for the new business and loaned it to the individual. Unfortunately, the new business failed quickly. Yet, my customer was able to retrieve the equipment and employ it elsewhere. Although he did lose some money in the transaction, it could have been much worse had this Samaritan invested cash rather than hard assets.

How to Get Money from Friends and Family

Locating likely investors among friends and family members should not be difficult. Most people have a pretty good idea of how much money their acquaintances and family own and who might be most receptive to a pitch. Heck, most people harbor dreams of owning their own business. An entrepreneur who asks for a loan or investment from someone gives that person a chance to become tangibly involved in a real business.

As stated at the beginning of this chapter, the key to successful financial transactions between business owners and their friends or family members is communication. Four topics must be discussed among the business owner and the prospective investors. Foremost is the simple fact that the investors must recognize that they may not get any of their money back. I would not accept one penny of assistance from a friend or family member until that person has told me, "Yes, I know I might as well flush this money down the toilet, but helping you means a lot to me."

The second important topic is to communicate the transaction. The loan application suggested in an earlier chapter should be the basis of this conversation. Since the potential investor is not likely to have financial expertise, it might be wise for all concerned if the investor invited his or her accountant to review the request. The accountant might raise concerns similar to those raised by a banker, like feasibility of the business, adequacy of capital, and so on. The accountant's primary job is to make sure that the investor understands the objective risks of the investment. The investor is free to disregard credit concerns and the advice of any professional counselor and may rely on subjective reasons to go ahead and make an investment.

The third topic to discuss is how the investment will be repaid to the investor. For loans, this means establishing interest rates, payment frequency and amounts, collateral, and how the business will report to the lender. For equity investments, this means determining voting rights at company meetings, dividend policies, conditions when the stock may be sold to outside parties, predetermined prices at which the company or main shareholder can repurchase the stock, and likely total return that may be expected by an investor. The last point is critical.

Too many people daydream about becoming wealthy by buying into a small company that later goes public and grows to enormous proportions. Not a day has passed in the last twenty years when I have not heard some purveyor of investment advice mention "the next McDonald's." Unrealistic expectations might be the worst enemy of an entrepreneur. In this day and age of IPOs (initial public offerings) where college sophomores who operate a rudimentary software company from their dorm room become instant billionaires, everyone dreams the big dream. Even if a business owner were able to reward an investor with consistent, healthy 10 percent gains every year, the investor, who might harbor the dream of turning his $1,000 investment in a franchise sub shop into a vacation villa in Bermuda, might be terribly put out. Returning to my main theme of this chapter, a happy investor is one who truly understands that his or her money might be gone forever.

The final topic to discuss with friends and family who decide to invest in a business is what happens if the business goes bankrupt. Many investors in these situations may understand that their investment may disappear, but they believe that the business owner will "make it right" eventually by repaying the debt from future salaries, refinancing homes, or future windfalls like the lottery or inheritances. Entrepreneurs must emphasize that even if the intent is to make everyone whole on their investments, it simply is not practical that it can be accomplished if the business fails. After all, the entrepreneur will have to provide for the personal living expenses of his or her own family and probably repair other credit that is more critical than friendly debt. If other debtors are involved in a business, each debtor must understand the mutual relationships. The priority of the debts must be explained to each lender or investor—that is, in a liquidation of the business, to whom does each successive dollar go. Investor-owners must know and trust that any proceeds left over after satisfying debtors will go to them first and the entrepreneur last. Investor-owners must also acknowledge that creditors have priority over them. Many people believe that ownership of stock in a company gives them more rights than those of mere lenders.

Everything should be well documented on paper. I highly recommend that each party to the transaction obtain a qualified attorney to draft agreements and other documents. The involvement of an attorney is more important in this type of transaction than in a bank loan transaction since bank documents are standardized and poured over by attorneys every day. Reducing every agreement and promise into the black and white of a document reduces the chances of any misunderstanding later. Never let a friend or family member sign a document and say, "I don't have to read it. I trust you."

Family Matters

There are several special considerations that entrepreneurs need to address when family members loan or invest in a business. The primary point is how the transaction affects estate planning for the investors. The refrain bankers hear frequently from parent-investors is, "Well, it is his inheritance. If he blows it all now, that's all he gets." That is all well and good and admirable; but if the consequences of the investment or loan are not considered up front, big problems could occur.

For example, if the lender passes away during the life of the loan, should the loan be deducted from any inheritance due to the entrepreneur-child? Should the entrepreneur continue paying back the loan to an estate or to co-inheritors and take a full share of the inheritance? Will there be an agreement that allows the estate to make demand for immediate repayment of the entire loan or investment so that the estate may be settled? Would repayment upon demand even be possible someday?

Another common concern is sibling rivalry. I have seen numerous occasions when siblings of a borrower discovered that Pop had helped out the entrepreneurial child with a loan. The siblings go ballistic and demand that Pop give them an equal amount of money right then and there. This happens in loving and trusting families, too! Money does strange things to the best of us. Holding a family roundtable discussion prior to any exchange of money is a great idea that will eliminate suspicion and fairness concerns.

Lastly, family members involved in a business transaction must promise that business is business and family is family. Too many people let business get in between more important aspects of life, including loving family relationships. An agreement to never discuss the investment at family gatherings, while carving Thanksgiving turkey, or taking a holiday at the beach, will preserve at least one successful thing in the respective parties' lives—family.

There are significant advantages to borrowing friendly money. Flexibility of terms and acceptance of the borrower's character faults are not the least of them. The disadvantages of borrowing money from family or friends usually result from poor communication and false expectations.

Bank on It

+ Pitch the transaction to friends or family members who are likely sources of investment just as if they were bankers.

+ Discuss alternatives to cash investment, like cosigning (guaranteeing) a bank loan or buying and then leasing a needed asset to the business.

+ Discuss and agree on the terms of the investment and reduce them to writing, preferably with the assistance of legal counsel. Emphasize how the loan or investment will be repaid and focus on realistic returns to the investor to eliminate any get-rich notions.

+ Discuss the worst-case scenario: What happens if the business fails?

+ Document everything, again, preferably with advice from a qualified attorney.

+ Family transactions need to be communicated to all affected family members, and unique issues like estate planning must be considered.

fourteen

The
Government

There are thousands of programs, funds, and grants available to small business owners that have been created by the federal, state, and local governments. It would be next to impossible to assemble a list of programs available through every state and municipality in the United States. This chapter will outline several programs available from the federal government and describe the types of programs that are typically found at state and local levels.

Whenever any business owner or banker thinks of government assistance, the United States Small Business Administration (SBA) is the first name that pops into mind. Let us be absolutely clear, though, right up front: The SBA does not make loans directly to businesses. In fact, most of the programs discussed in this chapter do not make loans or grant money directly to small businesses. The roles filled by these various programs are vital and can lead entrepreneurs to other, viable sources of funding. For this reason, they are included in this book.

The Federal Government

Largely due to the influence of the SBA, the federal government is often thought of as the primary source of government funding for small businesses. As mentioned, this is not true because the SBA does not make loans directly to small businesses. The SBA, though, should be on every business owner's Rolodex because of its phenomenal stockpile of information and reference material. A plethora of other government agencies and departments also play vital roles in the development of small businesses and will be discussed here as well.

THE UNITED STATES SMALL BUSINESS ADMINISTRATION

One of the first stops any businessperson should make after reading this book is the SBA's Web site at *www.sba.gov*. The site contains so much information that in five years of surfing the site, I still find new helpful information and links weekly. Of course, the SBA is best known for its loan guaranty programs. These programs actually guaranty partial repayment of loans made by participant banks to small businesses. This is key since the availability of the guaranty often permits a bank to make a loan it would otherwise not make to a small business.

SBA regulations do not permit the agency to guaranty loans that could or should be made under conventional terms by banks. This safeguards the budgeted funding granted to the SBA by Congress and ensures that the SBA-guaranteed loans are used to help businesses that otherwise would not get assistance. Until recently, any business that obtained an SBA-guaranteed loan was stigmatized by the fact that these loans were reserved for marginal applicants. The truth, today, is that many banks use SBA-guaranteed loans to make available terms or conditions it could not otherwise provide to the customer. These include maturities up to twenty-five years long, lower equity requirements, and long-term fixed rates. Credit quality often has nothing to do with the fact that a bank has offered to make an SBA-guaranteed loan to a client. In fact, famous companies like Intel, Nike, America Online, FedEx, and Callaway Golf have received SBA-backed assistance in the past. That is hardly a rogues' gallery of poor credit risk.

In order to qualify for the various loan guaranty programs, a business must be a small business as defined by the SBA. Nearly 90 percent of all U.S. businesses would qualify under the standards established by the SBA. For example, a manufacturing company could have up to 500 employees and still be defined as a small business under SBA guidelines. The following is a brief list and description of several of the more utilized SBA loan guarantee programs.

7(a) Loan Guarantee

This program guarantees loans made by banks to qualified small businesses. The maximum guarantee amount is equal to 75 percent of the loan or $750,000, whichever is greater. Maturities range from seven years for working capital loans to ten years for equipment loans to twenty-five years for real estate loans. Typically, the minimum owner's equity required is 10 percent of the total financing need. Interest rates may not exceed the current national prime rate plus 2 3/4 percent.

Low Doc Guarantee

The Low Doc program eliminates much of the paperwork required for the regular 7(a) loan guarantee program, but is limited to loans of $150,000 or less. The guaranteed amount is 80 percent of loans up to $100,000 and 75 percent for loans above $100,000.

SBA Express

This program is fairly new and available only through banks that have been designated as preferred lenders by the SBA. It eliminates all SBA application materials and most of the SBA closing documents. Unlike the other programs that require the SBA to review the application, this program relies solely on the discretion of the lender. Because the SBA does not have up-front oversight, it guarantees only 50 percent of the loan amount and loans cannot be more than $150,000.

CAPLines

Many businesses need short-term working capital and not term loans. The SBA created this program to meet those needs. There are several subcategories of CAPLines designed for different-sized businesses and industries. These lines of credit rely upon short-term assets for primary collateral, which is of tremendous benefit to service industry businesses that may not have a lot of other collateral.

Export Working Capital Loans

Many small businesses have difficulty financing international trade transactions. This program might be the solution. The SBA guarantees 90 percent of loans made for an individual transaction. The loans may be revolving and usually mature in twelve months or less. Businesses with less than twelve months of history are not eligible.

International Trade Loan Guarantees

In order to promote international trade, the SBA can guarantee up to $1.25 million for any combination of long-term and working capital financing. This is not a transaction-based program like the Export Working Capital program; it is designed to promote long-term involvement by small businesses in international trade.

Defense Loan and Technical Assistance Program

This program operates similarly to the regular 7(a) program but with higher guarantee limits. Eligible businesses are those located in communities that have been adversely affected by military base closures or downsizing.

SBA 504 Loan Program

This program is vastly different from the guaranty loan programs above. Bankers typically will use this program when a client has single-purpose real estate requirements or unusual equipment needs. It is also used for plant and equipment expansion purposes when other credit considerations are marginal. It is used only for acquisition or expansion of fixed assets. A bank loans 90 percent of the financing needs with the borrower covering the other 10 percent (percentages vary depending on whether the business is a startup or not and a handful of other factors). Once the assets are in place and ready to place into service, the SBA, through conduits called Certified Development Companies, funds up to 40 percent of the project costs. The total amount of funds provided by the SBA is usually limited to $750,000, with certain exceptional cases allowed to go as high as $1 million. Typically, this leaves the bank with a loan for 50 percent of the project costs and a very favorable collateral coverage ratio.

The SBA generates the funds that it loans to the business by the sale of debentures to investors. The effective interest rates, with fees included, are normally lower than competitive bank rates. Benefits to the borrower include a lower overall interest cost and lower equity requirements.

Microloan Program

The SBA has established a network of intermediaries that make direct loans to qualified small businesses from $100 up to $25,000. This program is designed specifically for small businesses that have had no luck in finding loans through conventional sources.

SBA's Other Programs

The SBA sponsors several other entities and programs outside the above loan guaranty programs. For the sake of organization, they are included here, with the exception of ACE-net and the Small Business Investment Companies, which will be covered later in the book under venture capital.

Minority Enterprise Development Program

This program delivers assistance to minority, nonminority, and disabled entrepreneurs who can demonstrate that they have been subjected to a cultural or ethnic bias. By definition, this would include African Americans, Hispanic Americans, Native Americans, and Asian Americans. Other groups may be eligible. The primary avenue of assistance is to help these business owners obtain business from the federal government, usually contract awards. The program also mandates that each SBA district office provide extra counseling and informational assistance to any qualified individual.

SBA Prequalification Program

Scattered around the United States, the SBA has developed several intermediaries that provide counseling to minority-, women-, or veteran-owned businesses in the loan application process. These centers help mold the loan application and obtain SBA's commitment prior to sending the applicant to a bank. The program is particularly helpful to entrepreneurs who are starting new businesses and have little business experience.

Small Business Development Centers (SBDCs)

The SBA has established at least one SBDC in every state; Puerto Rico; Guam; Washington, D.C.; and the U.S. Virgin Islands. There are more than 1,000 satellite locations, and they can be found in almost any moderate-sized city in the country. Each center is staffed by business experts and volunteers. The centers provide many kinds of business counseling services, including small business finance. Many of the centers sponsor a Lender's Assistance Program that affords business owners the opportunity to test-drive a loan proposal to a loan officer. The loan officer offers a critique of the presentation so that the client can fine-tune the application for his or her actual appointment at a bank.

SBDC offices also hold a wealth of information pertaining to local sources of financing, including loans, grants, and venture capital.

Business Information Centers (BICs)

Business information centers are similar to SBDCs but in a more, self-service environment. Besides on-site staff expertise, BICs offer software, video, and library services. Several major cities are home to BICs and some form the core of One Stop Capital Shops, a neat concept now being rolled out by the SBA. One Stop Capital Shops attempt to pull every resource that might be required by entrepreneurs under one roof.

Service Corps of Retired Executives (SCORE)

More than 13,000 retired business executives across the nation have volunteered to act as consultants to small business owners. Each SCORE office contains a diverse mix of executives who bring a breadth of experience to small business clients, including finance and banking. These volunteers have seen it all and provide advice grounded in decades of personal trial and error.

THE UNITED STATES DEPARTMENT OF AGRICULTURE (USDA)

A surprise to most anyone, including bankers, is the availability of loan guaranty programs from the U.S. Department of Agriculture (USDA). There are two distinct programs within the USDA. The first is geared toward farmers and is called the Farm Service Agency (FSA). The second program targets other businesses and is called the Rural Development Agency.

Farm Service Agency

The FSA provides guarantees to lenders who originate farm ownership and working capital loans. This is a crucial program in our country because the vast majority of banks classify agricultural lending as a very risky practice. Without it, the loss of small, family-run farms would be accelerated from its current alarming pace. Banks would simply not lend to small farms. Consequently, the big corporate farms everyone loves to hate would be the only entities able to structure the necessary debt to buy out or run farms.

The farm ownership program requires lower equity into a farm purchase by the buyer and provides terms or amortizations up to a maximum of forty years. A subprogram is designed for new farmers, young people, and succeeding generations of families who must buy out the preceding generation in order to hold on to the family farm. This program pays a healthy portion of the loan interest for the buyer. At the time of this writing, the net interest rate paid by the buyer was just 4 percent. This is a remarkable incentive for young people to take the risk of farm ownership since it obviously lowers overhead dramatically.

Lines of credit for farm operations have long been a bane for bankers. No banker wants collateral that has to be fed, milked, or mucked out after. What other business keeps its work-in-process inventory (crops) outside, exposed to the elements for months at a time? And when production creates a bumper harvest, prices crash so that total revenue is less than it would have been with a less than great crop. It is easy to understand why banks shy away from agriculture lending. The FSA guaranty program alleviates much of that risk. That is great for everyone. In many small towns around America, bankers and farmers are considered the salt of the earth and pillars of the respective community. It's nice they can cooperate and do business together!

The Rural Development Agency

The Rural Development Agency has four distinct branches: Rural Business Service, Rural Community Development, Rural Housing Service, and Rural Utilities Service. The main concern of this book is the Rural Business Service (RBS). As one can imagine by the nomenclature of the agency and its divisions, the purpose behind the assorted programs is to help rural areas develop. The Rural Utilities Service helps bring better utility services to backwoods communities with research, grants, loan guarantees, and consulting services. The Rural Housing Service helps to build, increase, improve, and maintain the stock of acceptable housing in rural areas. It accomplishes this largely with loan guarantees. The program makes an investment in an apartment building in a rural community very attractive to real estate investors. The Rural Community Development Service provides loan guarantees to banks for loans to municipalities for public assets like sewer and street projects, libraries, medical clinics, and recreation facilities. We recently completed a loan under this agency to a small northern Michigan community for the construction of a local United Way office.

The bread-and-butter program, though, for small businesses is the USDA Rural Business Service's Business and Industry Loan Guaranty Program. The program is available to most businesses, and there are no size eligibility concerns. The program is very similar to the SBA loan guarantee programs, but in many ways less restrictive. The program can be used for very small loans up to loans of $25 million. Loans up to $5 million are 80 percent guaranteed by the government. Larger loan amounts receive smaller guarantee amounts; the largest loans are guaranteed at 60 percent by the government.

The kicker for this program is that it may be used only in communities of 50,000 people or fewer. The term *community* seldom means just one municipality and is likely to include either an entire county or contiguous communities. Obviously, if a bank were to make a $20 million or $25 million loan in a small town, it would probably have enormous economic impact in job creation and the local tax base. The USDA people are a delight to work with. They exist to help rural communities, and every loan has tangible results for at least one small town or another.

More information on these programs can be found at the USDA's Web site, at *www.usda.gov*, at local USDA field offices, and at local banks.

OTHER FEDERAL GOVERNMENT DEPARTMENTS

If a person performs an Internet search of "federal government + small business finance," several hundred thousand "hits" are likely to appear. In my experience, every major government department offers some kind of assistance to small business owners. The United States Department of the Interior has many, very specialized programs. The most well known, though, are the loan guarantee programs for Native Americans available from the Department's Bureau of Indian Affairs (BIA). The Merchant Marine Agency offers loan guarantees and subsidies to fishing boat operators. The examples are endless. The best advice for a businessperson is to contact the most appropriate department or agency (or member of Congress) to investigate lesser known programs. The SBA's Web site contains several pages of links to other relevant government departments and agencies.

State and Local Governments

Battle Creek, Michigan, is located just down I-94 from the town where I live, but it seems to be in a whole other world than the rest of us when it comes to helping small businesses. Several years ago, the community, like many others across the country, faced a deteriorating urban core and job loss to other communities and states. The community came together and formed an economic development powerhouse called Battle Creek Unlimited (BCU). With a healthy investment by local corporate citizen Kellogg's and the foundation, which was endowed by the founder of the company, BCU's war chest was filled with dollars. Fort Custer, a nearby military base that had been in use since prior to the Civil War, was beginning to be dismantled. A big chunk of land from the base became available for development at bargain-rate prices. BCU used creative financing packages, including interest-free loans, forgivable loans, grants, free land, and tax savings incentives, to lure businesses to Battle Creek. Their plan worked, and it takes only a brief drive through the Fort Custer Industrial Park to see Japanese, German, Dutch, and American companies thriving. For every big-name plant to arrive, though, ten mom-and-pop businesses opened with BCU assistance. Two of my clients decided to relocate to Battle Creek from other spots only because of the attractive financing packages.

The point I hope to emphasize with this example is that owners of small businesses need to look over the horizon to other locations and municipalities not just for new market possibilities but also for financial incentives. Every state and most communities have some type of program or programs available to help meet the financial needs of small business. It is not only politically wise because small business owners have a strong unified voice, but also economically wise since small businesses create more than 90 percent of all new jobs.

Not this book, or any book, can possibly do justice to the programs offered by all fifty states, thousands of counties and parishes, and tens of thousands of individual communities. What it can do is point the reader in the right direction to help uncover any money that might be available in a particular state or municipality.

STATES

My first call would be to the state's department of commerce or business. Michigan even has a Small Business Ombudsman Office to help answer questions like these. State legislators would fall all over themselves to provide assistance and information to someone who, potentially, was going to add jobs to the specific legislative district. Most states also have a statewide chamber of commerce that would probably have information on available programs.

Many states now have a program called a Capital Access Program. The program is available through participating banks. It provides incentives to a bank to take more risk and extend loans to small businesses. Typically, a loan is enrolled in the program at the bank's discretion. The customer pays a fee based on the loan amount, which is matched by the bank. The state then matches that total. All the money is then deposited into a special account at the participating bank. For example, a bank makes a $100,000 loan to a company. The Capital Access Program fee might be 2%. The customer antes up $2,000, as does the bank. The state sends a check to the bank for $4,000. All the funds, in total $8,000, are deposited in a special interest-bearing account. As more loans are made in the program, the account balance grows. Any interest earned on the account is kept in the account, too. If and when a loan goes bad, the bank can take money from the account to pay off the bad loan. CAP programs, as they are called universally, are excellent vehicles for very small loans since the pooled interest concept readily covers the principal and there is no extra paperwork like that under loan guaranty programs.

LOCAL COMMUNITIES

The first stop that I recommend to people is the local chamber of commerce. It is the chamber's function to assist the business community. Chambers usually know about any available local resources or will have programs under the same roof. Most communities of any size also have an economic development office. It might be staffed part time by the mayor who also wears ten other hats; a single, full-time expert in small business needs; or a whole department of people dedicated to helping small businesses. Commission or council members at the county, city, or township level could also be of assistance.

The town in which I live has two interesting direct loan programs. One is provided by the city and is called the Revolving Loan Fund. The other is provided by a downtown authority and is called the Facade Improvement Fund. The former is designed to help entrepreneurs obtain the necessary money to open or expand a business. It is available in tandem with loans from local banks. The other is designed to help beautify the immediate downtown and is set up as a forgivable loan. After a specified number of years, the loan is forgiven if the business meets certain parameters (such as, still being in business downtown!). Unlike banks, neither program leans heavily on the six C's of credit; but both offer more generous terms like longer amortizations and lower interest rates.

Bank on It

+ The government, be it federal, state, or local, can be the small business owner's best friend in times of financial need.
+ Ask a banker if an SBA or USDA loan guarantee program would make the loan application viable to that bank.
+ Contact the SBA, via telephone at 1-800-U-ASK-SBA or on the Web at *www.sba.gov*, to gather information pertinent to the subject business or its owners.
+ Contact local state legislators to inquire about assistance available to small businesses that is made available by the state, including loans, grants, and guidance.
+ Contact local chambers of commerce, business authorities, or county or city economic development offices to ask about local sources of loans, grants, and guidance.

fifteen

Nonbank
Lenders

Nonbank lenders include savings and loan associations, credit unions, and commercial finance companies. Savings and loans and credit unions are familiar to most people. Commercial finance companies include well-known names like The Money Store, AT&T Capital, GE Capital, The Business Loan Center, and American Express. These companies make loans that are generally guaranteed by the SBA or asset-based loans.

Savings and Loans Associations

George Bailey operated a savings and loan in the movie "It's a Wonderful Life." Much of the World War II generation financed the purchase of their homes with loans from savings and loans. S&Ls, as they are called, were intended to be no-frills institutions that would concentrate on helping people to buy homes. After banking deregulation was enacted in the early 1980s, the rules changed and S&Ls branched out into other areas of finance, including commercial lending. Unfortunately, too many S&Ls branched out too far without the necessary experience or checks and balances in place. Hence, the S&L crisis that required the American taxpayer to cough up billions and billions of dollars to bail out the industry.

Savings and loans are allowed to keep a small percentage of their loan portfolio in commercial loans. Most of those loans are concentrated in commercial real estate and investment real estate deals, which allow the S&L to take advantage of its real estate lending expertise. Some S&Ls have become strong SBA-guaranteed loan originators; obviously, the government guarantee eliminates much of the risk of venturing into commercial lending. With just a few exceptions, savings and loans tend to be small operations limited to a handful of branches. Savings and loans can be owned by shareholders or mutually by all account holders. In any case, ownership is concentrated in the local community, which is a benefit to small business owners. The owners, depositors, and officers of a savings and loan live and work in the community and have a vested interest in seeing small businesses thrive there.

Credit Unions

Credit unions are financial service organizations whose customers share some connection. The connection might be employment by a common employer, membership in a common union, or residency in a single community. The customers own the credit union mutually. Credit unions are fascinating organizations. Some major banks even have credit unions set up for employees of the banks! They are classic examples of people helping their own kind. Generally, credit unions are able to pay higher interest rates on deposits and charge lower interest rates on loans because of their unique structure. Without outside ownership and Wall Street to please, credit unions basically could survive happily by just breaking even each year. Credit unions, with a captive market, so to speak, do not need to throw huge sums of money into expensive marketing campaigns. Quite often, the credit unions are located on-site at the business that spawned them. Credit unions, because of these and other savings, are able to pass the savings directly to their members.

Credit unions cannot, however, provide services to businesses. Think about it for a moment. Businesses do not qualify to be members of credit unions; they are not employees, labor union members, or residents of any community. The one exception is sole proprietors. By definition, a sole proprietorship is an individual who does business under an assumed name. The sole proprietor may open accounts in his or her own name at a credit union. Depending upon local bank competition, this may be advantageous for businesses with deposit accounts. It is an absolute advantage for small business borrowers who need small loans for miscellaneous business purposes. Credit unions can often provide highly competitive loans for vehicles and working capital to sole proprietors. Since the sole proprietor's business income (or losses) flow through to the individual's personal tax return, the loan decisions are based on personal income. I know several small business owners who mix deposit and loan transactions between banks and credit unions in order to custom-fit their financial needs.

The single largest advantage of credit unions is the common denominator between members. This is a distinct advantage when a person applies for a loan. Applicants automatically receive the benefit of the doubt that accrues to all members of a larger group that holds common characteristics.

It is not difficult to become a member of a credit union. Many towns and cities around the country are home to community credit unions that are open to anyone who resides in the specific locale. Relationship to a primary member of a credit union might also qualify a person to join one. The yellow pages are a good place to start. Local chambers of commerce will have a list of the available credit unions within their territory. Remember, the first step in working with a credit union is to become a member of a credit union.

Commercial Finance Companies

Commercial finance companies are enjoying a great era. The more prominent ones have branches or representatives in every corner of the United States. The unprecedented growth of the U.S. economy has created enormous demand for business loans. Because these firms are not subjected to many of the rules and regulations that are imposed upon banks, in particular the Community Reinvestment Act, they are able to concentrate on building their businesses without government interference.

The Money Store, AT&T Capital, GE Capital, and The Business Loan Center are four of the top SBA loan producers in America—even outpacing the largest banks. The companies sell the loans to investors and reap huge premium income from the sales. Selling the loans is necessary in order to maintain liquidity with which to make more loans since these companies do not collect deposits like banks. The companies also issue commercial paper (corporate bonds) to investors to generate pools of money to lend out to small businesses.

The loan officers for these firms are typically compensated 100 percent by commissions. That means the loan officers have every incentive to try to make a loan application work. It is not unusual to see a loan that had been declined by a bank approved by a commercial finance company. Both the incentive-driven loan officer and the fact that the credit risk is passed on to investors or the government via an SBA guarantee raises the chances that a marginal loan application will be approved by one of these companies.

The previous paragraph should not be construed as derogatory toward the commercial finance industry or any company in particular. These are blue chip companies with excellent management and systems in place. Most are years ahead of banks as far as computer technology and remote application processes (Internet applications). The major drawback is the lack of a local contact person for most business owners unless the business is located in a metropolitan area. The commissioned loan officer has no incentive to service an account post closing; the officer wants to be out and about to root out the next loan and commission. Despite any slick marketing, commercial finance companies do not provide relationship banking.

A common practice within this industry is to pay finder's fees to people who refer business to the companies. The finder's fee might range from $500 to a flat 1 percent to 2 percent of the loan amount. Business owners should bear that in mind for negotiation purposes. If an applicant's accountant, attorney, or business or real estate broker made the referral, it is likely that person will receive a finder's fee for the referral. Several independent real estate brokers in our area refer the clients from every transaction to one specific commercial finance company. The finder's fee pads the income that the brokers receive in commissions or fees from the applicant in the transaction. Applicants should ask the person who has made the referral about any finder's fee that person may earn from the referral. Applicants should verify the answer with the commercial finance company representative, who must provide a truthful answer.

If a referral fee is to be paid, ask the person who referred the business to knock an equal amount off the underlying commission or fees. Fair is fair. If no referral fee is to be paid or if the applicant found the commercial finance company independent of a referral, the applicant should ask the loan officer if the normal finder's fee, which would ordinarily have been paid to a third party, could be used instead to reduce closing costs on the loan. Many commercial finance companies (and some banks) will eat a portion of the closing costs. This is especially the case with SBA loans that will be sold into the secondary market. The wise applicant will also give the finance company the opportunity to use some of the hefty premium income generated by the sale to offset closing costs.

Utility Companies

A well-kept secret is that utility companies are great sources of money for businesses. Telephone, gas, and electric companies are unique in that they have vested interests in increasing business development within their territories. Some of the major companies even have captive finance companies that will provide fairly standard small business financing. Rural cooperatives are good bets, too. Part of the rural cooperative movement is geared toward helping develop rural areas.

Much of the available financing is project related. The more utility services the project will eventually use, the better the chances of finding funding. For example, I am aware of a furniture company and lumber company that were both in need of a gas-fired kiln to dry raw materials. The respective gas companies—one is a major midwest company and the other a small rural cooperative—jumped in with attractive long-term financing for each project. Of course, the kilns will use thousands of cubic feet of gas, which will help the utility more than make up for the up-front financing.

Because utilities are highly regulated, most have a public affairs office or liaison who can be reached at the respective home office. This person will be knowledgeable about any available programs and specific qualifications for each.

Where to Find Them

The growth of nonbank lenders during the last decade has paralleled the skyrocketing American economy. Local-based nonbank lenders like savings and loans and credit unions offer easy credit terms and on-site decision makers who live and work in the same community as the entrepreneur. National commercial finance companies have developed state-of-the-art systems to deliver loans and other products to small business owners. They have expanded across the country and have representatives standing by to assist business owners.

A quick perusal of the yellow pages will yield a list of local nonbank lenders to contact. An Internet search or referrals from local real estate or business brokers, attorneys, and accountants can lead an applicant to a reputable commercial finance company.

Bank on It

+ Investigate local savings and loans or membership-based credit unions.
+ Even if a business is bankable, a credit union may offer other services or benefits that are to the advantage of the sole proprietor.
+ Commercial finance companies are structured to take more risk and to work hard to make individual deals work.
+ If the nonbank lender pays finder's fees, try to get price concessions either directly from the lender (in lieu of paying a fee to someone) or from the person who referred you to the nonbank lender.

sixteen

Seller Financing

Seller financing plays an integral role in the change of owner-ship of businesses. It takes the form of a promissory note, a land contract, or a combination of the two. Seller financing is often more creative and flexible than bank financing, but beware, it also confers preferences to the seller that a bank does not get in conventional financing.

Why Seller Financing?

There are four reasons why seller financing is used to fund change of business ownership. The first and most typical reason is that the business simply cannot be financed by a bank. This might be due to any number of things like poor earnings, environmental issues, legal problems, and industry. The seller's only hope of moving the business (in order to retire or move on to other irons in the fire) is to finance the deal. The second reason is that the purchase price exceeds the business's lendable asset base. This occurs when a successful business is sold. Successful businesses own an intangible asset called goodwill. Goodwill is the presumption that the business will continue on as before with the new owners. Banks cannot loan against that presumption; yet, sellers deserve to get paid for their years of providing good service and building a reputation that should succeed them if handled properly by the new owners. Generally, in these cases, a bank will propose a maximum loan with which it is comfortable and suggest that the difference between owner's equity and loan, and sales price be financed by the seller. This is a great deal for a bank since the seller is motivated to collect all that is due to him or her. Should the buyer not be successful, the former owner, in order to protect the balance of the seller's note, can step back into the business and return it to its former glory (while bailing the bank out of trouble).

The third reason is that the buyer does not have enough cash equity to satisfy a bank. The bank may suggest a combined amount of cash equity and seller's debt that would be acceptable to it and allow it to structure a conventional loan for the balance of the purchase price. The rule of thumb is that banks like to see 25 to 30 percent cash equity into a business purchase; more on startups. Obviously, there are many times when a seller finds an acceptable buyer with the necessary interest and talent but who lacks adequate cash. Seller financing for a small portion of the price can bridge that gap.

The fourth reason that seller financing is used is when the seller views the financing as an income-earning investment. Many people make a living by buying and selling assets, in particular investment real estate properties and financing the transactions themselves. They turn a profit on the sale, earn interest on the land contract, and have collateral with which they are intimately familiar. Since land contracts typically carry interest rates slightly higher than conventional bank rates, many people eagerly buy land contracts from sellers, at discounted values, to earn above-market interest rates on their investments that are secured by real estate.

Seller Preferences

Depending upon whether a promissory note or land contract is used, whether ancillary collateral documents are used, and who drafted the documents, sellers can accrue tremendous preferences in seller-financed transactions.

Most standard land contract forms give sellers the right to evict the buyer and repossess the subject real estate if one payment is past due. Banks usually need one year to get to the same position. Similarly, if property taxes are delinquent, insurance policies not kept current, or maintenance deferred, the seller can repossess the property and regain ownership.

Promissory notes, if drafted by the seller or seller's attorney, can also include extreme preferences. Any documents to be used in a seller-financed transaction should be reviewed by legal counsel engaged by the buyer.

The biggest drawback that I have witnessed, time and again, in seller-financed transactions, is the continued presence of the seller. A former client of mine bought a recreation business that was financed by the seller. The seller spent every waking moment at the business to make sure the buyer was taking proper care of it. Any time the buyer made a decision that did not sit well with the seller, the seller sued in court to get the business back "before the buyer ran it into the ground." These suits sprang from some pretty innocuous events like redecorating the office, transplanting trees on the grounds, advertising expenses, and the like. The transaction ended up costing my client tens of thousands of dollars in legal fees. Finally, my client was able to refinance the whole land contract and pay off the seller. Unfortunately, the seller continued to file suit after suit under the pretense that decisions made after the payoff affected his family's good name and reputation.

That is an extreme example, but a true one nonetheless. The buyer needs to construct a firewall between the seller and the business. A good attorney can be worth his or her weight in gold in these situations.

Buyer Beware

Overall, seller financing is a good deal for the buyer who probably could not acquire the business otherwise. The aforementioned meddlesome seller is something that can be addressed in legal documents and should not be a concern post closing. Buyers, though, should be wary of preadvertised, seller-financing opportunities or sellers who press buyers to accept seller financing to the exclusion of any other lender.

As soon as a seller mentions the availability or the desire to directly finance a transaction, the buyer must assume that something is amiss. The SBA discovered so many problems with loans that it guaranteed for changes of business ownership that it implemented new rules to govern those situations. The basic problem is greedy sellers who want to sell their respective businesses for far more than they are worth. To combat that problem, the SBA now requires participant banks to obtain or perform valuations of businesses that are subject to sale. The dream of entrepreneurialship is so strong that many would-be entrepreneurs have tunnel vision and ignore the obvious fact that the price of the business might be out of whack with reality. The second problem is that sellers sometimes are aware of situations that they fail to divulge to the prospective buyers. This may be criminal, such as using fraudulent tax returns to portray rosy profits when in fact the company is losing its shirt. It may be unfair, such as the hardware store that knows that Wal-Mart is going to build right across the street. The SBA requires banks to verify seller's tax returns with the IRS to make sure the seller is fairly representing the business's history. Further, the SBA requires the seller to sign a statement that details the reasons for the sale of the business. If the seller of the hardware store in the example states "health" or "retirement" and the deal goes through, the seller had better watch his or her rear end because the SBA's inspector general will be looking him up. Indeed the seller's health better have deteriorated or he or she had better be living in a trailer park in Florida, or else the inspector general will assume that the seller had knowledge of Wal-Mart's plans.

For conventional loans, banks do not consciously follow the same rules. But remember that the SBA is an advocate for small businesses. What's good for the SBA is good for small businesspeople. Potential buyers should heed its example and get a good commercial attorney before signing any purchase agreement or seller's financing documents.

Bank on It

+ Seller financing is a convenient way for many buyers to obtain a business.

+ Always inquire about the availability and terms of seller financing up front.

+ Ask a banker if some combination of equity and seller financing would make the transaction bankable.

+ Find out why a seller would offer to finance the transaction. Is the business, as portrayed by the seller, too good to be true? Is there a large amount of goodwill? Does the seller want a steady stream of income for retirement purposes?

+ Prior to reaching any decision and prior to signing any documents, engage a qualified attorney and an accountant to review the situation for legal protection and tax consequences.

+ Make sure that the contract is assignable and can be paid off early without penalty.

seventeen

Asset-Based Lenders

There are three types of asset-based lending: equipment lending, leasing, and factoring. All three are available avenues for small businesses. Some lenders specialize in one facet or another; some provide all three or in combination with other services. Major banks may have divisions dedicated to these services, too. This chapter outlines each type of asset-based lending.

Equipment Loans

Asset-based lenders almost disregard cash flow in their analysis of loan requests. Typically, an asset-based lender will be involved with fast-growing companies that have not had time to build up an acceptable equity position, or with deteriorating companies that need cash fast. Basically, asset-based lenders are pawn shops for corporations. The main difference is that the customer gets to keep the asset working in the business and does not have to exchange it for a pawn receipt. As one can imagine, asset-based lenders are often the lender of last resort for businesses and are able to charge higher-than-conventional interest rates.

The main criterion used to determine whether a loan is to be made or not is collateral value. Asset-based lenders develop expertise in order to accurately gauge the value of specific types of equipment. In

Michigan, asset-based lenders have strong levels of expertise in lending against original equipment manufacturing (OEM) machinery in the automotive industry. The key question boils down to this: Can the asset-based lender repossess the asset and sell it for enough money with which to pay off the loan?

Most asset-based lenders are interested in big-ticket assets, mainly production equipment and machinery, and loans of $1 million or more. That shuts out most small businesses. Yet, there is a growing niche of asset-based lenders that specialize in smaller transactions. A commercial loan officer at a bank should have a list of asset-based lenders at the ready to provide referrals to small business owners.

Leases

Leasing simply means that an asset is rented from some other entity and is not owned by the small business. Leases generally require little or no money up front, which gives them quite an advantage over conventional financing that might require down payments up to 30 percent of the asset's cost. A typical lease contract calls for just the first and last months' payments at the time the lease is signed, which is just like a lease on an apartment.

There are two basic types of leases: capital leases and true leases. A capital lease has a built-in mechanism for the ownership of the asset to pass from the leasing company to the small business at the end of the lease. This usually calls for a last payment of $1. Assets held under capital leases are depreciated like any other asset on a company's income statement. The lease payments are not considered tax-deductible expenses.

A true lease allows the small business to deduct, dollar for dollar, the lease payments as expenses. Ownership does not pass to the small business at the end of the lease automatically although the business can usually buy the asset at some predetermined fair market value.

Leasing companies are extremely flexible in the structure of leases. Most can be customized to fit the needs of the individual small business customer. Two recent innovations are the master lease and trial lease. The master lease acts like a line of credit under which the business may acquire equipment, up to a certain value, during a certain time frame. This removes the burden of locating, negotiating, and setting up a separate lease every time new equipment is added to the business. The trial lease is a short-term lease that allows a business to test a piece of equipment to see if the equipment meets the needs of the company or performs as promised.

Leasing companies abound all across the country. Bankers and accountants can provide entrepreneurs lists of reputable leasing companies. Most equipment dealers have access to captive leasing companies or can refer the customer to a leasing company that is likely to make the dealer's sale work.

SALE AND LEASE BACK

Leasing affords small business owners with a convenient source of capital through a transaction known as sale and lease back. In this transaction, the business sells an asset to a leasing company, which immediately leases the asset back to the business. The major reason this tool is used is to provide cash to the business. It is also used for tax purposes that are best discussed with a qualified accountant prior to entering into a sale and lease back.

This process is of particular significance to older, more mature companies that need cash for working capital or expansion purposes. Any asset that is unencumbered by liens (owned outright) may be sold and leased back. Commercial real estate is a common type of asset that is subject to sale and lease back.

LOWER CREDIT STANDARDS

Leased equipment and sale and lease back options are available to businesses that are considered poor credit risks by banks. It is not uncommon to see companies that are emerging from bankruptcy fund their restart with leased assets. Why? Leasing companies enjoy one distinct advantage over banks; the leasing company owns the asset. If a payment is missed or if a bankruptcy is declared, the leasing company can pick up the asset to sell or lease to another business. Banks, in similar situations, must muck through months of legal wrangling before, if even then, it can get its hands on collateral assets that are owned by the business, not the bank.

For this reason, leasing companies accept higher credit risk. Leases, in general, are more expensive than conventional bank loans. Leases cannot be compared to loans solely on borrowing costs. Tax consequences must also be considered to gain an overall picture of the benefits and costs of each method.

Factoring

Factoring is the act of selling accounts receivable to generate immediate cash. Factoring companies discount the book value of the receivables by a predetermined factor—hence the name. Factoring is an expensive proposition for the small business since the amount of the discount usually eliminates any profit from the sale that generated the account receivable. In fact, it probably turns that particular sale into a loss for the business.

For example, let's assume a business has $100,000 of accounts receivable. Of that amount, just $60,000 of the receivables are acceptable to the factoring company. The remaining $40,000 may be past due, offset by payables, or otherwise tainted. The factoring company has decided, based on the specific business and its customers, to pay at the rate of 80 percent. That means the small business will sell $60,000 of receivables for just $48,000. The accounts are notified that their payments should be sent to the factoring company.

For all this, the small business owner sees the gross profit on the underlying sales drop by 20 percent and risks scaring off customers who now must be asking themselves, "what the heck is going on at my supplier?" Chances are those customers will begin to find backup suppliers, if not primary suppliers, that promise to be a steady source of goods or services. So, why use factoring at all?

Cash is the lifeblood of business. Without it, no business can stay in business for long. Struggling businesses, small fast-growing businesses with all the initial investment capital tied up in receivables and inventory, and businesses that have not been able to handle bank lines of credit properly are all candidates for factoring. Factoring is not a death knell for small businesses. I have had many customers resort to factoring for one reason or another and survive to tell about it. One customer had decided that money in his payroll tax account would make a great short-term source of working capital until he discovered the penalties (both monetary and prison) that might be incurred if Uncle Sam uncovered the diversion. Factoring looked jolly good to him in comparison.

Factoring companies are located throughout the United States. Referrals to reputable companies can be made by bankers, accountants, and bankruptcy attorneys.

Bank on It

+ Find asset-based lenders through referrals from bankers or other professionals.
+ A tax accountant should always review any asset-based lending transaction prior to close to determine any potential tax liability problems or benefits.
+ Asset-based lenders take much greater risk than other lenders.
+ Factors buy any qualified account receivable regardless of the business's credit and financial situation.
+ Asset-based lenders are prime sources of money for businesses that are emerging from bankruptcy or financial difficulties.
+ Execution of a sale and lease back can turn fixed assets into hard cash quickly.

eighteen

Venture Capital and Initial Public Offerings

Venture capitalists are affectionately called "the VC" in the finance industry. Any comparison to the Viet Cong from the Vietnam War era is purely coincidental. When venture capital is mentioned, most people think about Silicon Valley and the hundreds of companies that have sprouted there with investments by venture capital firms. Indeed, that form or level of venture capital is not the realm of this book. The venture capitalists that we read about in the newspapers and business magazines look to invest in companies that hold the promise of quick returns of 1,000 percent.

No matter how successful the mom-and-pop corner grocery store or how many quick-print franchises a person can open, those returns are not to be found in small business finance. Yet, several sources of venture capital have been created specifically to assist small business owners. It has become a crucial source of money as entrepreneurs rush to open or expand businesses that are not yet on sound enough financial footing for conventional bank financing. The small business owner should not look to Wall Street or to Silicon Valley for this type of venture capital. This chapter discusses five types of venture capital, including initial public offerings that are common today and available to most small businesses. The loan application that was developed earlier in this book is the perfect document to present to any venture capitalist in order for the entrepreneur to make a conceptual sale.

ACE-net

The U.S. Small Business Administration, in cooperation with the U.S. Securities and Exchange Commission and the University of New Hampshire's Whittemore School of Business and Economics, has developed a system to match investors with small businesses in need of equity capital. ACE-net is an abbreviation for Access to Capital Electronic Network.

ACE-net builds a pool of accredited investors who are able to review the business plans and proposals of qualified small businesses. Investors must meet minimum net worth and income levels in order to be accredited. They may be private individuals or investment businesses. Unlike any other scheme available via the Internet or other channels, ACE-net provides unparalleled protection to investors. This was achieved by the involvement of the North American Securities Administration Association (NASAA), which is made up of every regulative body that is devoted to investor protection. Thus, potential investors have a structured arena in which to participate.

Small businesses must qualify to participate in ACE-net, too. Businesses must be able to sell a security interest in the company, which means that the business must be a corporation or limited liability company. Certain businesses are disqualified from participation, and those include oil and gas businesses, partnerships, joint ventures, and sole proprietorships.

Businesses may raise up to $5 million using ACE-net. Red tape and other burdensome requirements dictate that companies will find it much easier to raise $1 million or less. To learn more about ACE-net, visit its Web site at *www.ace-net.sr.unh.edu.*

Angel Investors

The term *angel investor* first gained notoriety during the greenmail days of the 1980s when corporations sought out "angels" to save their companies from corporate raiders bent on hostile takeovers. Today, the term has expanded to include any person or company that provides the necessary capital to start or grow a business when no one else will take the chance.

Angel investors can be neighbors, anonymous local benefactors, ACE-net investors, Internet connections, or anyone with money and a penchant for buying into small businesses. Frequent sources of information about who might be willing to become an angel investor are accountants and attorneys. It is not uncommon for the professionals to have a wealthy client or two who are always on the lookout for a potential investment. Bankers, too, keep a confidential stable of names of people who like to look over opportunities to invest in businesses. The idle rich or trust fund kids are great sources of angel capital—it gives them something to do during the day.

Local or regional networks of angel investors are popping up all over the country. The oldest group in my neck of the woods is located in Grand Rapids, Michigan. The network comprises wealthy people who want to make investments in small businesses. These people tend to be successful businesspeople in their own right who wish to help other people achieve the same dream of business success. The group meets once a month, and prospective business owners are scheduled to make pitches to the entire group. If any investor's interest is piqued, a later face-to-face meeting is arranged. If all goes well, the investor writes a check, and the business is launched or expanded.

It is difficult to locate such a network. Accountants, lawyers, business brokers, and chambers of commerce are great places to start the quest.

Small Business Investment Companies (SBICs)

Congress legislated Small Business Investment Companies into existence way back in 1958. Through all these years, SBICs have yet to gain the recognition that other programs enjoy. SBICs are licensed and regulated by the SBA. They invest directly into small businesses and are for profit; that is, they hope to see their investments appreciate. Funding for the SBICs is derived from loans to the SBIC backed by the SBA or sale of preferred stock to the SBA.

Businesses must meet the SBA's size standard criteria in order to qualify for SBIC financing. Unfortunately, many SBICs limit their investments to particular industries or types of companies. A roster of SBICs may be found at the SBA's Web site: *www.sba.gov.*

Business Investment and Development Companies

Business Investment and Development Companies, commonly called BIDCOs, are available in many states. Some states may have similar entities approved for the same purpose. BIDCOs are similar to SBICs in that they are privately owned corporations that wish to make a profit through appreciation of capital investments. BIDCOs, however, receive capital for financing small businesses from private investors and the particular state rather than the federal government.

BIDCOs are owned by local businesspeople and investors. They seek out opportunities to make equity investments or to provide debt to small businesses. Unlike their rich cousins in Silicon Valley, BIDCOs seek total returns slightly higher than that yielded by conventional investments. Debt may be structured in several flexible ways, including subordinated to a bank or convertible to equity. Bankers and local chambers of commerce are good sources to obtain a referral to BIDCO.

Initial Public Offerings (IPOs)

Similar to the giant venture capital deals that the financial media banter about, we are inundated daily with news of the most recent initial public offerings and the owners who have become instant millionaires. The good news is that just about any business can "go public." The bad news is that most owners of those businesses are not going to get rich.

The U.S. Securities and Exchange Commission (SEC), through its Regulation A, allows small businesses to raise up to $5 million by offering stock for sale to the public. The securities offering must be registered in the state where the stock is to be sold, and some states have more restrictive rules and lower limits on the amount that may be raised. An acquaintance of mine recently went this route to raise money to open a microbrewery. An IPO for a small business is usually prohibitive given the amount of red tape and expenses necessary to navigate to a successful sale of stock. A good commercial law attorney can refer small business owners to a securities law attorney who specializes in this type of stock sale.

EXIT STRATEGY

As a rule, venture capitalists will peg a total return that they want from each transaction. An exit strategy will be interwoven with that figure in mind. The exit strategy tells the small business owner exactly what it will take to remove the venture capital company from the picture. Normally, the longer a venture capitalist is involved with a business, the higher the number. For example, if a venture capitalist injects $100,000 to buy stock in a business, it might establish the following buyback figures for the next three years: $125,000, $140,000, and $160,000. The agreement might simply state a percentage of total return that would be applicable at any future point in time.

The key is for the entrepreneur to know exactly what hurdles are ahead. Without a well thought-out, objective exit strategy, the business owner might find himself or herself shooting at a moving target and saddled with a permanent co-owner.

It's a Partnership

Venture capital or equity is available from many sources for small businesses. The benefits include adding expertise and financial acumen to the business's management team, securing proper capitalization, and frankly, the chance to salvage a business idea that might otherwise sink. The disadvantage lies in the fact that a portion of the business will be owned by someone else. Sometimes it means giving up legal control of the business to an outsider. It always means giving up effective control of the company since any venture capitalist worth his or her salt will shadow the entrepreneur's every move. That is a bitter pill to swallow for most small business owners—but that pill may be just what the doctor ordered.

Bank on It

+ Investigate local sources of angel investors with inquiries at accounting, legal, and commercial real estate firms.
+ Get on the Internet and surf the site of ACE-net and the SBA.
+ Contact state legislators to inquire about state-backed equity investment programs like BIDCOs.
+ Always have an attorney review a venture capital proposal and documents prior to entering into an agreement.
+ Always know your exit strategy before you accept venture capital investment.

Suppliers
and Customers

Besides the owner of a business, who has the most vested interest in keeping the business viable? Its suppliers, who desire to continue to sell products and services to the business, and its customers, who desire a consistent supply of products and services.

Suppliers

Almost every business in the land uses supplier financing already. Whenever a purchase is made "on account," the seller has financed the sale. A business's accounts payable ledger is a listing of creditors who readily provide credit to the business. The easiest way to increase supplier, or trade, credit is to add suppliers that will each provide credit terms to the business or to ask existing suppliers to extend current terms. This may mean stretching payables from 30 days to 45 days or longer. The simple addition of a few weeks can have immediate, positive impact on cash positions.

Entrepreneurs need to remember that suppliers have their own competitors and that they will sharpen the pencil in order to get or keep customers. Many suppliers have special programs designed to assist new or young businesses. A business owner needs only to ask the field representative of the supplier or to call the supplier's credit department to find out what standard or custom programs might be available.

Suppliers of big-ticket items usually have captive finance arms that can provide attractive financing terms to buyers. Whirlpool Credit finances inventory purchases for appliance dealers. Some captive finance companies offer rebates or other incentives for their customers who achieve higher sales levels. Most suppliers of brand-name inventory will kick in money to help the business market the product. Petroleum companies will kick in huge sums of money to help start new gas and convenience stores in exchange for a long-term supply contract.

If a business gets behind the eight ball and gets seriously delinquent on accounts payable, many suppliers will come to the table and show creative flexibility. This is more to preserve the debt that is already owed them than to add credit, but it is all the same to the struggling business owner. They can't say yes if you don't ask.

Customers

A bakery in my hometown struggled for years. It specialized in old-world breads the likes of which could not be found on the shelves of our middle-America grocery stores. The bakery built a loyal clientele but never seemed to get over the hump of its debt burden. The owners announced their decision to close the bakery; however, a groundswell of assistance poured in from the clients. The clients not only pitched in cash but also rolled up their sleeves and provided volunteer labor until the business got back onto its feet.

I can think of a score of examples where customers put their money where their mouths were and helped out small businesses. In many instances, it was a case of the customer not wanting to lose a product or service that he or she highly valued. In others, it was an unspoken bond between customer and business owner that had developed over years of nickel-and-dime transactions. Short of placing a sign over the counter that begs for financial help from clients, a business owner might be wise to collar a few discreet clients and mention the current financial condition of the business. It might be surprising how events snowball into a full-fledged campaign to put the business on sound financial footing again. (This, by the way, is a good reason to employ honest, fair, and ethical business practices and to treat every customer like a king.)

OUTSOURCING

The trend to outsourcing has also been a boon to customer-financed business startups. Many large corporations with which I am familiar have sought out individuals or businesses to take over production or processes that were formerly done in-house. Frequently, the larger corporation turns over the necessary equipment to the new business and agrees to sign a long-term contract with the company. The contract itself may be enough to back conventional bank financing.

Small towns, especially, are home to companies with paternalistic instincts. Employees of these companies may find that a smaller company may be able to provide a product or service to the company more efficiently than the company can provide internally. Sometimes a quick informal pitch to senior management is all it takes to launch that employee into entrepreneurialship. One well-known company in Holland, Michigan, spawned a dozen such companies, largely because the company's owner wanted to reward key employees in a way that he could not do if they remained employees.

Most often, customer financing is available to a lucky few who are in the right place at the right time. Budding entrepreneurs can ferret out opportunities by contacting purchasing agents and supplier management people at larger companies. The simple question, "What could be improved upon by your suppliers?" may open the door to opportunity.

OTHER IDEAS

If the small business's products or services are vital to a customer's business, the customer might back up its purchase orders with a letter of credit. A letter of credit can be used to borrow more money from a bank or other lender. Customers with special needs might foot the bill for the cost of new equipment, dedicated lines, new tooling, and so forth.

A direct cash loan from a corporate customer is not an unheard-of event. Repayment of a loan can be flexible and even derived from reduced sales prices over a certain term. A customer might also be persuaded to prepay for a purchase; the proceeds can be used as working capital to help deliver on the order. Businesses with specialized skills or products stand the best chance of obtaining customer financing. If the same product or service is available across the street, the customer has no incentive to take any risk. Therefore, the trick is to convince the customer that keeping the small business afloat is in the customer's best interest.

Bank on It

+ Suppliers and customers might be eager to help small businesses out.
+ They can't say yes if you don't ask.
+ Ask suppliers and customers if they have any programs designed to assist small companies.
+ Everything is negotiable. Postponing payments to suppliers or asking for early payment from customers are two easy and common examples of ways a business can speed up cash flow.
+ Exercise caution when soliciting customers for help. Don't send an S.O.S. signal that might send customers to the competition.
+ Employees of large companies have the opportunity to start businesses that allow the former employer to outsource functions. The former employer might provide assets, financing, or guarantees to help launch the business.

Employees

Any company, no matter the industry or size, can reap wonderful benefits when employees invest in the company. Many publicly traded companies offer employee stock purchase plans and use company stock to match the retirement plan contributions made by the employees. More and more companies are issuing stock options to employees. Although these plans all provide an immediate tangible reward to an employee, they also increase employee motivation.

If I own stock in the company for which I work (and I do!), I am going to do whatever I can in order to push the stock price higher and to increase profits. I will do so by making decisions that benefit the company and not me. I will put in longer hours and keep my hand out of the company's cash register. And I will use every opportunity to promote my company to neighbors, friends, and fellow PTA members.

Informal Arrangements

I know a couple of men who owned a pharmacy. They made the decision to expand and open several more locations. The new locations were basically two-person operations that required a full-time pharmacist and a pharmacy technician. The first hurdle the two entrepreneurs faced was finding people who would go to work for them. Given the choice between major chain or discount store positions that pay fairly high salaries and offer good benefits and this small-town operation, prospective employees always chose the former. And once people were hired, turnover exceeded the industry norms and interrupted business.

The second hurdle was making the new locations profitable. The employee pharmacists, content to draw their set salaries, had no incentive to build a strong business. Most were just killing time until they could find a job at a better paying, bigger name pharmacy. All the new locations struggled.

Finally, the gentlemen came up with a brilliant idea—one that I share with every business owner with whom I come into contact. They would recruit the brightest pharmacy school grads and in-town pharmacists with good reputations for customer service and management skills. In order to lure the cream of the crop to their company, they offered to give 10 to 20 percent of the particular store ownership to the employee. What a difference this made. All of a sudden, the locations were staffed with motivated, customer service–oriented people. The employee-owners were driven to build sales and lower expenses since a percentage of every dollar of profit went directly into their own pockets.

This was also done by a soft goods retailer that is a former client of mine. The business had been limited to one very successful location. Hoping to copy that success, the owners opened two new stores in different towns. Neither of the new stores got off to profitable starts. The owners were spread too thin and were not able to maintain the flagship store's profits since talent and inventory were drained to help jump-start the other stores. The expansion came close to bankrupting the whole operation. But, then, the owners decided to let the branch store managers and assistant managers buy into the company. If the individuals did not have the required cash to make the investment, the company created a promissory note between it and the individual. The note was structured to be paid back by the individual's share of profits. Voilà! The two branch stores enjoyed immediate turnarounds of their business. The difference was the vested interest the on-site employees had in seeing that the stores made a profit.

I have seen this kind of success happen time and again in industries as varied as investment brokerages to pizza chains. It works. I simply do not understand why any small business owner would not provide this opportunity to his or her employees. The amount of ownership that must be transferred is often negligible and is never enough to transfer control of the business. The intangible benefit of employee-owner motivation is well worth it, but the ability to raise cash from this structure provides a more important reason to consider it.

A customer of mine once faced ruin if he could not come up with a large sum of cash. His wife had divorced him, and the settlement called for him to pay her an amount equal to half of his ownership in the business that he ran. At the same time, his co-owner (not his spouse) and he fell out with each other. The co-owner demanded to be bought out or else he would file suit. Unfortunately, the business's financial statements had weakened since I had last made a loan to them, and there was nothing more that I could do for the company. In desperation, he asked his trusted assistant, half joking, if she had a nest egg she could use to buy into the business.

The assistant about leapt out of her chair! She had just received a good sum of money in an inheritance and had been thinking about what she could do with it. She loved her job and co-workers and thought it would be great to own a piece of the pie and, in a sense, become her own boss. With the quick help of an attorney to document the removal of the spouse and former co-owner, the deal was sealed. The company has gone on to record sales and profits since then, and both owners have greatly increased their personal wealth.

Another client of mine found his business on the ropes. His industry, office supplies sales, was experiencing rapid consolidation. The big boys, the national office supplies stores, had come to town and were in the process of blowing all the old local shops out of the water. As a prelude to closing down the business, he held a meeting of all the employees of the company. He explained the problems, the losses, and the lack of light at the end of the tunnel. The company's existing line of credit with the bank was fully extended. The bank would not lend more money simply because of the changing complexion of the industry (it, too, was afraid that the big stores would soon drive all the smallfry out of business). Without more working capital, the business could not buy its inventory in volumes sufficient to get price breaks. Besides, customers were flocking to the new stores which were spending big advertising bucks.

Less than an hour after the meeting, an employee stopped into my client's office. All the employees had gathered back in the warehouse to talk about the situation. He produced a legal pad of paper with every employee's name penciled in. Next to each name was a dollar amount. Some of the figures were $100; some were $25,000. This was the money each employee would come up with to buy into the company to keep it going and to salvage their jobs. All told, it added up to more than $75,000—more than enough to accomplish what needed to be done. An attorney and an accountant helped the company recapitalize and redistribute ownership.

The company slowly climbed back from the brink. The new co-owners attacked their jobs with enthusiasm and hunger. Customer service reached new levels and the business began to bring customers back from the larger stores. Even though it still could not compete on price with its larger competitors, it outperformed them in every other category to the extent that customers did not mind the minor price differences.

A last example contrasts employee ownership with employee loans. Yet another client of mine was a small wholesaler of parts to manufacturers. The company always needed to borrow working capital in order to keep its vast inventory well stocked and up to date. The office manager was one of those little old ladies who revel in minutiae. She ran a tight ship and could rattle off account balances owed to and by the company. She was authorized to call the bank and request advances on the line of credit, and she monitored the timing of the advances to the minute. I spent many hours manually calculating interest charges that did not match her own (she actually used "quarter days" dependent upon what time of day the money appeared in the company account!). The poor woman was also a widow who had been alone for more than thirty years. Conservative to an extreme, her own savings were invested in short-term bank certificates of deposit. The rates the bank paid her were approximately half what it charged the business for working capital loans. Long ago, she had put one and one together and figured that she could just as well loan money to the company. She would get more in interest and at the same time charge the business less than the "usurious" bank rates. It wasn't until the boss was given a once-in-a-lifetime opportunity to acquire a large block of in-demand inventory at fire sale prices that she spoke up. The company would have to go to the bank and go through the machinations of increasing its line of credit before money would be available to make the purchase, and by then, the opportunity would have passed by, lamented the boss. The lady offered to be the bank on this occasion and loan her personal money to the company. She saw no risk in the loan; after all, she knew the business as well as anyone did. Within months, as CDs matured, she completely replaced the bank!

These examples are informal structures devised by smart and sometimes desperate business owners. Anyone who contemplates raising capital by selling part ownership to employees or borrowing funds from employees needs to exercise prudent judgment in the process. Let's face it, some employees are simply bad apples. An announcement tacked to the break room bulletin board is not the way to ask for financial help from employees. The opportunity should be presented only to those individuals who will be positive forces for the company after recapitalization.

Formal Arrangements

Yes, even the informal arrangements must be formalized to a certain extent by attorneys in order to eliminate any possibility of a misunderstanding. Employee stock purchase plans, 401k and pension plans, and stock option plans are other formal ways that ownership in a company can be passed or transferred to its employees. For the most part, though, those plans are limited to publicly traded companies and are not realistic for privately owned small businesses.

One formal plan of which every business owner should be aware is an ESOP, or employee stock ownership plan. This is distinguished from regular stock ownership plans where employees buy or sell company stock on an after-tax basis. ESOPs come with favorable tax treatment for both employee and employer. The plans can be used as an additional form of employee compensation that rewards employees over time with gradually increasing ownership in the company. The ownership grows through further company contributions, appreciation, and dividends on a tax-deferred basis. ESOPs can also be used to raise immediate capital or to fund the complete buyout of the current owner.

ESOPs can borrow money from banks and use the money to make a lump sum purchase of all or a portion of the company stock. Normally, company profits are the source of repayment for ESOP loans rather than monthly payments out of the pockets of the employees. The SBA even has a special loan program designed specifically for ESOPs. If a company needs to raise cash quickly for expansion or asset acquisition, an ESOP could be formed to borrow money and inject cash into the business. Likewise, when it comes time for the owner of a business to retire or sell out, who better to sell the business than its own employees who have worked to build the business? When ESOPs are used to fund the complete buyout of an owner, the owner does not pay taxes on the windfall if it is immediately reinvested in common stocks. This is a great benefit in that the seller can invest money in income stocks from which dividend income can be drawn to fund retirement. The stocks continue to appreciate on a tax-deferred basis until they are sold. Admittedly, I am in way over my head on the taxation implications of ESOPs. The bottom line is that ESOPs should be fully explored by every small business owner if only in preparation for the day when it is time to hang it up for good. That means finding an experienced attorney and accountant who can provide the right advice for each particular situation.

Bank on It

+ Employees can invest in the business by owning a piece of the business or by extending loans to it.
+ Employee ownership has benefits other than to raise needed cash. Benefits include increased enthusiasm and motivation and tying together the best interests of the business owner and employees.
+ Employees know your business better than any outsider.
+ ESOPs can provide awesome benefits to the company, the employees, and the principal shareholder.
+ Be cautious about how you invite employees to participate in ownership of your business.

21

Cooperatives

This chapter discusses a type of financing that is mainly employed, in the United States, by foreign nationals who have immigrated here. Yet, for anyone with patience and a strong work ethic, cooperatives might be just the ticket to business ownership and success.

The Asian Model

I'll never forget Sohi. A citizen of India, he walked in for an appointment unannounced one day. He introduced himself, giving his full name, which I had no prayer of repeating owing to my untrained ear for Indian names and accents, and bowed to me. We exchanged pleasantries and sat down at my desk to discuss his needs. All the while, my mind's eye is giving him the once-over. My conclusion based on first impressions of his dated wardrobe and his dirty hands was that however long this interview would take, it was a waste of time for me.

Fortunately for Sohi and me, his story was an interesting one, and I listened intently to his remarkable saga. His extended family back in India had scrimped and saved enough money several years earlier to purchase a defunct egg factory in rural Ontario. His "brother" was sent to Canada to operate the new business. With sheer determination and more elbow grease than most Americans have ever applied to any enterprise, his family built the egg business back up and into profitability. As the business grew, so did the resident population of family members. Soon, though, the business's ability to support family members was saturated, and it was necessary for some members to strike out to find new ventures.

Sohi was one of the first to leave Ontario. He found his gold mine in a contaminated, derelict gasoline station in downtown Gary, Indiana. Now, Gary is about the last place in the world I would ever want to go into business, but Sohi was able to acquire the property from the owner for pennies on the dollar and obtained fantastic terms from the gasoline distributor. The small cash stake needed to purchase and open the station came from the family farm back in Ontario. Sohi personally worked at the station during every open hour. In off hours, he drove into Chicago to tobacco and convenience store inventory distributors to find the best prices for inventory. He saved on delivery costs and odd lot purchases. Within a matter of months, the Gary business was operating at a steady profit.

The Gary store was a springboard to bigger and better gasoline stations for Sohi. I eventually helped him acquire four more in southern Michigan. Over the course of our relationship, he had introduced me to more than one dozen "brothers," none of whom looked alike or bore any resemblance to Sohi. I finally asked him what was up with all these so-called brothers. He explained that in his culture, everyone with any connection, whether it be blood or simply having been raised in the same vicinity, is called one's brother. Sohi's niche in the family business had created more than twenty business opportunities for brothers.

Sohi's enterprise was and is based on the Asian model for cooperatives. Comedians joke all the time about how every 7-Eleven in America is seemingly owned by Pakistanis. Cooperative action is the reason that perception exists. The best examples are Chinese restaurants. In my hometown, we have one Chinese restaurant for every ten citizens (well, it does seem that way)! Entire Chinese families will immigrate to the United States and secure low-paying jobs as waitresses, busboys, and dishwashers in Chinese restaurants. Often, the whole family will live in one small unit of a down-on-its-luck motel or apartment building. Nearly every nickel earned by the family members is stashed away until enough is saved for the family to open its own restaurant. Lifestyle is an integral part of this proposition. There are no discretionary purchases or expenses. Only the bare necessities are allowed. And elbow grease plays a most important role, too.

One of my former customers brought his entire family over from China more than a decade ago. He worked two shifts as a cook at an established Chinese restaurant in town. After a few years, the family had saved enough money to purchase a vacant parcel of property. Shortly thereafter, he spent much of his eight free hours each day constructing a new restaurant on that spot. It took five years, but he finally opened the doors of the restaurant and employed each of his family members. A large apartment above the restaurant provided living quarters for them as well. Stories like this one and Sohi's just about bring tears to your eyes; it's the American dream achieved by the most unlikely people.

Once, only a few years ago, in the loan committee at a bank for which I formerly worked, a lender presented an application by a group of Punjabi Indians. The group was formed of about twenty different people scattered all across the United States. They wanted to borrow money to buy a rundown hotel in the metropolitan Detroit area. None of the financial information on the individuals or their related business ventures reported enough cash, combined, to form the necessary down payment on the subject transaction.

The vice chairman of the bank, who ran the loan committee and had veto power on every deal, asked the loan officer, "Where's the down payment coming from?"

The loan officer answered, "You have to understand the culture of these people. Once they have a closing date established, the money will be gathered from their network of family and friends. They assure me that they won't have a problem making the down payment."

At that, the vice chairman launched into a tirade, "I'm not approving the loan. You tell these guys that this isn't the Punjab and if they want to do business like that to go the hell back to India. This is America and we do business like Americans." Too bad Americans have not adopted the Punjabi way. We are wasting too much talent and too many lives in the "me first" race for riches. The numbers of our citizens fighting poverty could be greatly reduced, and many, many people could find the daily motivation to bootstrap themselves to a better life.

Americans, with good paying jobs and existing networks of family and friends, should excel at cooperative business success. They don't. What factors influence this failure?

Impatience—Americans do not have the patience to save for years and to start small. An unfortunate part of our culture is the common thought that we can have it all and we can have it now. Studies show that the lack of immediate gratification is one of the big reasons lower-income people turn to crimes like burglary and the drug trade. It is also why our rate of savings is the lowest in the developed world; we can't wait to consume our money with material pleasures.

Lack of trust—Americans do have an independent streak and lack a basic trust in others. Heck, churches even assign two or three people to watch over the shoulder of the person who passes the collection plate to ensure no slippage occurs. One of the first hurdles in forming a cooperative is to place complete and unfettered trust in the person who will hold the communal kitty. Since cooperative members will eventually run businesses far and wide, trust must also accrue to them. I have had scores of American business owners tell me that they operate their till "two for me, one for Uncle Sam." In other words, they are skimming cash so as not to report it for taxes. Cooperatives wring every cent for maximum return. If a member is not truthful about his or her earnings, the cooperative's ability to generate new business opportunities slows.

Paying dues—How many people do you know would gladly take over a defunct, polluted gas station in inner city Gary, Indiana? None of my acquaintances would do it. Let alone the location, how many people do you know would want to work twenty-hour days for several months or years to reach success? Americans, sorry to say, usually prefer an easier route than that taken by immigrant entrepreneurs.

Lack of identity—Unlike Chinese or Indian immigrants, Americans
do not have easily segmented identities. There are natural divisions like race and religion, but the mobility of Americans dif-
fuses extended families or other subgroups. Further, by the time
that an American reaches adulthood, too many bad habits or
ideas have been indoctrinated in them. Even with a few motivated participants, it is unlikely a cohesive group could be
formed. Back in their native lands, would-be immigrants dream
of the chance to come to America. It is a privilege for them.
Once here, they bust their tails to take advantage of the opportunity. It is easier to assemble a group when all are motivated
toward the same goal.

The American Model

Cooperatives of another sort are common in America. The two best
examples are utility cooperatives and agricultural cooperatives. Neither
is designed to create wealth or generate new business ownership for
its members. Utility cooperatives were formed to bring electricity to
rural areas deemed unprofitable by the big utility companies. Individuals and businesses joined together and either bought power from
another source or developed their own generation plants in order to
provide electricity to the members. Since availability of power was the
goal and not profits, the cost of energy provided by cooperatives is
usually less than that from mainstream utility companies. Thus, the
benefits provided to members of energy cooperatives are availability of
energy and lower energy costs.

Agricultural cooperatives are primarily marketing entities. In
Michigan, The National Cherry Cooperative purchases cherries from
small growers throughout the state and is able to better market the produce because of strength of sheer volume. The cooperative employs
professionals to negotiate better prices, which are passed on to its
members and used to develop new markets and uses for its products.
Dried cherries are one of those new products that did not exist several
years ago, and they have created new uses and demand for the abun-
dant cherries grown in Michigan. Agricultural cooperatives also use the

collective power invested in them by members to negotiate better prices on inputs, like fertilizer, seed, and fuel.

We in the banking industry often run into small groups of people who have banded together to buy fixer-up houses to rehabilitate and sell—they hope—at a profit. This is cooperative action. The people search out opportunities to buy houses cheap. Once the house has been acquired, the partners roll up their sleeves and repair or update the house to increase its value. They then sell the house or convert it into a rental property. Income from either choice is then plowed back into more houses. Unfortunately, this "industry" falls into the "get rich quick" schemes that are the subject of late-hour cable television infomercials. Rarely does anyone make any long-term money in this business. Sooner or later, something goes awry. Either a rehab project cannot be sold for enough to cover costs or a few vacancies cause rental income to drop below the monthly mortgage payments. Then the mini-real estate empire collapses like a house of cards.

None of the foregoing American cooperative models really fits the need that is the topic of this chapter. There is one model in existence, not generally identified as a cooperative, which does provide an excellent blueprint for entrepreneurs: the investment club.

Investment clubs have sprouted all across the country and have grown in proportion to the bull market of the 1990s. These clubs are all managed very simply. First, members are recruited. An organizational meeting is held where the club's purpose and goals are established. The method and type of investing may be defined or limited by majority vote of the members, and a fixed investment amount is determined. Typically, members will invest $25 or $50 per month. Periodic meetings are held to make investment decisions that may include stocks, bonds, mutual funds, and real estate. Over time, the mutual nest egg begins to add up to meaningful dollars.

I suggest that the investment club model is an excellent "Americanized" version of cooperative action geared toward business ownership. Can you envision a group of college graduates who decide that they want to own their own businesses someday and form an investment club with the sole purpose of acquiring businesses for each member? This method has many advantages over the informal cooperative employed typically by immigrants to the United States. First, a partnership, club, or corporate agreement governs all aspects of the venture. The group acts as a board of directors in making all decisions and overseeing existing savings. Members could be required to invest sweat equity into each successive venture.

This makes great sense for a group of people who each want to own a Subway Sandwich franchise, for example, someday. They each gain experience while opening each store, help reduce costs until each store is open long enough to support itself, and endear themselves to the franchiser. If the earnings of each store are plowed back into the investment fund, the rate of new business openings will accelerate. Whether the group comprises middle-income executives or the poorest of the minimum wage-earning laborers, this is a model that will work. The only difference between groups is the time it takes to save the initial investment. And time is something everyone can invest.

Forming a Cooperative

Cooperative action makes great sense for people who do not have much money either saved or in income. Younger people or people from disadvantaged backgrounds should especially consider forming a cooperative if business ownership is the goal. The pooling of capital by a number of people will hasten the time to business opening, and the mutual support of the group will be educational and motivational. The first step to be taken in forming a cooperative is to decide what is your own business objective. If it is to own and operate a franchise pizza store, then you must search out others with the same dream.

Check with friends and family. Talk about your dreams and see if it fits with anyone else's goals. If you strike out with the people close to you, then investigate people who should have a natural inclination toward your idea. Contact the managers of pizza shops already in existence in your vicinity. A few are bound to want to own rather than simply manage a store.

We see a lot of foursomes—two husbands and wives—join together to open a business. It would be a natural for a group of more than two couples to form for the purpose of owning businesses. Think of neighbors, fellow school parents, church friends, and the like who might be interested in a project. Once you have a number of interested people, it's time for a formal meeting.

In order for a cooperative to be successful, its goals and expectations must be crystal clear from the get-go. What is the ultimate goal of the group? Is it to create an opportunity for each member to operate a separate business? If so, will the businesses be identical or from different industries? What is the financial commitment of each member? How will the business of the cooperative be overseen? How many hours per day, week, month, or year will each member be required to contribute in labor? What happens if one of the early ventures does not perform or even loses money? How much money can the operator of a business take in compensation, or will every dollar be reinvested until everyone has a business up and running? The questions will fill hours of discussion.

Once a basic plan is decided upon, the cooperative must get legal counsel to formalize the agreements between members. In this sense, a cooperative is like a partnership. However, partnerships are capitalized up front and do not depend on the future pooling of funds or energy. Please, even if you think the ties between members of your group are stronger than the familial ties of Asian immigrant families, get your original understandings down in writing in a legal document. It won't prevent broken hearts, misunderstandings, or bad blood between members, but it will provide a clear roadmap of necessary steps or action to be taken in every conceivable situation. And do not try to "do-it-yourself" when it comes to legal agreements. Even if you do an incredibly professional job of it, you still stand open to accusations of self-serving language long after the agreement has been in force.

Once every member has legally signed-on, the easy part starts. Pooling startup capital is very simple. Everyone sends in his or her required amount, and it is saved in a safe place like a bank savings account. The difficulty of this phase is preserving the collective patience of the group. It is vital to constantly reiterate the group's goals and to communicate with each other to keep all the members motivated. Depending upon the amount and payment periods, it could take years for the necessary sum of money to build to the point where the first business can be opened.

Once that magic moment arrives, enthusiasm is rekindled and everyone works toward the acquisition or opening of the first enterprise. The periodic payments continue, and the pool is supplemented by excess cash flow from the first business. If all goes well, the second business can be opened in a much shorter time frame than the first one. Suddenly, the third and fourth stores are opened, and the rate of new businesses established accelerates because the cash being generated by the earlier businesses exceeds the individual payments. Soon, there is a business open for every cooperative member. Now, did your original agreement call for the businesses to be owned and operated by the cooperative forever or for the cooperative to dissolve so that each member has his or her own shop? Either way, congratulations, you have achieved the American Dream of small business ownership!

Bank on It

+ If you belong to any group that shares common goals, you may be able to form a cooperative.
+ Choose members carefully and pay close attention to work ethic, trustworthiness, and motivation.
+ Define your goals and set out a plan to achieve it step by step.
+ See an attorney to put your plan into a legal framework.
+ Have patience and regularly reiterate the common goals and progress.
+ Sit down with an immigrant entrepreneur to find out that there are plenty of brass rings . . . and that you only have to reach high enough to grasp one. Share these stories with your own cooperative members or have one of these successful immigrant business owners speak at one of your gatherings.

twenty-two
22

Barter

Bartering harkens back to medieval times; yet it is alive and well today. It is the process of exchanging one's own goods or services for those of another. It is a fabulous way for small businesses to finance the acquisition of needed goods and services. This brief chapter provides an introduction to bartering.

Direct Bartering

At its basic, business owners would agree to a direct exchange of products or services of equal value. Unfortunately, the goods or services required by most companies cannot be reciprocated in trade because the other party has no current need for the customer's goods or services. This is like exchanging time-shares at vacation spots. People who own a time-share in Hawaii can usually find someone else just about anywhere in the world with whom to exchange vacations. People who own time-shares in French Lick, Indiana (as do some of my colleagues), might never be able to find someone who owns a condo in Hawaii who is willing to trade a week in Hawaii for a week in Indiana—particularly in November.

It can be difficult and impractical to try to barter directly with any vendor or customer due to the problem of finding an acceptable match. Direct bartering is best accomplished on a transaction-by-transaction basis when the opportunity presents itself. The time and effort that might be expended to try to manage and track old-fashioned direct trading might use up so much of a business owner's time that the business suffers for it.

Indirect Bartering and Barter Exchanges

Fortunately, formal exchange agencies exist to ease these transactions. My colleagues who own a time-share can "bank" that week with a national exchange and trade it for a week somewhere else. Similarly, at a business barter exchange, a business can bank an amount of its goods or services in exchange for goods and services it currently needs. In practice, businesses join these exchanges and sign contracts that promise to provide a specified amount of goods and services. The promise is banked, not actual goods and services.

The obvious advantage is that a business that does not have cash can make purchases from other members of the exchange. Another advantage, almost always overlooked by those who do not participate in business exchanges, is the fact that the amount of credit a business receives at an exchange is based on the normal prices that the specific business would charge for its goods and services. Yet, when the time comes to honor the promise to provide the goods and services to other exchange members, the member is out only the actual cost of meeting the promise. For example, let's assume a woman starts a plumbing service. She needs PVC pipe for a job but has no money or credit with which to buy the supplies. She joins a business exchange and signs a contract promising to provide $10,000 of plumbing labor, priced at $100 per hour, to other members. She uses this credit to buy supplies from another exchange member. Weeks later, the exchange contacts her and tells her that another member would like some plumbing work done at home. She performs the work, which takes five hours. The exchange reduces the amount of labor she has promised to it by $500, although the plumber is out only her time and no real money. That's real sweat equity.

Naturally, even barter has its drawbacks. Each exchange has its own rules of the road, but reputable exchanges are careful to spell out all the advantages and disadvantages to prospective members. My promise to provide a dozen 186 Megahertz computers to an exchange is worthless to its membership; the exchange has to be on its guard to deal with reputable businesses that will be around long enough to cover their promises.

More information on bartering through business exchanges and where to find local exchanges can be found at the National Association of Trade Exchanges. Its Web site is at *www.nate.org*, and its phone number is 216-732-7171.

Bank on It

+ Barter can be a great help to new and small businesses.
+ Direct bartering is best left for isolated, individual transactions.
+ Barter exchanges exist throughout the country and offer a method for small business owners to borrow or earn credit for bartered services and goods.
+ Bartering is cost effective since exchanges use the market value of your goods or services while you are out only the actual cost of them.

twenty-three

Credit
Cards

The use of credit cards to fund small businesses and in particular, startups, seems to be the method of choice these days. It is a dangerous ploy, but one that can be pulled off. No matter how many credit cards, credit card account checks, or lines of credit land in an entrepreneur's mailbox, these are absolutely last resorts after all other avenues have failed.

And let's be right up front: It is a violation of most consumer credit card agreements to use credit cards for business purposes. That rule is intended to eliminate the credit risks inherent in business finance. Obviously, anyone forced to resort to credit cards to open or run a business is so far off the risk scale that no other form of finance was available. We must acknowledge that people will use credit cards despite our advice and the warning that using them for business purposes is not permitted; so, this chapter will discuss the advantages and disadvantages of using credit card debt.

Advantages

Ease of credit is the number-one advantage. Last week, I counted six offers for new credit cards in my own mailbox. The pace never seems to slow down. An old client of mine thought it would be cool to see how many credit cards he could obtain in a six-month period. He ended up with thirty-two credit cards and a total credit limit exceeding $150,000. He sliced them up, unused.

I really feel for a person who is struggling to find financial backing for a business venture and has credit card offers wafted in front of his or her face every day upon returning home from the salt mines. How easy it would be to take cash advances on them and to be on my way, he or she must think. It is like a person on a diet forced to walk the gauntlet of shelves in a chocolate shop.

It is not unrealistic for anyone, even those that have blemishes on their credit records, to accumulate $10,000 or $20,000 of credit card limits within a few weeks. Many popular franchises can be opened for that kind of money. The amounts would certainly buy a computer and put someone into an Internet business well capitalized.

Since the credit cards are issued and administered at faraway locations, businesspeople feel empowered to make their own decisions and to take their fate into their own hands. There is no banker to call to ask permission for a cash advance. There are no forms to fill out. Just make the minimum payments and no one will bother the owner. This sense of self-control is a definite advantage over other types of credit.

The credit card business is highly competitive today. In order to gain new market share or to hold onto existing customers, credit card companies offer unbelievably high credit limits (I have seen some as high as $100,000) and incredibly low interest rates. The most attractive rate that I have been offered in my mailbox recently was 3.9 percent. In some cases, these terms are advantageous over other sources of money, including banks.

A major advantage and the one cited by businesspeople who do not need to resort to credit card debt are the perks offered by credit card companies. Of course, the biggest perk is the accumulation of mileage for air travel. The use of credit cards for everyday business purchases can rapidly add up to enough air mileage to circumnavigate the globe. We have all heard of favorite scams pulled on credit card companies that are used to build up air miles. The latest one passed along to me was a person who bought traveler's checks for the maximum credit limit of his cards each month. He then used the traveler's checks to pay the credit card balance during the grace period. He never accrued any finance charges or used his own money. Apparently, he built up quite a bit of free travel before the credit card company caught up to him and altered its policy on the purchase of traveler's checks.

Credit cards can be accumulated while a person is still employed and before the business is launched. Since credit card companies lean heavily upon employment history to set credit levels and approvals, people can open up a lot more credit while still employed. Once the card is issued, there is little the card company can do even if it discovers that the cardholder is no longer employed gainfully.

Finally, the proper use of a card credit or juggling of several cards can demonstrate to a bank that the business owner is capable of managing a less costly line of credit.

Disadvantages

The primary disadvantage is that the illegal use of the card will be found out and that the user may be sued for immediate repayment or other compensation. Ouch. I have never heard of that happening, but it would be my luck if I were to use cards for a business purpose.

Once money is advanced on the card, the cardholder is committed. Payments have to be made. Late or skipped payments show up almost immediately on credit bureau reports, and that can all but eliminate the possibility of later obtaining more appropriate financing, especially from banks. Many credit card-funded entrepreneurs immediately fall into a near Ponzi scheme, whereby they must take cash advances on new cards to make payments on older cards. As soon as the new cards stop arriving in the mail, the whole house of cards collapses into bankruptcy.

Although credit card companies may lure people with attractive initial interest rates, those rates may soon balloon into unserviceable levels. Most credit cards, after special introductory periods expire, carry rates between 15 percent and 18 percent. That is expensive by any measure and means that, if just the minimum payment is made monthly, the principal balance is likely to never decrease.

Things to Keep in Mind

If a businessperson is determined to use personal credit cards for business purposes, a detailed record should be maintained of all purchases made with the cards. Later, if the business can refinance at a bank, the bank will need the itemization. In fact, if the loan ends up as an SBA-guaranteed loan, the SBA must receive proof that the credit card debt was used for business purposes.

Many banks now issue credit cards to businesses. It is less expensive to issue credit cards than to set up small lines of credit. These cards, unlike consumer credit cards, may legally be used for all sorts of business purposes. Likewise, major credit card companies have designed products just for business use. Some of these cards carry benefits similar to the consumer versions. These perks include mileage accounts, purchase protection, no-fee traveler's checks, and so on.

American Express, especially, is at the forefront of the business credit card movement. Combined with its other small business services, it presents formidable competition to all other segments of the small business finance industry.

Bank on It

+ Credit cards are the last resort for small business owners.
+ Exhaust all other sources of capital prior to tapping credit card lines.
+ Credit cards are easy sources of money.
+ Don't throw good money after bad—never use credit advances to make payments on other credit card balances. This is a sure-fire sign that bankruptcy looms ahead.
+ Refinance conventionally as soon as possible. Keep detailed records of the use of the cards in order to prove to a bank that you can handle a line of credit and to show that the money was used for business purposes.

twenty-four

Staying out of the Box for Keeps

Today, business owners have more options than any time in history for where and how to finance their businesses. Banks, by far, are still the preferred choice owing to lower costs, more services, and convenience. Nonbank lenders and nontraditional sources are multiplying, though, and giving banks a run for their money (literally!). Even successful, bankable business owners need to keep other avenues open and in mind.

Nearly every successful client, with whom I have had the pleasure of working at one time or another, claims: "If I knew then what I know now about banking and finance, I never would have started a business." That should not scare anyone who is contemplating starting or expanding a business; however, it is a basic truth that must be overcome. This book, I hope, goes a long way toward that end. Too many would-be entrepreneurs get trapped in the box by the old ways of banking. They never peer out of the box to see what else is available to them. Likewise, many existing business owners never quite reach their potential simply because their ideas do not fit in the box. Just the simple knowledge that there is a whole other universe outside the box gives a businessperson a leg up on the competition.

The Future of Banking

Banking has changed as much as any other industry in America during the past twenty years. The culture within the industry has turned 180 degrees in recent years. Rather than stodgy operations reminiscent of Mr. Mooney's Bank of Danville, banks today are proactive, sales organizations bent on gaining a bigger share of the consumer's pocketbook. Competition from the investment and insurance industries, nonbank lenders, and others has and continues to force changes in banks.

When automated teller machines hit the street years ago, my boss thought they were just a fad and refused to make the investment needed to keep up with our competitors. There are dozens of Internet banks available online. Who would have thought that possible just a few years ago? Several huge banking organizations are very near to being true national banks. Soon, tellers in thousands of branch offices all across America will have up-to-the-second access to our financial records. That will be a huge convenience to this mobile nation of ours.

I cannot help thinking that the next wave of bank mergers will leave the country with a handful of giants and thousands of community banks with no middle ground. How soon, too, will international mergers take off? It is occurring in every other industry, including the staid world of utility companies. Will my boss be American, British, German, or Japanese?

One change that I believe banks will begin to make during the next ten years is the elimination of loan officers. Loan officers will be jettisoned to become loan brokers, compensated purely by commissions. Banks will cultivate attorneys, accountants, and business brokers to build a stable of steady referral sources. These same professionals will be able to complete loan applications on behalf of their clients. The applications will be faxed or e-mailed directly to the bank's credit-scoring department—there will be no need for a loan officer to act as a middle man. This may be dangerous for small business owners simply because of the conflict of interest that confronts the loan broker or professional who makes the referral. What is more important to them: serving the client's best interests or pocketing a commission or finder's fee?

Technology

The Internet has opened a whole new world for consumers. It is only a matter of time before a company like Microsoft, America Online, or Disney decides to enter banking in a big way. Banks built of ether will have enormous overhead cost savings compared to traditional brick-and-mortar banks. These banks will have access to, and the ability to maintain, state-of-the-art technology. Their innovative abilities will knock consumers for a loop when compared to banks that usually have systems several generations old because the cost of updating infrastructure is prohibitive. How soon until one of these technological powerhouses takes over a major bank and converts it to a state-of-the-art technobank?

The fundamental roadblock to merging the abilities of today's technological marvels with banks is the simple fact that the financial rewards of banking (return on investment, dividends, and so on) pale in comparison to the returns being generated within the tech industry itself. If and when growth in that sector slows or falls into line with traditional investments, we may then see wholesale mergers. It will definitely be exciting.

Economic Cycles

The experience of farmers during the 1980s taught us a lesson that should be carried forward for decades. Prices for farm land exploded. It was easy money to borrow to the hilt and buy more land. Inflation drove the value of the land skyward and dwarfed the underlying loans on the land. That was the idea, anyway. When the agriculture industry crashed, thousands of farmers were trapped with loans that exceeded the value of their lands. On top of that, crop prices plummeted, and farmers could not even make minimum payments to keep their farms out of foreclosure. The crisis was so severe that dozens of farmers took their own lives in order to free up life insurance proceeds for their families to use to pay off debts. More than one farmer took the life of a banker, too.

Business is cyclical. There are good times and bad times. The bad times can be really bad if the business owner has not prepared for them. This means making prudent decisions during good times. That is tough to do especially when the golden ring seems just beyond reach. Bankers and other lenders do not roll up the sidewalks as soon as the economic cycle heads south, but they do become more choosy about with whom they will do business.

Small business ownership is the average Joe's best route to personal wealth. It is a tortoise-versus-hare thing. Bankers would much rather deal with the tortoise than the hare. A lack of planning and care may forever doom a businessperson to imprisonment in the box. While times are good, the smart entrepreneur will line up the best available advisors, attorneys, and accountants. As a team, good practices and contingency plans can be implemented to make sure that the small business stays out of the box for good.

Glossary
of Terms

Accounts Payable: Trade accounts of businesses, representing obligations to pay for goods and services received.

Accounts Receivable: Trade accounts of businesses representing moneys due for goods sold or services rendered evidenced by notes, statements, invoices, or other written evidence of a present obligation.

Accounting: The recording, classifying, summarizing, and interpreting in a significant manner in the terms of money, transactions, and events of a financial character.

Balance Sheet: A report of a firm's assets, liabilities, and net worth on a specific date.

Bankruptcy: A condition in which a business cannot meet its debt obligations and petitions a federal district court for either reorganization of its debts or liquidation of its assets. In the action the property of a debtor is taken over by a receiver or trustee in bankruptcy for the benefit of the creditors. This action is conducted as prescribed by the National Bankruptcy Act, and may be voluntary or involuntary.

Break-Even Point: The break-even point in any business is that point at which the volume of sales or revenues exactly equals total expenses—the point at which there is neither a profit nor loss—under varying levels of activity. The break-even point tells the manager what level of output or activity is required before the firm can make a profit and reflects the relationship between costs, volume, and profits.

Business Information Center: One-stop locations for information, education, and training designed to help entrepreneurs start, operate, and grow their businesses. The centers provide free on-site counseling, training courses, and workshops and have resources for addressing a broad variety of business startup and development issues.

Business Plan: A comprehensive planning document that clearly describes the business developmental objective of an existing or proposed business applying for assistance in SBA's 8(a) or lending programs. The plan outlines what and how and from where the resources needed to accomplish the objective will be obtained and utilized.

Capital: Assets less liabilities, representing the ownership interest in a business. Also, a stock of accumulated goods, especially at a specified time and in contrast to income received during a specified time period; accumulated goods devoted to the production of goods; and accumulated possessions calculated to bring income.

Capital Expenditures: Business spending on additional plant, equipment, and inventory.

Cash Discount: An incentive offered by the seller to encourage the buyer to pay within a stipulated time. For example, if the terms are 2/10/N 30, the buyer may deduct 2 percent from the amount of the invoice (if paid within 10 days), otherwise, the full amount is due in 30 days.

Cash Flow: An accounting presentation showing how much of the cash generated by the business remains after both expenses (including interest) and principal repayment on financing are paid. A projected cash flow statement indicates whether the business will have cash to pay its expenses, loans, and make a profit. Cash flows can be calculated for any given period of time, normally done on a monthly basis.

Charge-Off: An accounting transaction removing an uncollectible balance from the active receivable accounts.

Charged Off Loan: An uncollectible loan for which the principal and accrued interest were removed from the lender's receivable accounts.

Closing: Actions and procedures required to effect the documentation and disbursement of loan funds after the application has been approved, and the execution of all required documentation and its filing and recordation where required.

Collateral: Something of value—securities, evidence of deposit or other property—pledged to support the repayment of an obligation.

Collateral Valuation: The systematic calculation of the value of an asset that has been or will be pledged to secure repayment of a loan. The valuation may be market value or liquidation value.

Contingent Liability: A potential obligation that may be incurred dependent upon the occurrence of a future event.

Contract: A mutually binding legal relationship obligating the seller to furnish supplies or services and the buyer to pay for them.

Corporation: A group of persons granted a state charter legally recognizing them as a separate entity having its own rights, privileges, and liabilities distinct from those of its members.

Credit Rating: A grade assigned to a business concern to denote the net worth and credit standing to which the concern is entitled in the opinion of the rating agency as a result of its investigation.

Credit Scoring: Method used to numerically approve or decline loans based on credit history and financial measurements.

Debenture: Debt instrument evidencing the holder's right to receive interest and principal installments from a named obligor. Applies to all forms of unsecured, long-term debt evidenced by a certificate of debt.

Debt Capital: Business financing that normally requires periodic interest payments and repayment of principal within a specified time.

Debt Financing: The provision of long-term loans to small businesses in exchange for debt securities or notes.

Defaults: The nonpayment of principal and/or interest on the due date as provided by the terms and conditions of the note.

Documentation: The written record of the agreement between lender and borrower including promissory notes, loan agreement, and security assignments.

Electronic Commerce: e-Commerce denotes the ability to transact business via electronic means.

Entrepreneur: One who assumes the financial risk of the initiation, operation, and management of a business.

Equity: An accounting term used to describe the net investment of the owners or stockholders in a business. Under the accounting equation, equity also represents the result of assets less liabilities.

Equity Financing: The provision of funds for capital or operating expenses in exchange for capital stock, stock purchase warrants, and options in the business financed without any guaranteed return, but with the opportunity to share in the company's profits. Equity financing includes long-term subordinated securities containing stock options and/or warrants.

Financial Reports: Reports commonly required from applicants that provide specific information about the applicant's financial condition. These include the balance sheet, income statement, and cash flow statements.

Financing: New funds provided to a business, either by loans or capital stock.

Foreclosure: The act by a mortgagee upon default in the payment of interest and/or principal of a debt secured by a mortgage by forcing payment of the debt or selling the underlying collateral.

Franchising: A continuing relationship in which the franchisor provides a licensed privilege to the franchisee to do business and offers to provide assistance in organizing, training, merchandising, marketing, and managing the business in return for consideration. Franchising is a form of business by which the owner (franchisor) of a product, service, or system obtains distribution through affiliated dealers (franchisees). The product, service, or system is identified by the owner's name and the franchisee is normally given exclusive access to a defined geographic area.

Guaranty: The legal promise by a person or entity (guarantor) to repay a debt of another person or entity.

Holding Company: A legal entity formed to own separate banking companies.

Hazard Insurance: Insurance required by lenders that shows the lender as loss payee for losses from defined risks on real and personal property.

Incubator: A facility designed to encourage new and small business enterprise. Shared support staff, on-site counseling and professional assistance, and other services are normally provided by the operator of the incubator.

Insolvency: The inability of a borrower to meet financial obligations as they mature or the lack of financial assets to pay legal debts.

Investment Banking: Businesses specializing in the formation of capital. Usually, reserved for corporations with large capital requirements.

Lease: A contract between an owner (lessor) and the tenant (lessee) stating the conditions under which the tenant may occupy or use the property.

Leg Loan: Loan made to a business purely due to loan officer's personal interests in the company or the company's owner(s).

Lending Institution: Any institution, including commercial bank, savings and loan association, commercial finance company, or other lender qualified to legally make loans.

Letter of Credit: A guarantee by a bank to pay, under certain conditions, debts owed by its customer.

Leveraged Buy-Out: The purchase of a business with financing secured by the assets of the purchased company.

Line of Credit: A loan to a business that acts much like a credit card. Principal may be borrowed or repaid at will and interest is paid monthly.

Liquidation: The disposal, at maximum prices, of the collateral securing a loan.

Liquidation Value: The net value realizable in the sale of a business or asset.

Loan Agreement: An agreement between borrower and lender that establishes the pertinent loan terms, covenants, and restrictions.

Maturity: The date when all unpaid principal and interest is due and payable.

Mortgage: An instrument giving legal title to secure the repayment of a loan made by the mortgagee (lender). A mortgage normally places a lien upon the property in favor of the mortgagee.

One Stop Capital Shops: The SBA's contribution to Empowerment Zones. The shops provide a full range of lending and capital assistance.

Ordinary Interest: Simple interest based on a year of 360 days, contrasting with exact interest having a base year of 365 days.

Partnership: A legal relationship existing between two or more people contractually associated as joint principals in a business.

Proprietorship: The most common legal form of business ownership. The liability of the owner is unlimited in this form of ownership.

Ratio: Denotes relationships of items within and between financial statements.

Referral: An introduction to a person or institution that may be of assistance to you.

Secondary Market: Those who purchase loans from the original lender.

Service Corps of Retired Business Executives: SCORE is a 12,400-member volunteer association sponsored by the SBA. The volunteers offer expert counseling to small businesses.

Small Business Development Centers: SBDCs offer a broad spectrum of business information and guidance to business owners.

Term Loan: A loan that is repaid with periodic installments of principal and interest.

Turnover: The number of times that an average inventory of goods is sold in a one-year period.

Uniform Commercial Code: The code of uniform laws concerning commercial transactions.

U.S. Small Business Administration: The government agency chartered to act as an advocate for small businesses which accomplishes its mission through loan guarantees and informational programs.

Usury: Interest that exceeds the legal rate charged to a borrower for the use of money.

Venture Capital: Money used to support new or unusual business undertakings. This funding is usually reserved for firms with above average growth rates and significant potential for market expansion.

Index